ADVANCE PRAISE FOR *DESIGN FOR A NEW EUROPE*

"This book is a remarkable account of the most recent developments in the European Union. Professor Gillingham rethinks the process of European integration and offers an original prescription on how to reconfigure it. His *Design for a New Europe* calls for a mandate from the citizens, the return of power to the states, further enlargement, substantial reform of the EU's institutions and policies, and abandonment of the EU's attempt to harmonize laws. This work should be considered in any serious debate about the further course of European integration."

— Václav Klaus, President, The Czech Republic

"At a time when clear thinking about Europe's political and economic future is urgently needed, John Gillingham has provided a convincing diagnosis of the EU's present malaise and a challenging set of prescriptions which deserve to be taken seriously by Europhiles as much as by Eurosceptics. While praising the EU's achievements, not least in promoting and sustaining democracy in previously undemocratic countries, Gillingham condemns the drift towards bureaucratic centralism, which has produced an ever-widening gap between institutions and the people. Moves to slim down the Brussels bureaucracy and to transfer some responsibilities to the member states, he rightly argues, do not imply dismantling the EU, but rather rebuilding it on sounder foundations."

— Sir Geoffrey Owen, Senior Fellow, Institute of Management, London School of Economics, and former editor of *The Financial Times*

"By combining the objectivity of the outsider with his insider's knowledge, Gillingham succeeds in painting a persuasive and compelling portrait of the European Union after the rejection of the Constitutional Treaty. This insightful study brings the major developments in Europe to life and puts them into a global perspective. *Design for a New Europe* is a lucid, well-written account of what is wrong with the EU and how it can be fixed. It is a must-read for Europhiles and Eurosceptics alike."

— Tom Zwart, University of Utrecht School of Law

"John Gillingham has established himself as one of those very rare commentators who can read European historian in three dimensions. He knows it very well but is never overwhelmed by it: he can appreciate the creativity of 'Old Europe.' Now, he looks at the strange phenomenon, why Europe has stagnated and why it has so much less to offer to the ambitious young than the USA. The reason? Partly institutional, in the sense that the institutions designed to make Europe work in the 1950s now have become a or even the problem – a necklace of skulls. This is a very readable and extremely knowledgeable book."

–Norman Stone, Bilkent University, Ankara, Turkey

DESIGN FOR A NEW EUROPE

This is a book not only about how the European integration process broke down, but also about how it can be repaired. That it should be fixed is obvious. Europe's long-term movement toward closer economic and political union deserves credit for two immense historical achievements. One is to have created a single-market economy across the continent, the overall benefits of which continue to mount. Even more importantly, the European Union has in the past strengthened democracies in places where they already exist and helped spread them to where they do not.

The four chapters of this penetrating, fiercely argued, and often witty book subject today's dysfunctional European Union to critical scrutiny in an attempt to show how it is stunting economic growth, sapping the vitality of national governments, and undermining competitiveness; explain how the attempt to revive the European Union by turning it into a champion of research and development will backfire; and demonstrate, finally, how Europe's great experiment in political and economic union can succeed if the wave of liberal reform now under way in the historically downtrodden east is allowed to sweep the prosperous and complacent west. The European Union will then have proven worthy of its immense responsibilities and renewed Europe's spirit in the process.

John Gillingham is professor of history at the University of Missouri, St. Louis. His previous books include *European Integration, 1950–2003* (Cambridge, 2003), and *Coal, Steel, and the Rebirth of Europe, 1945–1955* (Cambridge, 1991), which was awarded the George Louis Beer Prize of the American Historical Association for the best book on European international history published that year.

Design for a New Europe

John Gillingham

University of Missouri, St. Louis

Harvard Ukrainian Research Institute

CAMBRIDGE
UNIVERSITY PRESS

D
1060
.G44
2006

CAMBRIDGE UNIVERSITY PRESS
Cambridge, New York, Melbourne, Madrid, Cape Town, Singapore, São Paulo

Cambridge University Press
40 West 20th Street, New York, NY 10011-4211, USA

www.cambridge.org
Information on this title: www.cambridge.org/9780521866941

© John Gillingham 2006

First published 2006

Printed in the United Kingdom by Biddles Ltd.

A catalog record for this publication is available from the British Library.

Library of Congress Cataloging in Publication Data

Gillingham, John, 1943–
Design for a new Europe / John Gillingham.
p.   cm.
Includes bibliographical references.
ISBN-13: 978-0-521-86694-1
ISBN-10: 0-521-86694-4
ISBN-13: 978-0-521-68664-8 (pbk.)
ISBN-10: 0-521-68664-4 (pbk.)
1. European Union.   2. Europe – Politics and government – 1945– .   I. Title.
D1060.G44   2006
341.242'2–dc22   2005037361

ISBN-13   978-0-521-86694-1 hardback
ISBN-10   0-521-86694-4 hardback

ISBN-13   978-0-521-68664-8 paperback
ISBN-10   0-521-68664-4 paperback

Автор присвячує цю книжку українському народові.

Contents

Introduction: The End of the Beginning

It almost had to happen. The crisis, which broke out across Europe in early summer 2005 after the French and Dutch people repudiated the proposed federal constitution, had been mounting for years: the European Union (EU) had somehow lost its legitimacy, and no one could do much about it. The EU was never democratic; it had always been a project run by an elite, which in turn justified its existence by results. For most Europeans this was enough. The public had been led to believe that the EU was a new kind of political and economic organization, for which no substitute existed or could be found; it accepted the claim that history had conferred special responsibilities upon this unique institution for directing an irreversible process of development, which would strengthen Europe both morally and materially. This discredited teleology was the foundation of the EU's existence. To save the EU, one must rethink the whole integration process.

The dead certainties of yesterday ring hollow because the EU has long since broken down. The fallout has been widespread. European diplomacy has degenerated into a free for all, revived old grudges, rekindled ancient enmities, and fouled the political atmosphere. Civility has subsequently disappeared. Cooperation, even on simple matters, has become much more difficult. The US-EU friendship has been another casualty. The rise of demagogic public rhetoric and the popularity of a destructive pseudo intellectual literature, on both sides of the Atlantic, strengthen the absurd impression that Americans and Europeans belong to separate and mutually antagonistic civilizations. The chattering has now become really nasty. The hostile ranting is both malignant and contagious.

The EU's problems run deeper than most experts realize. They are not merely a matter of inefficiency and waste, or even of bad policy, but of design. The malfunctioning Brussels institutions are now out of control. Much like a slow-moving juggernaut, they continue to reduce economic growth, usurp authority from the member states (thereby weakening them), misdirect resources on a grand scale, set conflicting priorities, and generate unrealistic policies. The EU even strangles in its own red tape, undermining the very purposes it was meant to serve. As a result, Europe cannot cope with today's challenges. Failure to repair or replace the EU's institutional machinery will bring the integration process to a halt – or worse if no Plan B exists.

This book explains how the European integration process broke down and also how to repair it. That it should be fixed is obvious. The EU is sometimes likened to a coral reef, which grows in ways understood only by trained specialists and cannot be pared, cut back, or otherwise reduced in size without being destroyed. Such an idea is mistaken. The EU is more like a Rube Goldberg machine: an unnecessarily complicated contraption for performing a simple task. Goldberg's contrivances, however, would always work. The EU no longer does. The EU can nevertheless be dismantled systematically and reassembled intelligently to perform satisfactorily. What's required is less a heroic feat of engineering than a new principle of construction – democracy instead of elitism.

Europe's long-term movement toward closer economic and political union deserves credit for two immense historical achievements. One is to have created a market economy across the continent, the past benefits of which have been considerable. It is an open question whether, in a global economic world, this will continue to be the case. Even more importantly, the EU has, over time, strengthened democracies where they are in place and helped establish them where they are not. This is a worthy contribution to peace, prosperity, and human dignity, whose value can increase in the future.

We are living in an era whose greatest blessing is only now – and episodically – becoming clear: it is the rediscovery of freedom. The ideals for which the EU stands are still alive and well within the often slighted and ill-represented electorates of modern Europe – among people like you and me – as well as in long misgoverned and corrupt nations surrounding it. Europe will not only do mankind a service by nurturing these neighbors' political and economic development, it will also enrich and renew its own spirit.

There is no turning back from the verdict of the constitutional referenda. The European public is for the first time now a player in a drama in which it was never assigned a role. Weak, inflexible, and overstretched, the EU has reached the limits of its strength and must be overhauled to survive. This is not a matter of choice but of method. Forget past shibboleths. The grand project of European integration is dysfunctional and in public discredit. Its rescue will require returning power to the states, restoring growth, and strengthening democracy both within the EU and on Europe's borders. Leaving things as they are today will likely result in slow decline. This, however, would be the lesser evil. Inaction could also trigger panic. A design for a new Europe is needed now.

This book will explain what has gone wrong with the EU, why present remedies may make things worse, and how the EU can rediscover its civilizing mission. The author's purpose is to salvage the integration process in the only way possible: by jettisoning the Brussels institutions and rebuilding something different on a new platform, a democratic consensus anchored in a new vision of a future Europe. Such a proposal would have seemed radical a year ago. Today it is simply necessary.

ONE

Governance

The legitimacy crisis currently facing the European Union (EU) may
be partly the consequence of human error or even the result of folly,
but at the heart of the problem is structural breakdown. For decades,
Europeans overlooked the high-handed and spendthrift ways of the
Brussels technocracy out of trust, believing that, in spite of it all, over
the long run the EU was an indispensable and irreplaceable engine of
progress. The public repudiation of the proposed European constitution has shaken this complacent belief to the roots. No matter how
emphatic the rejection, the episode is only a symptom of a deeper malady. The EU should no longer be imagined as a nascent political structure suffering teething problems: it is unsound and unraveling. The
design is flawed, and the machinery needs repair. Coordination is lacking. There are no clear demarcations between its main institutions –
the European Commission, the European Council, and the European
Parliament (EP) – or between these institutions and powerful affiliated
bodies such as the European Court of Justice (ECJ) and the European
Central Bank. The relationship is equally blurry between the public
and private spheres, both of which influence policy making. The dense
thicket of snarled transnational structures that inextricably binds the
twenty-five member states to Brussels is the cause of endless jurisdictional conflict between the central authorities and the states and among
the states themselves. One never knows who or what can speak or act
in the name of Europe. Confusion is endemic, and the threat of chaos
is seldom absent.

The EU chronically overshoots and has been vastly oversold. Its
vaulting ambitions far exceed its paltry resources. This will not likely

change soon: contributing member states refuse to pay more into the common kitty and beneficiaries decline to settle for less, even as the EU's appetites continue to grow. It is as a result becoming very hard for the EU to make credible commitments. The EU also lacks feedback loops and subsequently cannot correct its mistakes. The EU has trouble keeping track of its money and makes little effort to stem corruption. The sorry state of affairs is hard to set right: the operating methods of Brussels are arcane, opaque, and – being neither checked nor balanced – simply out of control.

European institutions were created fifty years ago in a world where democracy and capitalism had broken down and had to be reconstructed from the top down. Their original design made little provision for the development of open markets and almost none for self-government. The founders' era has long since disappeared – thanks in part, albeit ironically, to the integration process itself. Many of the politicians, bureaucrats, and policy experts who have built Europe in the past, and who would do so in the future, do not yet realize, however, that their out-moded methods are often counterproductive: they debilitate represen-tative government, impair the market economy, and weigh each of them down with the heavy hand of excess regulation. Such methods deserve much of the blame for the present unpopularity of many of Europe's governments, the anemic economic growth of the past twenty years, and the pervasive malaise from which the continent currently suffers. Europe's malady may require a convalescence spanning decades.

The cure will have to be found in the public forum. Democracy, devo-lution, and open markets are needed to heal the Brussels institutions: a future EU must rest on popular consent, the sovereignty of the nation-state, the subsidiarity principle, and competitive economies. Only then can Europe have a real government instead of the peculiar form of gov-ernance from which it now suffers. "Governance" is the standard EU buzzword for the perplexing maze of order and edict, directive and regu-lation, and administrative law and judicial interpretation that comprises the purportedly sacred and irreversible corpus of law and administrative fiat – the *acquis communautaire* – by which Brussels tries to rule Europe. It must be disentangled to be understood.

This will not be easy. Official Brussels, as *The Economist's* astute columnist, Charlemagne, once noted, is a club – something formed to exclude outsiders – predisposed to adopt insider jargon. Among administrative and governmental bodies, bureaucracies, the EU indeed holds a commanding lead in the cryptic art of inventing unnecessary acronyms, using numbers in place of words, and adopting locations to refer to events – all of which give the impression of having been scrambled through an Enigma machine to prevent de-coding. This misuse of language poses, as intended, a barrier to transparency.[1] Many scholars have been infected with the EU virus. The time has come to talk turkey.

The EU is truly in a sorry state of affairs. The European Commission, which is supposed to lead it, cannot do so. Over the past few years, power within the EU has not been exercised constitutionally – or within any framework of written agreement or implicit understanding. It has rather been seized extra-legally and, until recently, wielded irresponsibly from behind the scenes by France, a nation intent upon projecting power on the world stage. In the meantime, the Brussels governance machinery grinds on, operating according to its own wasteful and perverse logic, which mainly privileges insiders. Both powerful and fragile, the EU's only remaining source of authority is what survives of the myth that sustains it. The loss of its shredded legitimacy may prove fatal unless a new rationale for the EU can be found or an old one rediscovered.[2] How did Europe get into such a mess?

Current problems date from the attempt of Jacques Delors, president of the Commission from 1985 to 1995, to transform the EU into a superstate.[3] His intention was to introduce a European-level socialism like the one he had tried in vain to build previously as French Minister of Economics in the cabinet of François Mitterrand. Delors was the most influential figure in the history of integration since Jean Monnet, but his ambitions collided with the very different ones of the British Prime Minister of the day, Margaret Thatcher.

She envisaged Europe as a large free-trade area. A compromise, the Single European Act of 1986 (SEA), emerged from their numerous clashes. The SEA removed impediments to internal trade but also vested new powers in the Commission. It left unresolved the question of whether the future EU would be organized horizontally though marketplace competition or vertically by means of strong, centralized institutions.

Delors exercised his new authority to maximum advantage. The result is the present structure of the EU. He brokered a deal, first of all, whereby the largest single program of the EU, the Common Agricultural Policy (CAP), was reduced from three quarters to about half of the total budget. The remainder went into so-called regional funds, which fostered the loyalty of the new Mediterranean member states. He also introduced the practice of budgeting in seven-year cycles, which strengthened the executive power at the expense of the embryonic EP. Delors was also midwife to the proposed European Monetary Union (EMU), something designed to lead the way to a federal superstate. He feared that without it, US-driven globalization would undermine the "European social model."

The EMU was the product of the Maastricht conference of 1992, the scene of Delors' greatest triumphs. The ensuing treaty included provisions for two other vast new "competences" (jurisdictional claims), one of them, "pillar two," for home affairs (the police force), and the other, "pillar three," for security and foreign policy (diplomacy and defense). These pillars were, however, hollow and not expected to become solid until the future. Only the first pillar, the Single European Act, had any substance whatsoever. How the three pillars related to one another, or to the EMU, was unspecified in the text of the treaty. The unresolved problems stemming from Maastricht would whiplash EU development for many years and give rise to mounting conflict between those who, like Delors, were intent upon "deepening" EU institutions and others, like Margaret Thatcher, who sought to "broaden" the union by bringing in new members. Before real progress at the EU is possible, Delors' legacy must be settled.

The seriousness of the EU's problems became apparent for the first time at the Nice Summit of December 2000. It had been convened in order to adapt EU institutions to the impending accession of ten new members, eight of them from eastern Europe. Lorded over by the magisterial Jacques Chirac, who then occupied the European Council's six-month rotating presidency, it degenerated into a donnybrook. For the first time a still unwary public was exposed to the fierce animosity existing at the summits of power. Nice also produced an egregious patchwork treaty, which overloaded the already creaking governance machinery, left everyone unhappy, and bore the stamp of impermanence. Within a month, a movement was afoot to replace the tangled skein of prior treaties and agreements with a new constitution designed to enable the EU to operate more like a state.[4] The various pros and cons of this much-discussed but little understood document count for less today than the ratification procedure. It brought the public into the policy-making forum for the first time. Eurocrats and politicians can no longer treat the EU like private property.

A Sorry State of Affairs

The Nice debacle also marked the definitive eclipse of the European Commission, the agenda-setter for the European project. The Commission could no longer lead. Neither Delors nor any of his three successors managed to either staunch the burgeoning problems created by his projects or clean up the Commission, which remains riddled with fraud and shot through with bad practice. Jacques Santer, Delors' successor, had to step down as the result of a scandal. Called in as a white knight in 1999, Romano Prodi proved himself to be pathologically windy at the podium, ineffective in Brussels turf wars, and unfocussed. Prodi's authority soon evaporated. He was an impotent bystander at the Nice brouhaha.[5] His successor, Jose Manuel Barroso, has yet to get his own agenda off the ground.

The new millennium has not been kind to the Commission. It is no longer a cohesive body. An inverse correlation exists between the sizes and strengths of most of its twenty-plus directorates. There is little coordination between them, and they often work at cross-purposes, when working at all. Some do almost nothing. Only a few directorates have real policy-making authority, and even the ambitious programs of the Commission's most successful units, competition and internal market, are no longer headed anywhere. Financial controls at the Commission are inadequate, and corruption is rampant. Private parties often make public decisions. Important projects have been launched without either mandate or supervision. The Commission must also compete against other institutions with vague policy mandates. One of them, the EP, is an expensive and meddlesome talk shop. Another, the European Council, representing the member states, is in disarray. All the components of the Brussels complex vie with the member states. Although the Commission counts for less and less, its pretensions remain undiminished.

Romano Prodi knew he had a problem after the Nice shoot-out. In the latter months of his ineffectual and openly ridiculed Commission presidency, Prodi belatedly recognized the gravity of the growing split between what the public demanded and what the EU was delivering, but his efforts to close the breach were pitifully inadequate. Published in July 2001, "European Governance: A White Paper" set out a master plan for the Commission's reform agenda. It recognized the urgency of "connecting Europe with its citizens" by means of "democratic institutions and representatives of the people." To narrow the gap, the paper – a characteristic Eurocratic amalgam of the trite, the apocryphal, and the bewildering – proposed taking recourse to more "network-led initiatives" such as the "Telecoms Package." This epiphany of regulatory success grew out of lengthy consultation with relevant stakeholders on the basis of a Commission working paper rather than in open public debate. To imagine using lessons learned from utility regulation to create democracy boggles the mind. Reading the white paper's pretentious conclusion, "From Governance to the Future of Europe," is like watching someone try to steer a drifting ice floe. Called for in the white paper are "structuring the EU's relationship with civil society," enlisting local and regional governments in the process, and increasing inputs of "expert advice." Other recommendations include dovetailing official and unofficial policy making, strengthening EU regulatory agencies, and forcing "citizens to hold their leaders [accountable] for the decisions that the Union takes."[6] Such an imposition of authority from the top down not only reflects a novel form of representative democracy; anyone outside of the Eurocracy would recognize it as an exercise in futility.

After Nice, the Commission's projects and proposals are often difficult to take seriously. A green paper on entrepreneurship (or more specifically the lack of it in Europe) pointed to a serious problem but amounted to another iteration of the banal: "Entrepreneurship is first and foremost a mindset.... Entrepreneurship is about people, their choices and actions in starting, taking over or running a business.... Risk-taking should be rewarded rather than punished."[7] Prodi could have done little to change embedded risk-averse mentalities. Yet where he might have acted, he did not.

Prodi's economic plan for 2003, the "growth initiative" called Quick-Start, amounted to little more than a massive public works proposal. Heavy-handed and unimaginative, it elicited a joint protest of the Big Three, Schröder, Chirac, and Blair. They griped that "the Commission is pursuing not one but many policies in the context of the Lisbon strategy and that they are at best juxtaposed and at worst contradictory.... Declarations are being made on various sectors: the hydrogen economy, ship building, textiles and clothing, photovoltaic solar power, arms, airspace, biotechnology and soon automobiles and steel. There are, however, no overall guidelines."[8]

There were, however, policy surrogates: a number of new zippy-sounding bureaucratic organizations such as the Competitiveness Council set up in February 2002, which housed separate sections for the internal market, research, and industry. At its meeting in February of the following year, the Council begat a new European Research Area (ERA) ("a true internal market for science and knowledge") before, in a rousing conclusion, introducing as a remarkable administrative break-through the "open method of coordination" based upon an organizational principle only recently discovered in Brussels. This deep insight was that individual member states could better implement policy when using customary methods rather than when responding to Brussels' diktats. If this new initiative was not enough of a snore, the internal market commissioner presented to the Council Communication IP/03/214 as a follow-up to the previous year's "Action Plan on Better Regulation" as well as documentation on several other tedious outstanding matters. The voluminous churning of paper produced scant results. In a September 2004 press interview, Laurens Jan Brinkhorst, chairman of the Competitiveness Council, denounced his forum as "Mickey Mouse" and lacking "any team spirit and focus on an issue."[9]

The Sapir Report of July 2003, which Prodi had commissioned, should have provided the tonic needed to invigorate the Eurocracy. It subjected the Brussels institutions to the most rigorous insider criticism ever. Noting that the end of the long-term slowdown in economic growth was not in sight – and specifically that the ambitious growth targets set at the Lisbon Agenda of 2000 for 2010 were completely unrealistic – the author, a prominent economist and EU consultant, and his expert team concluded that far-reaching reform would be needed to sustain the "European social model." The Sapir group recommended eliminating the CAP, reducing regional funding sharply as well as limiting it to the poorest members of the community, and plowing the savings from these two programs into research and development, which could then develop into the centerpiece of a reformed EU. It also proposed reforming tax and fiscal systems to stimulate innovation, increasing funding of state-of-the-art research, and improving university education. The report also advised that only projects that boost growth should be supported and the practice of *juste retour* (proportionate shares) halted; that regulatory agencies be given independence and shielded from national pressures; and that EU funding be made less dependent on member state contributions. The Sapir team also recommended, for the first time in any official document, loosening the growth and stability criteria governing the EMU.[10] The report triggered heated protests from several commissioners. Prodi refused to endorse it. No matter: this was the *fin de regime*, and for months he had devoted much of his time to becoming the standard bearer for the Italian Left's campaign against Silvio Berlusconi in the next election. Their contest would be like a street-corner brawl between two wheezing middle-age drunks.[11]

The incoming Barroso Commission, which replaced Prodi in October 2004, should have had a chance to do something constructive. The auguries for reform were generally hopeful. The Dutch, who then held the rotating presidency, had recognized the inescapable reality that "Europe has lost ground to both the US and Asia, its societies are under strain, and ... ugly political forces are beginning to manifest themselves.... At risk in the medium to long run is nothing less than the sustainability of the society Europe has built, and to that extent the viability of its civilization."[12] A report by a committee headed by former foreign minister Wim Kok contained these sobering words. It had been set up to guide the incoming president, Jan-Peter Balkenende. Lest its message not be clear enough, the Kok Report emphasized that "if Europe cannot adapt ... [its] working population will be unable to sustain the growing army of pensioners, economic growth will stagnate, [and] institutions will all face contraction and decline." Officially aired in November, the report drove home the fact – obvious to anyone with a working knowledge of business or finance – that the European economy was in a deep hole and someone should start shoveling quickly.

The Dutch presidency focused single-mindedly on this objective. Social Europe would have to sit in the rumble seat. It has stayed there ever since.[13]

The Kok Report nevertheless arrived too late for the new Commission president, Jose Manuel Barroso. Demagogues in the European Parliament had already tripped him up. The EP exercised a single important decision-making power: it could vote down an incoming Commission by rejecting not the president but the entire slate of his candidates. A former Maoist turned economic liberal, Jose Manuel Barroso was Britain's choice as Prodi's successor and distinctly not the candidate of either France or Germany, which preferred the buck-toothed Flemish Francophile Guy Verhofstadt, the Belgian prime minister, or the compliant backroom politician from dinky Luxembourg and patron saint of Europe's tax cheaters, His Excellency Jean-Claude Juncker.[14]

Barroso never got the honeymoon he wanted, even after bending over backwards to appease hostile Franco-Germans and embittered Socialists. Not even an avowal of "hatred for US arrogance and unilateralism" did him any good; his acceptance as vice president for economics, a new office, of Günter Verheugen, a German advocate of industrial policy, also failed to change the picture. Nearly 300 Members of the European Parliament (MEPs) voted against his investiture.[15] The worst was yet to come. Barroso's proposed cabinet – allocated as always by national quota – was stacked heavily with promarket nominees, including those for the crucial economic directorates, internal market and competition. It also included Rocco Buttiglione, Italian Prime Minister Silvio Berlusconi's designated candidate for the justice directorate.

Buttiglione made an easy target for antineoliberals keen on knocking Barroso down a peg – not to mention for underworked and overpaid MEPs thirsting for a power grab. A traditional Catholic, Buttiglione admitted in testimony to viewing homosexuality as a sin and, more grudgingly, to preferring that women stay home rather than go to work. Such beliefs are apparently politically incorrect in secular postmodern Europe, where infidelity is considered an adult privilege and "Catherine M." gets honored as a Lindbergh of sex. Faced in November with the prospect of having his entire slate rejected, Barroso sent Rocco packing. This was the fate of someone from a Christian civilization who adhered to values held by the Pope! The cheap-shot parliamentarians turned Barroso into one of recorded history's earliest lame ducks, while making themselves look like fools.[16]

All this nonsense made little difference. The Commission Barroso inherited was intellectually stifled, pervaded with institutionalized corruption, and nearly immobilized. The problem was long term and structural; it began with the existence of 30,000 or so unionized civil servants who could not be moved, let alone fired, and who could count on support from their home countries when things got a bit hot. Unlike national civil servants, they had no real political masters but answered only to political appointees of different nationalities, many of them mediocrities and most of them isolated from one another. Some directors-general, according to Alisdair Murray, "[ran] their departments as virtual fiefdoms."[17]

These officials currently earn up to $300,000 per year, pay taxes of only 16 percent on their base salary and net three times as much as – and in poorer countries many times more than – their national counterparts. The perks are even better. They include cash bonuses (16 percent) for living abroad, monthly household and child allowances ($200 per month plus 2 percent of basic salary), free private school tuition for kids (up to $8,000 until age twenty-five), cash rewards for becoming a parent (at an annual per child rate of $5,000), and moving and settling-in costs. Medical coverage is generous, and pensions pay up to 70 percent of the final salary. It's a secure package that a senior executive of a multinational corporation might envy and that almost anyone would be reluctant to lose. This perhaps helps explain what is demurely referred to at the Commission as the "politeness conspiracy": friends don't snitch on friends. The wink-wink attitude runs from the top down. There exists, in the words of the Commission's former chief auditor, a "dominant monoculture that allows those responsible to bluff their way through the numbers."[18] This is hardly an ethic of *omertà*, but it does produce an environment that does not suffer whistle-blowers gladly.

Jacques Delors is responsible for many of the Commission's problems, but they have since gotten worse despite half-hearted attempts to correct them. Delors brought new money into the Commission but established neither the necessary control nor the compliance machinery needed for accountability. Payments for both the CAP and the regional funds pass through national disbursement agencies, which leave no records behind. How such transfers – 80 percent of the total EU budget – are made is hard to determine; why so much of them remain unspent and pile up in bank accounts is difficult to understand; the beneficiaries of the interest they bear are hard to find; and the legality of the expenditures in question is often murky. Foreign aid is a special problem. No one has yet been able to explain how the monthly payment earmarked for the Palestine Liberation Organization (PLO) somehow ended up in the hands of the Al-Aqsa Martyrs Brigade, which is on the EU's list of terrorist organizations.[19]

In 2003 only 10 percent of payments "faithfully reflect[ed] budgets and expenditures"; the remaining 90 percent of the $130 billion could not be accounted for. In 2002 more than $10 billion remained unspent. Estimates of graft run from 7 percent to 37 percent of the budget. The accounting firm of Deloitte, Touche managed to uncover $7 billion worth of fraud in the 1997 budget in a study done for a committee of the EP. The Commission's feeble anticorruption unit, "Olaf," which lacks enforcement machinery, uncovered 10,000 cases of larceny in 2002 – theft from the EU amounting to $1.5 billion. Little of this lost money is collectable. Only 17 percent of the $1.8 billion stolen by Italians from the CAP between 1971 and 2002 was ever recovered. By its own reckoning, Olaf collected less than 2 percent of the 5.34 billion euros it could account for as missing between 1999 and 2003. The actual amount of the unrecoverable money was suspected to be far greater.[20]

No one knows the full extent of graft and corruption in the EU because the community's accountants work with hands tied. For eleven consecutive years, the EU's Court of Auditors has refused to sign off on the Commission's books. Its experts cannot rely on modern accountancy systems for their audits but must rather cut through a "convoluted spaghetti" of words.[21] The Commission has, moreover, failed to provide proper balance sheets for over a decade. Until the necessary technical reform is completed by about 2009, third world standards will remain the rule in Brussels.

Olaf, the antifraud investigative body, is also a part of the accountability problem. Even though its staff had been doubled since 1999, the number of investigations taking over a year to settle has risen from 51 percent to 62 percent. Lacking official legal powers, it turns increasingly to snooping in order to dig up dirt and, according to critics, protect its turf. No less than three reports presented in July 2005 to an investigating committee of the EP complained that the "lack of direct judicial supervision" had given rise to serious abuses. One anonymous senior official griped that "we are always being tapped ... especially during periods of conflict. ... There is an eye [sic] to everything you write and say." Noting that "the legal situation was unclear as national laws did not apply on the territory of the European Commission," an Olaf spokesman admitted that "[the investigative body] had the power to check the content of e-mails, phone call records, and employees' hard drives without their permission." Condemning such "Vichyite" methods, the Tory MEP Chris Heaton-Harris noted in disgust that eavesdropping by the Commission security service could only have the effect of deterring potential whistle-blowers.[22]

Prodi could hardly take a pass on cleaning up the graft that had brought down the Santer Commission and swept him into office. He indeed declared a policy of "zero tolerance," created a special new agency for administration, and appointed the former Labour Party wheel-horse Niel Kinnock "Sleaze Commissar" to direct it. Unfortunately, Kinnock "did absolutely nothing to stem corruption. In fact fraud [soon] doubled." He did, however, "do his utmost to gag the officials who tried to blow the whistle on the crooks."[23] Not a single official resigned under suspicion of fraud during Kinnock's reign as anticorruption czar.

When chief accountant Marta Andreasen, an Argentine-born Spaniard, warned Kinnock and the rest of the Commission in May 2002 that the EU budget was "an open till waiting to be robbed," the antichiseling chieftain suspended and eventually sacked her for disloyalty – something virtually unheard of at the Brussels Eurocracy. Even after an internal audit had justified her allegations, Kinnock refused to reinstate her. Prodi stood by his man. Andreasen is still trying to get her job back. In July 2003, accountant Dougal Watt posted allegations of high-level corruption on his website; he was soon shocked to discover a pink slip on his desk even after a secret ballot of 205, or 40 percent, of his colleagues from the Court of Auditors supported his claims. His case remains on appeal.[24] Another Scot, Robert McCoy, was not fired but had to endure months of daily catcalls of "Gestapo," "Gestapiste,"

"Gestapista," and so on in several other languages from his erstwhile colleagues. Financial controller for a cost-ineffective and nearly impotent talk shop called the Committee of Regions (CoR), McCoy launched a three-year one-man campaign against grafters. His initial disillusionment resulted from the discovery that most of the 222 members of CoR, which held regional conferences six times a year at different places in the community, charged for first-class air travel without providing any documentation and sometimes even without attending meetings. The secretary-general of the ineffective body, one Falcone, actually rebuked him privately, as well as in an e-mail circular, for requesting spot checks for signatures on sign-in rosters. Separately, McCoy discovered that printing contracts, including one for about $500,000, had been placed without tenders. His attempt to void them was overruled. McCoy's complaints finally got action from the EP, which, within days, commissioned two separate internal audits. They substantiated his suspicions but concluded that no "substantial infringement" had occurred. The chiseling was apparently okay. The disillusioned McCoy soldiered on despite the daily harassment, resigned that "until there is a culture of doing and getting things right instead of a culture of 'What can I get away with?' this sort of thing will continue to happen."[25]

Dorte Schmidt-Brown, a Dane, was another unlucky whistle-blower. She got smeared by a contractor working for Eurostat, the EU's statistics wing, after reporting irregularities in his books, later suffered a nervous breakdown, and now receives lifetime disability. Kinnock refused to support her accusations of libel until, after years of rumors and finally the appearance of a muckraking article in a German glossy, Der Stern, by the journalist Hans-Martin Tillack, the scandal broke out in the open. Not even an extraordinary breach of press freedom could prevent this airing of dirty linen. The violation in question was a European Court of Justice (ECJ) ruling that the Belgian police were justified in raiding Tillack's home and seizing his notes on the grounds that they were based on documents belonging to the Commission![26]

Eurostat was too close to home to be overlooked. Founded with a staff of just seven, by 2003 it employed 700 officials and had an annual budget of $160 million. Eurostat was the source of the data used, for instance, to determine regional aid allocation and to enforce the EMU's stability and growth criteria – serious stuff. In 1996 Eurostat's director, Yves

Franchet, advised that the French government *could* legitimately transfer about $4 billion in pension transfers from France Telecom to itself in order to meet the crucial requirement that limited budget deficits to 3 percent of GDP; the amount made the difference. Eurostat had in fact been at the center of power for years, and Franchet, as he subsequently proved to an investigating committee, kept no less than three successive Commissions apprised of its activities and problems.[27]

Olaf investigated Eurostat no less than six times, uncovering in the process the existence of shell companies, slush funds, and rake-offs. The full extent of its malfeasance will probably never be known. One "cut out" at the center of the controversy, Planistat, received contracts worth over $60 million between the early 1990s and mid-2003, according to Pedro Solbes who as EU monetary commissioner during part of this period was deeply implicated in the scandal. Another shell company, CESD-Communautaire, received $32 million in contracts between 1995 and 2003, about $5 million of which disappeared. A third dummy, Eurogramme – as the unfortunate Dorte Schmidt-Brown discovered – had received $3.5 million in 1995 and 1996 in EU contracts, even though, contrary to its falsified books, it had had no turnover the previous two years. Eurostat often charged the Commission several times over for the same work and also billed it for data freely available on the Internet. Still another phony outfit, Eurocost – which like the rest of the implicated firms was directed by either Franchet or one of his associates – closed down on being investigated and refused to hand over the $900,000 salted away in a special bank account.[28] Where did all the money go?

The discovery by French investigators of a million-dollar slush fund in Luxembourg touched off the scandal in the first place. A subsequent report of an EP investigating committee uncovered evidence of lavish expenditure on travel, dinners, horseback riding, and (curiously!) volleyball, totaling another $6 million spent between 1996 and 2001. According to one of the then few Euro-critical MEPs, Jens-Peter Bonde, the problem was systemic: "This [was] not one crook, two crooks, or five, but a parallel system of financing" that continued until July 2003 when the whistle-blowing became earsplitting.[29]

The sleaze problem was indeed endemic. Even a Commission investigator admitted as much. "It appears," wrote the author in the usual contorted bureaucratese of Brussels, "that it was a relatively extensive practice at Eurostat to set up irregular reserves [known as 'financial envelopes'] through a number of contracts held with various specific contractors. According to the practice the value of contracts would have been artificially increased to allow the funding of other activities financed by the monies paid to the contractor." The report innocently added, "Some of these contracts seem to have been fictitious." Such practices began under Delors when the Commission, purportedly "groaning under a rapidly increasing workload that was often difficult to reconcile with budgetary constraints and the fine print of public accounting regulations," resorted to "creative financing."[30] While untruthfully denying that such double bookkeeping continued after 1999, once he had become antichiseling commissioner, Kinnock actually justified such fraudulence as "necessary to get the job done." Is there a more damning indictment of Commission methods?

The Eurostat scandal had no sequel. After enduring two months of intense media pressure, Prodi, who had been familiar with its questionable practices for years, stopped stonewalling, admitted that past abuses had existed, denied that either he or any of the three commissioners most deeply implicated – Kinnock, Solbes (monetary affairs), and Michaele Schreyer (budget) – knew about any improprieties until recently, and promised to undertake heroic measures of sleaze abatement. Prodi next let self-righteous EP committeemen blow off steam and then, in a closed-door session, got serious about pots calling kettles black. Neither big parliamentary faction was willing to press for another Santer-like resignation. There was indeed, according to the EU expert Thomas Rupp, a "kind of fraud which is tolerated because it is within the bounds of what is expected and therefore does not lead to any consequences."[31] The MEPs knew that while Eurostat had pushed the envelope, it still played by the rules of wink-wink. They indeed played by them too.

A Sad Situation

Two mighty towers of integrity stood proudly above the rest of the Commission, the directorates for competition and the internal market. These were places into and from which corruption did not seep.

They were also, as Carl Mortished of the *London Times* put it, "the only [ones] where the European Commission has any power to do [any] good." President Barroso placed them front and center in his official policy agenda, *Europe 2010: A Partnership for European Renewal*. Published in late January 2005, this document made no attempt to maintain a balance between economic expansion on the one hand and the preservation of the European social model on the other; the program "marked a clear break with the recent past, when environmental concerns and improving workers' rights were given the same priority as the need to govern growth."[32]

Over the next few months the Parliament would serve as a mouthpiece for the interests of Greens and Socialists as Barroso vainly tried to advance his probusiness program. It focused on two measures needed to complete the development of the half-finished internal market: the so-called Services Directive (SD) to improve labor mobility and the Financial Services Action Plan (FSAP) for a unified regulatory framework for the euro. Although Barroso admitted that little progress could be expected until the constitutional issue had been settled – which from the vantage point of January 2004 could well have meant never – his program was virtually dead on arrival.[33] From mid-2002 on, competition policy had met with a series of setbacks and reversals, which, at least in the near term, limited its development as a policy-making tool; worse, by January 2005 nearly every one of the ambitious initiatives from the internal market directorate had failed. The exception was the SD, soon to become notorious as the "Bolkestein directive," which – by purportedly opening the gates of Paris to a future invasion of Polish plumbers – provided the first big rallying point for the French *Non* campaign. The project has now been trashed beyond repair.

Competition policy – in many respects similar to US antitrust law – is at the core of the Rome treaty. Its purpose is to prevent the misuse of public and private power and to optimize the production and delivery of goods to the consumer. Rules to enforce fair play in the marketplace are essential to its proper operation; collusion between producers will take place in the absence of them. The competition directorate is the only branch of the Commission with real teeth – vested with investigative powers – and able (chiefly by moral suasion) to impose fines in order to enforce compliance. The Commission president, though not the Court, lacks the power to stand in way of such actions. Competition policy would be ineffective if those subject to it refused to accept the legitimacy of its verdicts. A high priority of the previous commissioner, Mario Monti, was therefore to strengthen national competition laws. His agency could also then concentrate on big cases, especially megamergers, while at the same time coordinating overall policy anchored in common principle yet tailored to local specifications. The future of competition law may depend on the strength of the national enforcement machinery.[34]

The EU competition directorate has suffered successive setbacks since mid-2002. Up to that point, Commissioner Monti, who built on the work of three powerful predecessors, could look back to a string of impressive breakups of cartels and mergers across a wide swath of industry. His streak culminated in July 2001 by ending the "corporate copulation" of two US giants, General Electric and Honeywell. The following year, three reversals of Commission dissolution orders by the ECJ brought an end to Monti's aggressive pursuit of colluding producers. He disbanded the Merger Task Force, hired a devil's advocate to vet for overactive prosecution, engaged a chief economist to strengthen casebooks, and slowed the pace of big operations such as the one against Microsoft for bundling its Media Player software with the Windows operating system. He also put up less resistance to political pressure.[35]

The impending bankruptcy of Alstom – French state champion, manufacturer of the famous high-speed train, and employer of 110,000 – in September 2003 was a turning point. Under intense pressure from President Chirac, Monti allowed the government a $2.5 billion bailout of the beleaguered giant with the stipulation that it replace the existing plan to inject cash into the company by stock purchases with a new one, which relied on the sale of government-backed convertible bonds. The change was a mere face-saving device. Member state bullying of the Commission would intensify over the following year, and state aid to ailing businesses would decrease only slightly, from $65 to about $63 billion and, over the three-year period from 2000–2003, from an average about 0.59, a two-tenths-of-a-point decline from the previous three years. The long-term reduction of state subsidies had ended. The French, Germans, and Italians (in that order) remained the most serious offenders. Today they account for over half of the payouts of state aid.[36]

It can no longer be ascertained whether Neelie Kroes, Barroso's candidate for competition commissioner, brought a handbag to her nomination hearings at the EP in October 2004 or, if so, what might have been stashed away inside it. She would have been well advised to carry Mace: the suspect Maggie-in-the-making got brutally mugged by an attack pack of angry Socialists. Was she not a capitalist tool? Her inquisitors were unimpressed that she had relinquished membership on company boards and placed her portfolio in a blind trust: She was rich and had earned her money in business! Unspeakable shame! Cover her with it! Neelie got nailed. The 63-year-old Iron Grandmother staggered but held her ground. The rough stuff was pointless. "Nickel Neelie" had already been neutered. She in fact stood under orders from Barroso to do nothing to threaten a French *Oui* in the constitutional referendum. Condemned to inaction, Kroes could only engage in third-order quack-quacking. In June 2005, she belatedly announced that state aid would indeed be the main target of future investigations.[37]

The internal market directorate has not only been weakened, it has been virtually put of business. This is a sad story of good intentions, high ambition, and poor judgment that proved in the end to be a monumental waste of time. The internal market directorate lacked the well-defined remit and established tradition of its counterpart for competition but held a general mandate to complete the construction of the still only partly built single market. The task facing it was less to enforce existing rules for the conduct of business than to make new ones. Discharge of this responsibility rested heavily on the person in charge, Frits Bolkestein of the Netherlands – a Commission titan.[38]

Seventy years old and with a background as an industrial executive (Royal Dutch Shell) as well as in Dutch politics (Liberal Party), Bolkestein had in abundance qualities bureaucrats often lack – vision, candor, and courage – as well as an overabundance of energy. Personally charming, he tackled his job ferociously and with considerable aplomb. He was among the first to warn the Commission that the EU was failing: the euro had not brought about price convergence, cross-border investment had dropped, and net capital export from Europe had risen. Policy, he insisted, had to focus on growth – stuck for years at less than 2 percent – and member states should be required to translate EU directives more promptly into national law. New initiatives were imperative above all: "a better regulatory framework [was] absolutely essential if [Europe's] companies are going to hold their ground in the face of global competition."[39] Frits Bolkestein lobbied tirelessly for long-range policies, such as pension and mortgage market reform, needed to restore competitiveness and also fought hard, though often unsuccessfully, for a wide range of important technical reforms. They included provisions for a single European patent (still under discussion), a new EU takeover law (a huge setback), a unified basic corporation tax (a nonstarter), unified accountancy standards (still alive), the parallel importation of pharmaceuticals (a success), the standardization of corporate reporting (still moving in the right direction), and the long-term spread of the mutual recognition principle (fate still unknown). Bolkestein also lobbied doggedly to make the "Lisbon Agenda" of 2000 the centerpiece of the Dutch and, later, Irish presidencies. He was, above all, the author of the most ambitious economic program since the Single European Act of 1986.

This was the Financial Services Action Program (FSAP). Its purpose was to create a single regulatory system for the EU. The adoption of the euro has had little impact on Europe's banking structure, which remains divided into national markets, is inefficient, and cannot keep pace with dynamic change in world trade and finance. This entrenched system retards growth but also prevents the euro from competing with the dollar in international markets. Bolkestein directed a massive campaign to turn the situation around. It involved the setup of no less than forty standing committees composed of experts and stakeholders tasked with finding solutions to a wide array of problems facing banking, finance, and insurance. Dealing with issues ranging from the mundane (the high cost of retail services) to the exotic (the regulation of new derivatives), they were directed to have programs in place and ready for adoption by January 2005. These committees worked intensely and, to all appearances constructively, up to the last minute. Then nothing happened.[40]

The City of London, which Bolkestein expected to support reforms from which it would be the chief beneficiary, dug in its feet. The Commission could do nothing about it. The merits or demerits of the FSAP need not be debated in order to explain the City's behavior. It was due, in a word, to asymmetry. As large as all other European financial markets combined, the City would have to bear disproportionate cost and risk for the introduction of any new system based on compromise, while having, at the same time, to compete with Wall Street. Its negative reaction was rational and should have been predicted. The City indeed complained incessantly about red tape, which had in recent years become the largest single drag on profitability. Bankers, brokers, and traders had to cope with a new set of regulations from the British financial services authority, faced unknown costs from the US Security and Exchange Commission sponsored Sarbanes-Oaxley (SOX) bill, and would have to adjust to the new requirements of the Basel II process. The City was in fact crushed by regulatory overload. Despite the flashing yellow lights, the FSAP ground inexorably forward to the very end of the Prodi Commission. Today, under Barroso, the FSAP has fallen beneath the radar screen. Bolkestein's successor as internal market commissioner, Charlie McCreevy, an Irish accountant, dropped the project with nary a word of explanation.[41]

The Services Directive (SD) – something of huge potential significance – turned out to be another dead loss. Compared to the FSAP, the SD was technically simple. It did not have to be thrashed out with representatives of concerned interests but required only a single enactment to enforce the "rule of origin," which eliminated restrictive national laws discriminating against job seekers from other parts of the EU. The SD, which concerned 70 percent of the economy in the services sector, would have done more to promote the single market than any measure since the Single European Act. The SD would have encouraged labor mobility, stimulated growth, increased professional opportunity, and given new meaning to the fourth and least respected fundamental freedom of the EU guaranteed by the Treaty of Rome – the right to live and work anywhere in the community. It would, of course, also have endangered livelihoods and threatened entrenched interests across the board.[42]

The SD was worth defending, even against unfavorable odds. Like the FSAP, the SD was expected to add a half point to GDP. A sweeping measure, such as the "Bolkestein directive," should not, however, have been slipped under the door: it would have affected too many lives in too many ways. The attempt to impose it without serious and protracted public discussion was a colossal misjudgment. Responsibility for the blunder must rest primarily with Barroso. In the same month in which he told Kroes to remain silent regarding state aids, he assigned high priority to enacting the SD. It would have been better, tactically, to sit still during the run-up to the referenda and deal properly with the matter later. The cat had, however, been let out of the bag – the SD was coming up for discussion in the EP. President Barroso only made things worse by vainly trying to defend the "Bolkestein directive" after the *Non* tide began to rise in March. Facing an angry French public and under intense pressure from a weakening Chirac, Barroso disowned what had been the main project on the Commission's agenda. A week later, a desperate Frits Bolkestein flew to Paris for a last-minute rescue of the SD, the *Oui* cause, and Jacques Chirac – and to defend his own good name after agitators and the gutter press managed to identify it with another "-stein," the crackpot Transylvanian medical doctor, whose infamous botched experiment took a singularly monstrous turn. Speaking meticulous French, Bolkestein bravely explained the purposes behind the directive to a mass television audience of critics – but with little effect. Public admiration of his evident good will and intellectual power neither turned the polls around nor stopped angry electrical workers from cutting off the current to his summer home in northern France. Bolkestein *did* manage to get his tarnished name off the front pages: the lowly Polish plumber soon replaced him as the symbol of France's woes.[43]

The liberal agenda of the Barroso Commission broke down even before the French and Dutch rejected the treaty. Opposition from the court and the member states had worn down the competition office. The grand plans of Frits Bolkestein were unpopular and unrealistic – and where he failed, no one else could have succeeded. The Lisbon Agenda had at least set sound priorities and crowded out the conflicting demands of the Reds and Greens, which were reduced to mere protesting. The EU had become both too weak and too inflexible to handle the vast tasks it set for itself. There will almost certainly be neither a sequel to the SEA nor another Jacques Delors at the Commission. As leadership from the center broke down, power within it devolved to one of the two big blocs of member states, a tight one headed by France and Germany and a large, looser, and more diversified one usually led by Great Britain. Until the double whammy of the two referenda, the Franco-Germans held the upper hand. How they used it bears close scrutiny: their misguided and even malign policy misdirected, weakened, and discredited the EU, antagonized the United States, inflicted damage in East Asia, and accomplished nothing in the process.

Empire by Stealth

The authority once exercised by the Commission under Jacques Delors but lost by Romano Prodi did not gravitate to the European Council, the other EU executive which was composed of heads of state and government. Since the Nice Summit, it has had little impact as a policy-making forum. The authority of its rotating president is limited and sometimes merely cloaks one of the two power blocs in the community, the Franco-German couple or the looser one generally headed by the United Kingdom. Although the Council can set priorities and influence outcomes informally from behind the scenes, it has had little impact on recent events. Consider the consecutive presidencies from mid-2003 to mid-2005. The Italian presidency, which featured Silvio Berlusconi's theatrics, cannot be held responsible for the breakup of the Brussels summit, where the treaty was supposed to have been concluded. The Irish presidency, generally thought a success because it revived the constitution, could not prevent the public rebuke given to the EU in the June 2004 elections for the EP. The Dutch presidency of the second semester got nowhere with its liberal agenda. The Luxembourg presidency of the first six months of 2005, a stand-in for the Franco-German duo, could not, finally, prevent the electoral repudiation of Gerhard Schröder in early May, the rejection of the treaty at the end of the month, or the humiliation of Jacques Chirac thereafter. The British presidency, which began in July 2005, would provide a unique opportunity to launch a reform campaign at a time when the EU faced upheaval and events were in flux – a chance to make a fresh start, collapse catastrophically, or drift away into insignificance.

Sitting in the driver's seat until recently, the French set the EU on a futile course of competition with the United States in 2004 and caused big trouble in Asia until mid-2005. The grandiose policy posed a potential long-term danger to democratic development in Europe and should provide warning of what can happen when political accountability is missing. After being humiliated at Nice, French President Jacques Chirac shunned the European Council and made a behind-the-scenes policy with Germany. Although Chirac hoped to preserve the "European social model" by strengthening national champions, his main concern was defense policy and, in particular, the projection of French power in Europe and European power in the world. Events have favored him. The 9/11 attacks and the war against (Islamic) terrorism provided an initial "beneficial crisis" (to use Brussels jargon) – a welcome opportunity to fill the heretofore empty "pillar two" (home affairs). Bush's War in Iraq presented an even more "beneficial crisis" – for Chirac, indeed a godsend. The French president's outspoken opposition to the unpopular venture had almost universal public appeal; in 2003 anti-Americanism would become the quasi-official European ideology.

Hostility to the United States provided excellent cover for pursuing, in a new guise, a traditional policy of the French political Right: Paris has managed, by projecting military power, to keep Germany in tow, Washington out of step, and Moscow, Tokyo, and even Beijing respectful of French status. Such foreign triumphs have confirmed and legitimized to the French nation its claim to European leadership. It's all make-believe, of course. The military power in question was not meant to be used in actual warfare but merely put on display. It was a stage setting in the politics of illusion, not necessarily something bad – only potentially dangerous. Illusion – claiming as verity something not known to be true – shades imperceptibly off into delusion – tricking others – and from there to self-delusion – tricking one's self, which in French farces often ends with cuckoldry. The pendulum swings back and forth between the three. The proposal for a European Defense Community (EDC) was a first notable effort to drape the exercise of national power in Euro-raiment. The French themselves killed EDC off in July 1954 after the fall of Diem Bien Phu. The second was the successive Fouchet Plans in the early 1960s, each of which featured French-dominated European supreme commands, but they got nowhere. The Cold War was too serious a theatre for such playground politics. Chirac would try for a third time to secure French military hegemony in Europe. The pendulum again began to swing.

France did not dismantle its nuclear capacity after the fall of communism, as did South Africa; nor were its missiles, like those of the United Kingdom, subject to a two-key control system with Washington, which deprived Britain of independence. Nor did France, like Russia and the United States, agree to a post–Cold War scale-down of nuclear weapons. Rather, the French proudly maintained three atomic submarines and began building a fourth. Also able to field about fifty aircraft armed with nuclear weapons, the French obviously intended to continue playing power-pool with the big kids. France has not, like Germany, cut back – but continues to increase – its military budget and remains the only real nuclear power in the EU. Chirac's ambitions did not, however, depend entirely on the existence of the standing French force. His intention was to expand and, in a manner of speaking, Europeanize it. The French Defense Minister Michèle Alliot-Marie has been a tireless advocate of this position. Her imagination is boundless. "At a time [after the constitutional referenda]," she intoned, "when a no in two countries raises questions, defense is a pole of stability and consensus, even among those who have said no." She added, astonishingly, that even though Europe spends half as much per capita as the United States for defense (1.5 percent of GDP), "we are currently at the same technological level as the United States – if we want to stay there we have to do a lot more. That is the price for being not just an economic power but a political power."[44]

In this scheme, France would retain ultimate control; its partners, Germany in particular, would supply the additional resources needed to modernize France's armed forces. Great Britain would be brought in as an outrider. Beginning with the St. Mâlo agreement of 1998, Prime Minister Blair would set Great Britain on an uncertain course of cooperation with the trans-Rhenanian couple by committing to the establishment of a multinational "European Rapid Reaction Force" (ERRF) and apparently agreeing to outfit U.K. elements with compatible equipment. This was nevertheless a small caliber development, which had little bearing on the larger strategic issue of the French bid for superpower status. It required an uncomfortable stretch but was not altogether undoable. What France wanted did not necessitate achieving strategic parity with the United States – the Soviet Union, after all, had never enjoyed it – but only making a threat credible enough to establish a blocking position.[45]

Technological breakthroughs put this dream theoretically within reach. Network-centric warfare holds the key to Chirac's ambitious grasp for geopolitical influence. According to one breathless description, the new strategy has led to a "growing conviction that the art of warfare faces as dramatic a change as that which consigned the horse, lance, and saber to the dustbin of history."[46] In Afghanistan and later in Iraq, the United States demonstrated that intelligence supplied by the Global Positioning System (GPS) enabled a handful of US troops to overwhelm a much larger enemy in astonishingly little time. The GPS leveraged effective military power like few other breakthroughs in military history. The French decided that Europe should build one: Galileo was born. This was, however, not the only military project afoot at the EU; indeed, it was part of a larger long-term one for outer space. The recently rejected constitution designated space as a new European competence. Under the general rubric of research and development, the EU plans to commit substantial funds to rocketry in the budget for 2007–2013. That both these related projects are officially described as being civilian in character could fool only fundamentalist believers in the Easter Bunny.[47]

There's not a snowball's chance in hell that the tax-strapped European public will accept a doubling of defense budgets so that in a decade or two, *Europe hyperpuissance* can stand toe to toe and nose to nose with the bully from across the street. The main threat posed by programs like Galileo is not strategic in character, but political – and it is not to the United States but to Europe itself. The pursuit of the superpower chimera could prove ruinously expensive, but that is the least of its dangers. It is reckless and irresponsible to build up a European security state in the absence of strong democratic institutions: the end result of such *folie de grandeur* would, if successful, be military dictatorship. The proposed European constitution would not have remedied this deficit in responsible government but significantly widened it.

Any policy governed by fear of US superpower domination is also wildly off the mark geopolitically. The unipolar world, which France and Europe dread, is rapidly disappearing. China is already an economic *hyperpuissance* and is planning to become a military one by 2015.

Arming it, as France and a compliant Germany apparently intended and might still intend to do, is seriously destabilizing and viewed, quite appropriately, with alarm in Washington.[48] Real European security cannot, in any case, be located in outer space or found by waging brushfire wars against failed states à la St. Mâlo. It depends on creating stable democracies on the EU's borders.

Troubling Waters

A man sits at a desk in a Brussels building. He shares office space with seventy others, some of them with lengthy titles. These individuals neither make nor sell anything. They buy very little. They command nobody. Although much is written about them, their files are mostly empty. Even though their jobs put them at the fulcrum of world geopolitics, they do not even officially exist. The man's name is Nick Witney. He heads the European Defense Agency. The men around him comprise his general staff. No theory of integration or history of politics sheds much light on how all of this came to be. A true fable may make things easier. In 1859, a man on a San Francisco street corner declared himself Norton I, Emperor of the United States and Mexico. He had no army, no followers, and not even a place to sleep. He was in fact a bankrupt rice merchant, but no one really cared about that. Norton found a gaudy uniform and put it on. He printed money, and people saved it. He defied Congress, proposed building a bridge over the Golden Gate, and even founded a new religion. Norton had standing seats at the opera. He ate in the best restaurants for free. When his dog, "Bummer," died, hundreds mourned. When Norton himself died, tens of thousands mourned.

Emperor Norton caused no real harm. The same is not true of the obscure men in Brussels with the big pretensions: the policy they represent could have inflicted real damage had the proposed constitution not been rejected – and might still do so unless their operation is either terminated or brought under some form of public supervision and control. The crisis in East Asia triggered by the new security policy may also have lasting repercussions. Unlike the comic Norton's empty claims, policy made in the name of Europe is backed by force. It is not, however, accompanied by responsibility. Unless Europe places limits to its ambitions, comes to a better understanding of its real needs, and recognizes the extent of its actual powers, it will create big problems for itself in the future. Its credibility will be shot altogether.

The force referred to earlier is French. Decisions regarding the use of this power will not be made in Brussels, Strasbourg, Luxembourg City, or any other European capital except Paris. Such matters are therefore subject to the vagaries of French politics and the cupidity of the current French head of state. That puts Europe at risk. The shadowy figures behind the mysterious desks in Brussels pose an even more deep-seated threat: How can Europeans – unable to hold even civilian Eurocrats accountable – control a future EU military establishment shielded by secrecy laws and supported by a multinational defense industry exempt from competition and disclosure rules?

The United States – the target of Chirac's wild shots – continues to hope that reinforcing and bulking up the hollow vertical tube of the Common Security and Foreign Policy (CSFP) will enable the EU to carry part of the peacekeeping burden in the European theatre. It also specifically endorsed the creation of an independent European rapid deployment force to implement this responsibility, because the growing disparity between US and European military proficiency would otherwise put American lives unnecessarily at risk in joint operations. Until recently, the Pentagon had no fear whatsoever of creating a European competitor, because the EU does not pose a credible threat to US security. The United States has long spent over twice as much per capita on defense as the EU, has a big single market for military hardware rather than many little ones, enjoys a virtually unsurpassable lead in high-tech weaponry, and plunges five times more money into advanced defense research than all the EU countries put together. Americans, unlike Europeans, approve of a strong defense policy and are prepared to pay for one in the future; it is a bipartisan matter.[49]

Europe's new security policy originated in an intra-European struggle rather than that between Europe and the United States. Its development can only be understood as part of a political strategy for containing Blair and the Brits. The policy is irrelevant to the current world conflicts and meaningless in military terms; it is, like Norton's empire, imaginary. Witney has announced plans "to boost Europe's defense, technological, and industrial base" by developing "unmanned drones, new armored vehicles, and advanced communications systems in a strategy to become a military superpower and close the defense technology gap with the United States."⁵⁰ At this stage, however, the striking power of the 60,000-man ERRF being prepared since 1999 to intervene in far corners of the world consists of a thirty-man planning staff in Tervuren outside of Brussels and a French army headquarters building under renovation in Lille. Europe is pursuing the politics of delusion.

The Nice Summit of December 2000 provides the background to the new emphasis on security policy. After the debacle, according to Thomas Pedersen, a series of intimate but informal monthly Franco-German meetings began to "strengthen cooperation."⁵¹ Starting out with agreement on the general shape of the proposed constitution, these talks produced unity on several divisive old issues and some important new ones. Set up in order to prepare common positions for forthcoming European Council meetings, they were a huge coup for France. Germany would move steadily toward French positions on both the CAP and Enlargement. The spring elections of 2002 in France resulted in the elimination of the Socialists in the first round and produced a thumping victory for Chirac over his septuagenarian challenger, the ultra-right wing Jean-Marie Le Pen, in the second. This victory was somewhat deceptive. Many wore clothespins on their noses at the polls. Others cried when voting for Chirac as the lesser evil. The outcome of the election, nonetheless, substantially strengthened the French president's negotiating hand. Unable at the Schwerin meeting of July 2002 to agree on CAP policy, which Schröder wanted desperately to reform, one of Chirac's guests – the obliging Belgian Prime Minister Guy Verhofstadt – proposed raising the organization of a European defense force to a top community priority as a way to break the ice. The French president seized the chance. The joint commitment to the new security policy would provide the adhesive for the trans-Rhenanian relationship.

A couple of important considerations spoke in favor of the policy. The French and Germans were partners in the aerospace field and jointly controlled the European Aeronautic Defense and Space Company (EADS), the manufacturer of the Airbus. The conglomerate faced big problems. Most European nations, including Germany, were slashing military budgets. EADS had been frozen out of the only important growing market for its products, the United States. It could not merge with BAE, the remaining big British aerospace firm, because BAE would not give up its privileged position on the US market and would probably soon be swallowed by one of the three big surviving American goliaths, in any case. EADS needed new business.[52]

A larger consideration was also in play. Schröder demonstrated in September that anti-Americanism could even win elections in Germany. The untapped appeal of the demagogic approach proved to be immense, especially with the United States mired in a foreign war. If Vietnam had given a foretaste of this reality, Iraq would provide enough to sate any glutton – a twelve-course meal with seconds readily available. Europe's politicians could prepare and serve up unlimited amounts of the sumptuous fare, if only President Bush, the reckless cowboy, could be provoked into supplying enough food. Proving exceptionally maladroit, Bush played the black-hat role to the hilt. The object of the Franco-German ploy, Tony Blair, would, it was hoped, have to either drop the "special relationship" with Washington or pay a heavy price for it in Europe. The European Commission housed, and is supposed to implement, the couple's new policy. The choice of location was a matter of convenience as well as ideology. What took place there could be kept out of view until sprung upon the public in the name of Europe.[53]

As so often, the United States provided a model for policy making. The United States had pioneered in the promotion and exploitation of a civilian space program for military purposes; this was the job of the National Aeronautical and Space Administration (NASA). The GPS put up in 1996 was only one venture to grow out of this civil-military collaboration. The GPS made terrestrial targets visible anywhere in the world, even at night and in bad weather. The system could thus provide instantaneous intelligence on troop dispositions, both friendly and hostile. Battlefield coordination took a quantum leap: commanders could now adjust to troop movements on both sides, and deployment could take place with unprecedented speed and efficiency. Otherwise costly and protracted military actions could be settled within a few days. A new kind of gunboat diplomacy had become possible but only if the United States could dominate space – from which weapons could be fired as well as guided. In 1996 President Bill Clinton declared the US domination of space a top national priority. US Air Force Space Warriors are wont to speak in awe of the realm as a "final frontier," which must be defended at all costs.

"Counterspace" weapons for threat elimination are a given of this strategy. Three such portable systems – involving microsatellites so small that "ten can be loaded in a reusable military orbiter" and built at an astonishingly cheap price of $5.2 million per unit from off-the-shelf components – are already up and running. The United States can, in other words, physically destroy or temporarily disable any deployable GPS-like system with electronic weapons costing mere tens of millions of dollars – chicken feed in space weaponry terms. After heated US protests that Galileo could interfere with US military operations, the EU agreed to shift prospective bandwidths in order to make interference with the GPS more difficult; if, however, such an event should occur and the United States found it necessary to take action, the EU also assented to accepting as legitimate what would amount to the chemical castration of Galileo. The concession ruled out any use of the system in future military confrontations with the United States. Galileo, if ever built, will be militarily worthless.[54]

Economically, the same thing is also true. In 1999 President Clinton opened the ample nonsecurity capacities of the US GPS system – a sunken cost – free of charge to civilian end users. There is, in other words, no commercial point to building a second system at present. Claims for the economic benefits of the Galileo program – that it will create 150,000 new high-tech jobs in a new industry, which by 2010 will produce 10 percent of GDP – seem wildly exaggerated. The real purpose behind the project is strategic. A confidential letter of February 2002 rejecting a US offer of help in building a second system fully compatible with the existing one said as much. It frankly admitted: "Galileo will give the EU a military capability."[55]

This was officially denied until 2005. The program itself was wrapped in a bafflegab calculated to confuse the public. It would protect endangered species, help locate lost children, enable nice little old grandmothers to drive safely home on rainy days, and so forth. Policy making now takes place on obscure ad hoc boards and committees housed in the innocuous transportation directorate run by Jacques Barrot, a former Chirac bagman once busted for violating campaign finance laws. German-led Socialists in the EP, overlooking his conviction for embezzlement, voted him into office. Barrot would be right at home in his new position. The Frenchman answers informally to Günter

Verheugen, the German Commission Vice President for Economic Affairs. Funding is now routed through the budget for Trans-European Networks ("TENs"), something set up innocuously to improve railroads and highways, as well as via the framework programs for research and development.[56]

It is impossible to get to the bottom of the control issue – to know who or what will be in charge of the future Galileo system. The unknown consequences stemming from the two constitutional referenda cloud the picture still further. A consortium dominated by the French and led by EADS, Alcatel, and Thales has now been designated the prime contractor. The Germans feel cheated, however, and squabbling continues. The project still must be approved by the Council. Scheduled for completion in 2010, Galileo may literally not get off the ground unless the EU gets its budgetary act together.[57]

Philippe Busquin, though now out of office, was the lead man for most of Galileo's life. In early 2003 the tireless Belgian bureaucratic entrepreneur conducted four months of "consultation" (discussion rounds for interested parties) to build a constituency for his program; struck a partnership with the European Space Agency (ESA), which disposed of the expertise the Commission lacked (in return for the political clout that the European Space Agency mistakenly assumed it to possess); and lobbied successfully for priority in EU policy making. By October 2003 he had broadened his mandate to include not only the heavens but a portion of the earth as well. Europe, he declaimed, "was paying a very high price for artificial and uniquely European [sic] separation between civil and military research." He demanded the creation of a new "security culture" in which, he expansively explained, "we should be able to foster co-operation between the traditionally distinct sectors of civil and security research by focusing on how to best ensure the security of citizens in an enlarging European Union and a globalizing world."

A white paper of November set out the requirements. They included, first of all, budgets from 5.4 billion euros in 2007 to 7.7 billion euros in 2113. Such funding, indeed the project itself, according to the paper, could skip authorization from an Intergovernmental Conference (IGC) of the European Council: "The need is to act now to create the key components of a European space policy, even if space is not included in the Treaty as a European policy." The lack of statutory legitimacy for such a program is a trifling matter, the garbled document proceeds, because "a number of legal bases can already be invoked which enable existing EU politics to call upon space as a relevant technology to support their implementation."[58] This was mission creep with a vengeance.

Although Busquin felt confident that Franco-German support could make up for the lack of an official mandate, he did face a short-run money problem; indeed he would have no funds until appropriations for the budget cycle for 2007–2013 had been agreed upon. To get cash flowing in the meantime, China, India, and other prospective Galileo partners would have to pay upfront. Bringing them into the project has set the EU on a parlous course. Although not yet worried about *Europe hyperpuissance*, the Pentagon gets grey hairs about China's expanding military budget – officially rated at 20 percent per year but probably twice as rapid. Access to the military "side" of Galileo could eventually enable the emerging Asian superpower to impair or disable the GPS system in the event of war, for instance over Taiwan, thereby risking American lives. The Joint Chiefs of Staff view the threat facing the US Navy – whose mission was to interpose itself between the two belligerents to stop an invasion – as especially grave. Chinese missiles now have enough range, moreover, to reach the American West Coast, which causes sleep loss in California suburbs.[59]

The architects of the Galileo policy view the spy satellite as a first step toward a strategic partnership, a global alliance with China formed to check what is still anachronistically referred to as "the world's only remaining superpower." Joint Sino-French naval exercises in March 2004 ("for Beijing...the most sophisticated ever with a foreign navy") marked the beginning of a distinctly new course. While visiting Hu Jintao to clinch a $12 billion arms deal for France in October, Chirac spoke often and quite openly about the need for China and Europe to work as a counterweight to the United States and "to build together the multipolar world which is in the process of being designed for tomorrow."[60] He also committed himself to lifting the arms embargo imposed after the Tiananmen massacre in 1989. The vice prime minister of China pledged in return to "continue to advance the...Sino-European comprehensive strategic partnership." This was serious business.

France had, to be sure, long cheated on the export ban – and is known, for instance, to have supplied China with silent propulsion systems for submarines and critical components for missile guidance. Ending the embargo would, however, amount to throwing open the floodgates to a flow of the high-tech weaponry China needed to modernize its armed forces – until, that is, it started copying it. French Defense Minister Michèle Alliot-Marie's flimsy excuse for the deal – that if the Chinese were supplied with this stuff, they would not have to produce it – met deservedly with loud guffaws. Marianne could turn this particular trick only once. Her pimp should have told her as much. But could Chirac speak for Europe?

"The world," reported the excited commentator Martin Walker, "has just dodged a bullet. A majority of the 25 members of the European Union agreed Monday [11 October] to ignore the urgings of the French and Germans and maintain the arms embargo against China. Had they not done so, the trans-Atlantic row between Europe and America would have become very serious indeed."[61] Lifting the arms embargo was not yet, however, a dead issue. The ludicrous Luxembourger, Jean-Claude Juncker, held the chair of the rotating president of the European Council for the first half of 2005. Savoring every unaccustomed moment in the international diplomatic limelight and happy when cuddling with Jacques Chirac, he pressed relentlessly for reconsideration of the embargo. The effort emboldened the Chinese, who – mistaking words for deeds – overplayed their hand on the Taiwan question. The embargo still stands.[62] This strange sequence of events requires a bit of explanation.

In East Asia, the EU fished in troubled waters. The sudden yet relentless rise of China, and the growing economic dependence of both Korea and Japan on its expanding markets, is shaking up the distribution of power in the region almost overnight, reviving ancient enmities, changing long-standing policies, and resulting in significant realignments. After an intense behind-the-scenes struggle in September 2004 ended with Chairman Hu Jintao in full control of the Chinese armed forces, a shift in policy ensued with far-reaching ramifications. It was manifest in a new aggressiveness toward Taiwan and Japan – to wit, the increased number of "incidents" involving the latter. They include violation of the waters around Okinawa in late November by an "unknown submarine," which prompted the first ever deployment of the post-1945 Japanese Navy against a hostile ship and resulted in a two-day chase; the (organized) anti-Japanese demonstrations of March and April 2005; the officially tolerated misbehavior at the Asian Games; the demands for more and more apologies, and so forth.[63]

Japan is now quietly but decisively breaking with the fifty-year-old "Yoshida doctrine" limiting military strategy to national defense, helping build and joining the new US "star wars" antiballistic shield and entering into mutual security arrangements with interlocking ground, air, and naval forces at an "unprecedented level of interoperabilily and intimacy." "This is," adds British foreign policy expert Lord David Howell, "going hand in hand with an extensive command and control makeover, adding up to a force structure second only to that of the Americans."[64] The new arrangements are calculated to strengthen Japan and draw the United States more deeply into the defense of the island nation.

The realignment of Japan and the United States in 2004–2005 may be less consequential for the EU's ambitions in East Asia, however, than the change in Taiwan's situation. Miscalculation played a large role in bringing it about. Expecting the victory of Lee Teng-hui, the leader of the pro-independence Taiwanese political party, in the December presidential election, the Chinese parliament rubber-stamped a brutal antisecession bill. It amounted to an ultimatum that invasion would result from any attempt to declare Taiwan's independence from China. A frightened Teng-hui quickly backed off, thereupon alienating the most fiercely pro-independence faction of his party. It cost him the election. The opposition party dominated by Mainland Chinese, the successor to the old Kuomintang (KMT), instead took office. Like its ancient communist enemy, it held fast to a "one China" policy, although there remained disagreement, of course, about which of the two should run China. The KMT victory nevertheless deferred the independence crisis.[65]

Events then took an unexpected – though historically not unprecedented – twist: a Beijing-staged reconciliation of the KMT and the Chinese government took place, which will probably serve as a prelude to an eventual relationship between the mainland and Taiwan like the one existing between China and Hong Kong. In other words, Taiwan will eventually become part of China. In East Asia, the implications of the secession bill crisis are not yet played out. In Europe, however, they are. Chinese aggressiveness shocked the European Council into belated recognition that the Franco-German plaything – the dilettantish new security policy meant to trip up the Colossus – could wreak severe collateral damage on innocent parties. The ultimatum to Taiwan killed the attempt to lift the arms embargo. It did not, however, chasten China. The state-controlled Galileo Industries (CGI) intends to gain full operational control of the surveillance system in the East Asia region by 2008, including targeting information for its new cruise missiles.[66]

Although shorn from the grand strategy it was supposed to serve, Galileo has survived, thanks partly to the appointment of the veteran EU Commissioner Karel van Miert as "mediator" of the increasingly bitter disagreements between the idled Franco-German experts assembled to build the future but unbudgeted space spy network. Militarily useless, commercially purposeless, and economically questionable at the least, yet seriously destabilizing, Galileo is merely the most recent European *grand project* to substitute for sound policy – a fitting companion to the unsafe Concorde and the oversized Airbus 380. Although provision would normally be made for it in the budget for 2007–2013, the necessary money can also be raised by means of a special treaty outside the EU framework. Born in the shades of policy making, the program may yet – along with the embryonic defense ministry, the European diplomatic corps now under construction, the proposed institute for gender studies, the nascent public prosecutors office, and the headquarters for the judicial training network – linger in a grey zone of public unaccountability with a host of other unauthorized and publicly unknown projects, which have developed at the interstices of EU institutions.[67]

On December 27 the first of a proposed 30 Galileo satellites was launched on a Soyuz rocket from the Cosmodrome in Kazakhstan. If all continues to go well, the system will be up and running by 2010.[68] For all of their lack of realism, the EU's high-tech projects are still alive and may even eventually see the light of day. More remains of them than the now defunct proposed constitution, the nonstarting agendas of Commissioners Prodi and Barroso, or the important recent Commission economic initiatives spearheaded by Frits Bolkestein's internal market directorate but now in tatters. The futile military and faltering civil programs all, nevertheless, have one thing in common: they were designed within the framework of institutions out of touch with their constituents. Unless this changes, the EU will become an appendix on the body politic.

A Dysfunctional Family

The development of the EU followed no master plan: it is the misshapen product of policy entrepreneurship, institutional inertia, interstate bargaining, and backroom deals. Why bother discussing the EU as if it were a government? It has no real parliament but only a legislature, which operates by means of convoluted procedures regulated by different sets of rules, depending on the issue. It has no single executive authority but two bodies aspiring to such a role – the Commission and the European Council – each outfitted with different sets of crisscrossing powers. It also houses the European Court of Justice, which can compel enforcement of its rulings at lower levels but refuses to set limits to its own power, lacks a democratic mandate, and cannot ultimately legitimize its rulings; the EU does not rest, in other words, on a firm legal foundation. Though treaty-based, the EU is not, furthermore, treaty-regulated. This is in fact the chief argument marshaled by proponents of the proposed constitution, or "constitutional treaty," as it more appropriately termed. No description of the EU would be complete, finally, that overlooks the vast amount of unofficial, and often invisible, policy making taking place at the interface of the public and private sectors.

It is off the wall to speak of a "separation of powers" as the guiding principle of the EU: the very thought of such a thing would make James Madison spin in his grave. A misshapen outgrowth of a process gone awry and a snare of confused but conflicting legislative, executive, and regulatory jurisdictions, the EU is a sui generis entity neither answerable to nor controllable by anyone or anything. There is no effective appeal from it to a higher court, parliament, or executive authority. No legal or constitutional mechanism exists for orderly reform; it never has been, and cannot yet be, constitutionally or administratively stripped of powers and responsibilities – unless the member states, acting jointly, should decide to undo the whole arrangement. Although shortages of money limit the EU's growth, the referendum is – short of outright rebellion – the only recourse for restraining its abuses of power. Reform will entail redesigning, reconstructing, and perhaps even recreating a functional new mechanism mandated by the public.[69]

The EU is also unlike any national government because it does not deliver services. The EU is unequipped to defend borders; keep public order; run hospitals or other civic institutions; maintain roads, rails, and waterways; and care for the aged or bury the dead. It does, however, dispose of two levers of power, one long and the other short, rule making and wealth redistribution. Since the EU is undemocratic and unrepresentative, policy making from Brussels can be justified on a cost-benefit basis only if it can produce otherwise unobtainable positive results. This is an unlikely, but still possible, outcome. The EU has the wrong priorities, executes poorly, claims responsibilities that could be better discharged at lower (or higher) levels of authority, and is wasteful. If there is "more to Europe" than can be captured in a weighing of plusses and minuses, the value added must be measured not only in narrow economic terms but, more broadly, in the less tangible form of moral payoffs. There is no guidebook for making such determinations. They are an individual matter, which can only be expressed collectively through the orderly processes of representative government. Such rewards would nevertheless have to be considerable to offset the high costs Brussels inflicts on the public. Such payoffs may exist but to find them will require rethinking the significance of the European integration project.

Transfer payments are the short lever of EU power. The Common Agricultural Policy is the biggest of them. It is the EU's original sin – which, by definition, it can neither escape nor outgrow. The crop support program has the first claim on EU revenues. If today it comprises about 40 percent of the total budget, for most of the more than forty years of its operation, it consumed about three quarters of it. Whereas the heavy economic costs of this monumental boondoggle have been the subject of an enormous literature, the political ones are less well known. They, too, are vast. The CAP privileges a small and shrinking group of constituents – wealthy land-owning foodstuffs producers – half of whom are French. The magnitude of the payments requires that – like it or not – no French government relinquish them without compensation, which would require treaty revision. The conclusion is inescapable that to break the present budgetary impasse, the EU will almost certainly have to be refounded.[70]

Serious progress toward CAP reform happened only once, under Jacques Delors. Thanks in part to huge one-time infusion of new German money, he created the program of regional funding – the second great transfer program. As intended, it created another powerful entrenched interest in the EU, the then recently admitted "Club Med" nations. The two big hand-out schemes, which together consume three-quarters of the EU budget, have warped the development of the Brussels institutions. The understandable reluctance of "net contributor" members to increase the modest community budget has, contrary to public impressions, led over the past decade to its shrinkage as a percentage to about 1 percent of GDP, or about a trillion euros, and ipso facto increased the importance of the longer of the two levers of EU power, the rule-making function.[71]

The privileged position of the CAP has also hindered the development of the EP as a legislative body. The EP has no authority whatsoever over the CAP portion of the EU budget. By re-jiggering EU rules in 1988 to deprive it of effective control over the rest of the budget, Commission President Jacques Delors eliminated the remaining chance that the EP might someday exercise the power of the purse, without which no legislative body can develop the authority needed to govern. Delors' move involved the introduction of the seven-year budgetary cycle ("economic perspectives"), which rested on Commission inputs and was negotiated (in closed session) within the European Council. The new method locked the EU into rigid medium-term planning, which – apart from being incredibly inefficient and wasteful – marginalizes legislative policy making. The subsequent so-called codetermination procedure loosened the straitjacket only slightly. The procedure allows MEPs to influence particular pieces of legislation, but not to draft them, set priorities, or shape agendas. Finally, the EP has no authority whatsoever over member state monetary and fiscal policy. (It rests with the European Central Bank.) The EP is, in fact, condemned to remain a 732-delegate talk shop.[72]

The only escape from this "irrelevance trap" is demagogy. The EP's only real full-time job (apart from protecting its perks) is to create constituencies for itself. This often interferes with sound policy making. Empty rhetoric, two well-known economists argue, can amount to more than meaningless words and indeed "can become justification for heavy and misplaced interventionist governments, [which] can mislead the public debate, generate unreasonable [public] expectations, [and] thus create obstacles for well-intentioned policy-makers facing tough choices."[73]

One bugbear the EP faces, according to David Bailey of the London School of Economics, is due to the failure of social democracy at the national level. Bailey explains that in the 1970s, leftist parties throughout Europe in everything but name abandoned polices of state ownership and central direction of the economy in favor of more effective promarket alternatives. At the same time, however, they also backed away from EU-hostile or neutral ideological positions and became, like Jacques Delors, champions of reviving socialism at the European level. The position is absurd. Politicians cannot deliver on such a policy for several compelling reasons: there is no European *demos* to provide solidarity; "negative" integration nearly always trumps "positive"; EU law has an in-built promarket bias, which erodes social protectionism nationally; and European institutions have too many veto points. Welfare states are, moreover, too expensive to maintain, let alone expand, and vary widely in structure and coverage. Finally, citizens of well-administered national benefits systems refuse to share them by merging with weak-sister outsiders. Bailey notes in concluding that welfare regimes have usually arisen in centralized systems, not in intrinsically more market-competitive federal ones, the only exception being authoritarian states such as Bismarck's Reich.[74]

Workable "bypass mechanisms" are, furthermore, rare; the trap really is iron. Things could only have been different, according to Fritz Scharpf, if in the original negotiations for the Treaty of Rome, which created the modern EU, the French had managed to "harmonize" wages and benefits. Instead, they put their weight behind the CAP. The EU is, to put the matter bluntly, a dead end for social democracy. The only choice open to their representatives in the EP is therefore, according to Bailey, obfuscation. It entails insisting upon the reality of a viable "European social model" and upholding the pretense that the EP is, in fact, a parliament.[75]

It is a myth, according to the Conservative MEP Daniel Hannan, "that we MEPs fiddle our expenses. We don't need to. All our allowances are handed over unconditionally without any need for invoices or receipts. There is, as it were, nothing to fiddle."[76] The "champagne and gravy train" that stops at the EP is as bounteous as the one waiting in front of the Commission. Benefits at the EP are normally greater than salaries, taxed at a flat low rate, and include tax-free daily attendance bonuses of about $300 per day even for nonattendance at meetings. Monthly staff allowances of $18,000 are often used to employ wives, mistresses, or boyfriends, and another $4,500 streams in to cover undocumented "general expenses." All efforts to link remuneration to actual expenditures were voted down until June 2005, when a new "Statute for MEPs" was tabled. It levels annual salaries at about $100,000 – reducing theoretical disparities between Italy (about $15,000 per month) and Hungary (about $1,000 per month). They will only take effect, however, after the next Euro election in 2009, and governments (read France and Italy) will be able to opt out, allowing reelected MEPs to maintain previous salaries. Reimbursement of travel expenses will in the future require receipts.

The June 2004 elections for the EP supplied proof, if any were really needed, of the low esteem in which the public holds its elected governments, the EU, and the EP itself. Turnout was at a record low, less than 50 percent Europe-wide and less than 30 percent in the accession countries of the East, which were voting for the first time. The high abstention rate signified disgust rather than neutrality. Across the board, publics repudiated governments of every stripe, all of which were committed to ratifying the proposed constitution. Where the Left held office, the Right gained votes – and vice versa. The popularity of Chirac's Neogaullists, Schröder's Social Democrats, and Berlusconi's Forza movement all plummeted to new depths. Spain's Socialists also took a licking. British voters turned on the Tories and the Labour government alike – and tripled the representation of the radically Euro-hostile United Kingdom Independence Party (UKIP). In Scandinavia and the Netherlands, new single-issue clean government parties walked away with more than 10 percent of the vote. In eastern Europe, populist and free-market parties of the Right emerged in several countries as the largest bloc of voters. Only in Greece and Portugal did electorates, for special reasons, support the parties in power: Greece had the Olympics, and Portugal the Commission.[77]

Nuanced interpretations of the results are unnecessary. In a staged and (by all the major parties) uncontested plebiscite on Europe – one structured to demonstrate symbolic support for the constitutional project – the public had failed to deliver as expected. Official explanations blamed the results on insufficient information and a weak defense on the part of national politicians against "Brussels Bashing." Incredibly, Pat Cox, speaker of the EP, hailed the results a "great success" and proof that 90 percent of the electorate had given a "green light to the constitution." Wiser heads, like the Oxford don Vernon Bogdanor, feared that "Europe is giving rise to that most dangerous of cleavages – between the political class and the people."[78] The proposed constitution was indeed turning the British itch of Euroskepticism into an eczema raging across the EU body politic. The more the public learned of Brussels, the less it liked of what it heard.

How would the public have reacted if fully aware of the importance of lobbying in "Europe's capital city"? Most of the real action in Brussels takes place in the gray area of public-private interplay. The elitist Commission is a body of "experts" only in a restricted sense. It consists chiefly of political-economist, lawyer-managers – technocrats – who make policy (in the form of administrative law and regulations) but lack the specialized knowledge of practitioners familiar with the issues actually dealt with. For this practical expertise, Eurocrats depend on outsiders as contractors and consultants. Lobbyists enter the picture at this point – as purveyors of information not otherwise available. Since most of the issues Brussels has traditionally dealt with are economic in character, business and finance are the source of the necessary know-how. Its providers are firms, associations, think tanks, professional and other types of consultants, and public relations experts – not to mention less formal, interest-based ad hoc organizations combining such elements. Official Brussels creates twice as many jobs indirectly for lobbyists than it does directly by putting officials on the payrolls of the Commission; the economic stakes are, indeed, very large. They turn less on the size of the EU budget than the exercise of its rule-making power. A directive or regulation can change competitive conditions across Europe, rewarding some interests and punishing others, enriching well-positioned "players," and jamming up less-privileged outsiders against the wall.[79]

The word *corporatism* no longer adequately describes the relationship between big business and the Brussels institution. Over the past decade, so-called nongovernmental organizations (NGOs) representing the interests of consumers, the environment, and a variety of other good causes have challenged the power of the sectoral and umbrella associations of organized business. The NGOs lobby Brussels but also play constituency politics; they reach the public directly rather than, like business organizations, through national governments. The relationship between business lobbying and advocacy groups is issue specific and almost always complicated. The NGOs have outposts in the environment directorate and the EP, especially among Greens. Action in such forums tends to be highly verbal. Producers, according to a leading expert on EU lobbying, have more staying power: they control 70 percent of the total sum spent to influence legislation and dispose of the expertise needed to maintain long-standing relationships with all the relevant directorates. They can, thus, frequently "water down" directives or regulations detrimental to their interests.[80]

Success at Brussels lobbying is less often a matter of profit making than of loss containing. The game is not, however, zero sum: the benefits of legislation weakened downstream by business lobbies often disappoint their NGO advocates. It remains to be seen whether better "policy learning" will eventually reverse these negative outcomes. In the meantime, they raise the volume of rhetoric on one side and fuel the level of frustration on the other. The only real beneficiaries of legislative, administrative, and regulatory policy making in Brussels are, at the moment, the well-compensated players themselves.

The European Court of Justice is the only prominent "success story" among the so-called Brussels institutions – perhaps because its headquarters is actually in remote Luxembourg, far from the hurly-burly of EU politics. The ECJ was little more than an afterthought in the Treaty of Rome, which narrowly defines its powers as specifically limited to the minimum needed to force member states to comply with Commission rulings. In the 1960s, however, the ECJ developed the Supremacy

Doctrine, which, as the name implies, claimed that its judgments override national laws. It has been said of the EU with only slight exaggeration that "the Community's only weapon is the law it creates."[81]

No national supreme court has ever accepted the validity of this doctrine, yet none has seen fit to challenge it directly. The German *Bundesverfassungsgericht* in Karlsruhe has come the nearer than any of its counterparts to having a head-on confrontation with the ECJ. Its famous Maastricht judgment of 1993 denied its claim to *Kompetenz-Kompetenz* – the authority to define its own jurisdiction – and warned that German law forbade any encroachment upon rights guaranteed by the Fundamental Law (*Grundgesetz*). In the "Metric Martyr's" case of 2002, Lord Justice Laws ruled in a variation on a similar theme that the British Parliament may delegate but cannot assign sovereign powers to any higher authority. Courts in France, Italy, and Denmark have also set limits to ECJ power. At the same time, national courts continue to enforce European law; if they refused to do so, it would immediately become meaningless.[82] The *acquis communautaire* – the corpus of the EU treaty and administrative law – has now ballooned to the point that 70 percent of the legal rulings affecting British business are made in Brussels.

Jurists agree that European law rests on shaky legal foundations. The Treaty of Rome was not, as the ECJ claims, "special" or "original" but was no different from any other. Nowhere did it give individuals the standing to appeal state violations of European law to the ECJ, and nowhere did it say that national courts must enforce European over domestic laws. The Supremacy Doctrine, nevertheless, rests on precisely both such assertions. The very idea that the Rome treaty created a "new legal order of international law" was a fiction. A constitutional challenge to the Supremacy Doctrine could have far-reaching repercussions.[83]

The ECJ's always highly political approach has involved looking into the "purposes" behind, rather than examining the text of, the treaty and arguing for expansive doctrines as necessary to fulfill them. Although the European Court of Justice is, in theory, subordinate to the political institutions of the community as well as the member states and is empowered only to interpret laws they have made, it is, in reality, their superior. The ECJ's interpretations of treaties and EU laws have fundamentally affected the balance between the community and member states in part because it is not, as with administrative procedures, subject to cumbersome political processes required to make explicit amendments to the *acquis*.[84] The ECJ is highly politicized. A forerunner of economic liberalization, in the 1980s the ECJ issued a string of judgments promoting the development of the single market. More recently, the ECJ has favored industrial policy and tax harmonization. "It is no secret," admits its present president, "that the case law of the Court has been a major driving force towards European integration."[85] The ECJ has also changed legal and political contexts nationally, which has given further momentum to Europeanization.

The ECJ's interventions have predictably generated counterpressures from "integration losers," who have only recently discovered their voice. This is a dangerous situation, according to legal scholar Karen Alter. The difficulty of reforming European laws, she notes, "contributes to the perception that the EU lacks accountability. European law supremacy is partly to blame because ... [EU] policies [have] by-passed democratic elected governments and can be invalidated by the ECJ based on an interpretation of the Treaty which member states never accepted. This is not a price to be paid for a rule of law. Rather it is a sign that the political system needs to be changed."[86] Such change would entail tearing the whole cloth of European law. It is a frightening prospect.

A Consequential Constitution

The debate that swirled around Europe's proposed constitution may no longer be fraught with tension or charged with immediacy, but the project is not yet dead. It has in fact been revived once already – after the Spaniards and Poles refused to sign in December 2003 – and plans are afoot at the Commission and at the chancelleries of the Franco-German bloc to introduce it incrementally by stealth. Two Italian professors of law have argued cogently in a recent paper for the existence of three different legal scenarios, which can be followed to reverse negative referenda outcomes: one for an enhanced Europe, a second for a pact to coordinate action within the Union, and a third for a "refounded" Europe. Is it surprising that the public would object to conferring new authority to an institution where such machinations are possible? Thanks to the referenda, there will be less scope for such things in the future.[87] The Germans would like to reraise the constitutional issue in early 2007 during their presidency. Nothing, however, can seriously begin before the French elections of May 2007 and only if, of course, the electorate has a change of heart.

It is not fault finding to point out that the British Labour Government's deceptive insistence on characterizing the proposed treaty as little more than a "tidying-up exercise" presumed fathomless public gullibility. Every other member state government, one might add, took the opposite and equally dishonest position that failure to ratify it would result in catastrophe. In war, it has often been said, truthfulness is the first casualty. This was not war, just politics as usual in the EU. The crowning absurdity of the constitutional ratification is that in the course of two years of haggling over the process, Europe's would-be rule makers revealed themselves to be chronic rule breakers. They have deservedly lost the public trust almost everywhere.[88]

The treaty is of course so bewilderingly complex that no two commentators fully agree on what the 400-page document is all about; what one sees in it depends largely on the eye of the beholder. Perhaps it can be revived as a kind of Rorschach Test. The Convention for the Future of Europe was summoned, as the magisterial title indicates, for something that went beyond cleaning up after a bad party in Nice: it was meant to serve as the capstone of a new federal state equipped with a full-time president, a foreign minister, its own police, and armed forces – the internal fittings and external trappings of a state. Political realities ruled out announcing such an explicit goal – because the convention never had any sort of popular mandate – but if ratified, it could legally have been achieved within the treaty framework. To doubt the fact is to make nonsense of the EU's very history.[89]

The European Constitution asserts its primacy over national constitutions; declares that the EU has a "legal personality" and possesses the sole right to represent the member states internationally when it so chooses; binds these states by the principle of "solidarity" requiring compensation for any actions purportedly detrimental to the EU (like assertions of independence); and includes a sweeping and detailed Charter of Fundamental Rights, whose interpretation rests exclusively with the

ECJ. It also confers a number of specific new responsibilities on European authorities, the most important of them being a common asylum and immigration policy; the harmonization of civil procedures and the "mutual recognition of legal judgments," which would oblige one member state to accept the rulings of another's court even when national law is violated; the "coordination of economic policy," a buzzword for interventionism; the control of intellectual property; and a broad array of social matters.

The Charter of Fundamental Rights includes under the rubric a number of debatable public policy issues in several different fields. These include medical, biomedical, and scientific ethics; representation in the workplace and job security; affirmative action; and social assistance (childcare, housing, and other benefits). The proposed constitution also centralizes the decision-making process. To the 113 areas currently decided by majority voting, it adds 42 new areas. Thirty-six additional ones come under the "codecision" procedure. The Commission also gained the right to propose legislation in several new areas. Changes in voting procedure triple the odds of passing legislation and reduce the number of veto points and therefore also the power of blocking minorities. Reflecting its centralizing bias, finally, the Constitution assigns no new powers to the member states and includes nothing to protect or strengthen the principles of subsidiarity and proportionality.[90]

Ninety percent of the constitutional treaty (the most accurate name attached to the hybrid document) was the work of one man, the imperious former French President Valéry Giscard d'Estaing, who was born in 1926. Giscard had no intention of producing a framework for a democratic federal Europe. His purpose was to strengthen the EU. The delegates to the convention were not elected but appointed to reflect a balance of power between the various community stakeholders. Procedures were tightly controlled. The public remained sidelined and largely in the dark over the year and a half during which it was negotiated. The draft treaty, which Giscard and a presidium composed of allies rammed through stacked committees, angered ardent federalists in the EP, a vociferous Prodi, representatives from the smaller states (who felt bulldozed), and the growing number of skeptics among the 105 delegates.[91]

The sloppy draft was a huge disappointment to a business and financial community normally well disposed to the EU. The formerly supportive *Economist* recommended simply binning the document, which it ridiculed for having had accomplished the "incredible feat" of making the EU's "constitutional architecture harder to understand than it was before."[92] The draft met with public apathy when announced in June 2003 except in Britain, where an aroused majority firmly opposed the treaty by at least two to one. The government, however, firmly objected to holding a referendum on the disingenuous grounds that the Constitution was not important enough to merit one. A vain Giscard, on the other hand, welcomed such an opportunity. Confidently describing his literary handiwork as sufficiently "brilliant" for membership in the Académie Francaise, he was taken utterly aback by the French electoral verdict. No matter, however: the Constitution may be dead, but Giscard is now *immortel*.

The decisive Swedish rejection of the euro in the referendum of September 2004 should have shaken Brussels' complacent belief in European public compliance. It was no anomaly but a clear warning of the seriousness of the cleavage between the governors and the governed. The Swedish establishment had guided the nation into the EU back in 1995 to shift the onus for harsh but necessary reform of the country's bloated welfare state from Stockholm to Brussels. Since then, Sweden had successfully addressed these problems while remaining outside the Eurozone, but EU membership had become expensive, and Swedes had become sickened by the corruption and arrogance of the Eurocracy. All the main political parties, the central trade union, academic and informed opinion, and the major newspapers and media – indeed everyone but the public – nevertheless supported adopting the euro.[93]

In spite of outspending the *nye* side by five to one, the polls continued to slip as the election approached. A desperate Prime Minister Gøran Persson tacked erratically, untruthfully claiming that he had opposed a referendum in the first place and maintaining that it would be nonbinding. Only the popular Foreign Minister Anna Lindh might have saved the situation, but she was tragically murdered while shopping in a department store three days before the vote. With the public deeply in mourning, pundits tendentiously predicted that the Lady Di penumbra would save the *ja* cause. Instead, the pro-euro camp took an 8-percentage-point thrashing. In "core Europe," the outcome was widely attributed to the mental peculiarities of a people condemned to dwell on the subcontinent's frozen northern fringe.[94] Who were these odd Nordics to stand in the way of history's inexorable forward progress?

Certainly, Silvio Berlusconi wanted an answer. As Council president for the second semester of 2003, he planned a spectacular signing in Rome, quite appropriately, in the city bearing the name of the first treaty. Delegates arriving at the opening of the constitutional conference, held at the Pallazo dello Sport, were greeted by the statue of a muscular athlete giving the fascist salute next to a stone frieze of Italian heroes, including the short, "balding, barrel-chested figure of Benito Mussolini." Italy's present leader, the short, balding, barrel-chested figure named Silvio Berlusconi, pompously proclaimed, "This is the conference of European will, the will of Europe to be Europe."[95]

That was not the case either then, a few days later at the get-together in Naples, or at the final session of the Intergovernmental Council held in Brussels on December 12. The Brussels conference was a nonevent, broken off early to prevent another public scofflaw like Nice. It opened with Berlusconi's suggestion that the delegates talk about women and football. In his characteristic but deceptive self-deprecating manner, he admitted to knowing something about the ladies and even to having been featured in the pages of *Playboy*. Turning jovially to Chancellor Schröder, he remarked, "Gerhard, you have had four wives – what can you tell us about women?" The meeting went downhill from there, breaking up over the refusal of not only Spain but Poland – which had been promised EU accession on more favorable terms in the Nice treaty – to sign. The unpopular Polish government had little choice but to back out; it would otherwise have fallen. Most member states outside the Franco-German bloc were pleased to let the Poles and Spaniards bear the onus of failure. They, too, were getting fed up – and, alarmingly, so were their publics. Starting in January 2004, the Commission's private polls indicated that a majority across Europe opposed the Constitution.[96]

It was time to close wagons as quickly as possible in order to save the project, especially since, quite by chance, the well-disposed Irish held the Council presidency in the first semester of 2004 and were to be followed by the disaffected Dutch – now seriously troubled by flagrant Franco-German violations of the EMU's growth and stability pact. Rather than deliberate for another year, the key players tacitly agreed to have a document ready for signature by July. By then it was too late. Needled incessantly by Euroskeptical Tories desperately in need of a campaign issue, Blair finally relented and on April 20 agreed to holding a constitutional referendum for which he feigned enthusiasm. His only hope was to postpone the event, preferably until after his reelection or until one of the several other member states ratifying by referendum voted it down first. He would then have slipped the noose.[97]

There was a second problem facing the Constitution as well. No one had reckoned with the disastrous outcome of the June 10 elections for the EP. The message of profound public disaffection, which should have been conveyed, went unheeded; in several skull-knocking summit sessions, a compromise was eventually arrived at, which tinkered at the margins with Giscard's bloated document but did not alter it significantly. The constitutional project had been revived, but at a cost: the Franco-Germans apparently accepted Barroso as Commission president as a tradeoff for a British signature on the Constitution.[98]

A fatal decision would soon be made. After putting up with months of goading from his ambitious and popular finance minister, Nicolaus Sarkozy, Chirac announced grandiloquently on Bastille Day that the French people deserved a chance to vote on the Constitution. Was the decision rash or courageous? Chirac's party had nearly been swept away in the March 2004 provincial elections. Other countries with optional referenda ran scared. The Swedish government refused to risk another public rebuke. Belgium's party-politicians, fearing repudiation in Flanders, also preferred to keep ratification off the streets and safely in-house. Chirac – and many others – soon had reason to rue the decision. The collateral damage was considerable. The EU commitment to Turkey, made between October and December 2004, was highly unpopular across the political spectrum. As a supporter of Turkish accession, Chirac found himself isolated in his own party. To save what remained of his footing, he came up with the novel claim of France's right to block Turkish EU accession by referendum, thereby undermining the credibility of an EU commitment.[99]

Chirac, to be sure, soon won an ally in the hapless Socialist Party chief, François Hollande. In December 2004 Hollande managed to secure a sixty-forty victory from the 30,000 *militants*, or card-carrying members, voting in a party referendum. This turned out to be a disaster in disguise. Traditions of solidarity notwithstanding, Hollande could not carry the base – the voters – more than 60 percent of whom eventually followed the defecting Laurent Fabius into the "anti" camp. The Socialist Party, which had suffered a near-death experience in the 2002 elections, still had a chief but no longer enough Indians to present a credible alternative to Chirac's center-right UMP party. The specter of Le Pen thus reappeared. Worst of all, in a vain effort to salvage the referendum, the Commission jettisoned its own agenda by disowning Bolkestein and the Services Directive (SD).[100] Europe, nonetheless, owes the French president a back-handed debt of gratitude. His ineptitude had staved off catastrophe.

The Dutch "No" of the following day was in ways even more remarkable than what happened in France. The Dutch government, while not popular, was also not despised by much of the electorate. The government coalition partners also held together; there were no defectors to the "anti" cause as in France. With the exception of the *Elseviers* magazine, the entire media, moreover, supported the Constitution. There was in fact no real *Nee* campaign other than the raucous one-man band of the xenophobic Geert Wilders, who, although facing death threats from Islamic extremists, barnstormed the country in the two weeks prior to the election. The issue profile was even less clear in the Netherlands than in a France united by fear of Anglo-Saxon "ultraliberalism," which purportedly threatened jobs, benefits, and the special French way of life. The Dutch worried little about such things; the unifying bond of "anti" sentiment in that bellwether nation was belief that the EU had become remote, unresponsive, and unaccountable and had failed to live up to its promises. This, indeed, was the lowest common denominator of attitudes toward the EU in most member states.[101]

Torn initially between a desire for keeping the Constitution alive and the fear of public rebuke, beginning with Great Britain, successive national governments shelved plans for referenda over the summer of 2005. This did not end the story of the Constitution: a loophole was found to keep it legally alive for another two years. Yet, the likelihood that governments would go back to their electors for a constitutional mandate is nearly zero. The referenda brought to the surface wellsprings of dissatisfaction more powerful than almost anyone expected or any politician feared. These men and women must now go back to the drawing board, devise workable reform policies, and (as Jean Monnet would have put it) change the integration context.

Prime Minister Blair, finally, owes his arch nemesis a debt of gratitude. By taking the first fall, Chirac spared him certain defeat in the promised UK referendum and, quite possibly, forced early retirement. Blair should also be grateful to the Tories for fearing to make Europe a campaign issue. By overlooking the rising tide of EU skepticism on the continent and failing altogether to generate a constructive policy toward the EU, they handed a deeply mistrusted Blair the May election. With Chirac enfeebled and Schröder all but out, Tony Blair was the last big man left standing in the EU after June 2005. The challenge Blair faced was big: he would have to reestablish trust, create agreement about what Europe should or should not do, and set the EU on a course of reform. Was it worth the effort?

At the end of the day, the peoples of Europe must decide whether a future EU will be basically economic or political in character, centralized or decentralized, or shaped by rule or by market (or some combination of the two). They must also determine where its borders should run and how it should be fitted into the new global order. This responsibility requires a new understanding of what has gone wrong economically and politically in the EU, how things can be set right, and how innovation can be encouraged. Only then will Europe be able to move from governance to government and from bureaucracy to democracy.

TWO

Economics

Europe is shrinking in an expanding world, running in place while others sprint, and glancing sideways instead of looking forward. If things do not soon change, it will not only count for less in the future but miss out on much of the fun. Don't be morose: remarkable events are unfolding in our time. We are witness to the opening and self-realization of cultures, the birth of modern nationhood in various parts of the globe, and the spread of democracy – even on Europe's doorstep. An adaptive and economically robust European Union (EU) of vigorous nation-states can strengthen this global trend and benefit from it. The EU must first be overhauled, however. Having once been a spur to growth, the EU has become a brake on it, which must be released for Europe to prosper.

The world is enjoying the longest sustained growth spurt in history. In 2004 the international economy grew at the fastest rate in fifty years, more than 5 percent. Every region except Africa, parts of the Middle East, and Europe registered robust gains. Today less than a sixth of the world's population lives in poverty, whose eradication now seems within reach. Growth has been breathtaking in China, much of East Asia, and India, impressive in Latin America, and strong in the United States. Europe lagged behind last year at 2.2 percent, less than half the US rate – an improvement, at least, over the 1.4 percent over the past decade and 1 percent in the 1980s. In 2005 the Eurozone grew at a meager 1.3 percent, as opposed to 4.2 percent in the United States, and it is not expected to rise above 1.9 percent in 2006. Since 1996 US productivity growth has also substantially outpaced the EU's, and in 2004 it was more than a point higher. Persistently high levels of unemployment of about 10 percent in much of Europe have plagued the slow-moving economy. Not surprisingly, since the early 1990s, Europe's overall share of world trade has declined by nearly 10 percentage points to just more than 40 percent. At the present trends, China's GDP will surpass Britain's and Germany's by 2010, India will overtake both France and Germany by 2020, and Europe's share in world GDP will shrink from 34 percent to 25 percent over the next twenty years.[1]

To close these gaps, the EU will have to rethink its developmental model, according to "Global Europe: Full Employment Europe," a landmark policy pamphlet written by Chancellor of the Exchequer Gordon Brown and published on the eve of the EU's October 2005 economic summit at Hampton Court, London. Brown predicts, quite simply, that European integration will count for less in the future. Indeed, he all but calls the need for it into question. Brown believes that the "trade bloc era" of the post–World War II generation has come to an end or, more precisely, *given way* in the twenty-first century to globalization. Long-standing policy-making assumptions, he argues, are no longer tenable: a common market will not generate a single market, followed by a single currency, a federal fiscal policy, tax harmonization, and even a single state. Brown wants fresh approaches and emphasizes the need to upgrade skills, increase innovation, and encourage change nationally (rather than imposing it from above). He further recommends that the EU complete the deregulation of telecoms, open up the market for services, eliminate state subsidies, strengthen competition policy, reduce burdensome regulation, promote tax competition, and improve the transatlantic economic dialog.[2]

Adaptation to a globalizing world will not occur overnight. The *Financial Times* columnist Wolfgang Munchau is right: with the Federal Republic of Germany politically gridlocked, the French government obsessed with the 2007 elections, and the British presidency reluctant to assert active leadership, a European-level initiative is unlikely before the German presidency of 2007. If it is to succeed, the painfully constipated national economies of the big European nations must be freed up and economic growth resumed.[3]

The first priority must be, however, staving off a breakdown of the European Monetary Union (EMU). Launched as a step toward federal union, today but a remote prospect, the single currency has not lived up to expectations. In spite of yielding certain secondary benefits, the EMU has shaved annual growth by a whole percentage point and is intrinsically unstable. The burning question of the hour is, What will happen once bondholders start worrying about the "full faith and credit" of a state that has never existed and likely never will? The threat of financial panic must be dealt with immediately. One need not abolish the European Monetary Union, however, because by changing its operating principle the EMU can be saved.[4] The euro need not be taken out of circulation but can instead be allowed to find its value in competition with restored national currencies. Individual countries should have the choice of opting into or out of Euroland or of using both domestic and European currencies concurrently.

Reform of the Eurocracy must also begin. The EU's most costly and wasteful program, the Common Agricultural Policy (CAP), should be quickly phased out. The fraud-ridden regional funding scheme (designed to subsidize economically weaker member states) should be either altered so as to pay out exclusively to the poorest member states or be scratched. The third largest item in the EU budget, the deeply politicized and shambolic framework program (FP) for research and development (R&D), must be science-driven rather than politically directed if innovation is to spark future growth. Finally, the EU has got to stop swamping national legislatures with an endless stream of often unnecessary and sometimes harmful regulations, directives, and decisions, lest it, along with the rest of Europe, strangle in red tape.[5]

The dismal European growth record has several familiar causes in addition to the euro. One of them is demographic: the population is both shrinking and aging – something unlikely to change soon. According to the economic and monetary affairs commissioner of the EU, aging will increase public expenditures on pensions, healthcare, and long-term medical care by between 8 percent and 14 percent by 2050. At the same time the labor force will shrink by 48 million, or 16 percent.[6] Employment is also declining, both in absolute terms and as a percentage of the population, as is the total number of hours worked. High rates of joblessness persist.[7] These numbers, which compare unfavorably with those of OECD nations in other regions, derive from poor policy choices.

Reform will be difficult without a reduction in the size of the welfare state. A one-size-fits-all policy is out of the question. No single

European social or economic model, according to the current EU Commissioner for Employment and Social Affairs, Vladimir Spidla, adequately describes the many national varieties of the welfare state. Welfare systems are also notoriously "sticky": the decision to cut back on them is, as a rule, politically fraught. Effective reform thus presupposes a high degree of public trust not only in the governmental process but between citizens. According to the Austrian social critic Gunther Zichy, such trust exists at present only in Scandinavia – and specifically not in Germany, France, or Italy, where it must still be created. Restoring the sovereign authority of elected national governments – and especially monetary and fiscal autonomy – is therefore the essential first step toward reform of the welfare state, the revival of economic competitiveness, and the reconstitution of the EU. Forcing the pace of change by directives from Brussels is pointless.[8]

A Multipolar World Order

Exogenous pressure is the main catalyst to economic change in Europe today and will become stronger in the future. Its source, the expanding world market, can be resisted but is too strong to overcome. But why bother? Globalization works. According to Martin Wolf, "Broadly defined, [it] is a long-run process with powerful forces behind it. Economics, conventionally defined, is a crucial component of a wider range of positive-sum activities that drive ever-wider exchanges and, with these exchanges, create bigger and more complex political institutions."[9] Only since the 1980s has the volume of international trade approached the importance, in relative terms, of that before World War I. Globalization is more an old friend than a new threat.

Why panic? The net overall impact of globalization – huge gains in productivity and declines in cost – is positive. At the same time, globalization must be better understood in order to minimize undesirable political side effects. According to Wolf, globalization causes six fundamental ongoing changes: the production chain is being unbundled across frontiers and extending deeply into services and manufacturing; trade is rising in relation to output; foreign direct investment is soaring; commodity and energy prices are increasing, while those of information technology (IT), high-labor manufactures, and tradable goods are declining; both capital and brainworkers are becoming more mobile; and the supposed race to the bottom, finally, is not taking place, as indicated by the competitiveness of highly taxed Nordic economies. Wolf also notes three politically significant implications of the globalizing world economy, with which governments must contend: rewards will go to producers complementary to, rather than competitive with, the emerging Asian giants; policy making must be tailored to persons and corporations able to "exit"; and the demand for unskilled labor will fall, leading either to wage declines or unemployment.[10] Needed are investment in education, a market-friendly investment climate, and firewalls between the state and the economy.

China, it was said at last year's Davos gathering of the rich and powerful, holds the answer to every question. If so, it will be hard to find: China is big, China is deep, and China is still, by dint of such facts, almost unknown. A brief discussion of China must preface what Europe faces today. China already looms so large in international affairs that one tends to overlook that its adjustment to a world dominated by the West for more than two centuries is far more difficult than the West's adaptation to the rising new superpower. China's post-Mao opening has required nothing less than the continuous reconfiguring of the state, the end of which is not in sight. The Chinese government has thus far directed the process of change expertly and avoided revolutions, famines, and war. No one can predict how long this will remain the case: a world with a Chinese superpower will be unlike any other in history; there is no precedent for it. The United States or Europe can only influence China at the margin. Since convergence has its limits, mutual accommodation will be necessary.

Almost overnight, China has become the growth engine of an increasingly interdependent international economy; the welfare of the West now depends on the smooth operation of something beyond its control. Everyone stands to gain if the machinery can be kept humming. At the same time, China must be watched very carefully. Since September 2004, President Hu Jintao has eliminated any remaining obstacles to one-man control in Beijing. He intends to make the future China as powerful politically, and perhaps militarily, as it is now economically. In October 2005, the publication of a seventy-four-page policy paper titled "The Building of Political Democracy" eliminated any remaining doubt about the matter: it defined a democratic government as "the Communist party ruling on behalf of citizens with a view to perfecting 'the people's democratic dictatorship'."[11]

China's "peaceful rise" is producing a new worldwide multipolarity. China is the largest trading partner of both Korea and Japan, has displaced the latter as the hub of the East Asian economy, and has become the dominant party in a network of bilateral relationships with all the nations of Southeast Asia, with which it runs a substantial trade deficit. Memories of the meltdown of 1998 have faded as prosperity has returned to the region. China is now pressing for a reorganization of the Association of Southeast Asian Nations (ASEAN) as a free-trade area to include both Japan and Korea, but with itself as the dominant power. The settlement of border disputes with neighboring countries (like Vietnam), a high priority, is one facet of this current campaign. The Chinese oppose including India, Australia, and New Zealand in the group – the latter two as alleged Trojan Horses for the United States. In such a reformed ASEAN, China would play a role similar to Germany's in the original European Economic Community (EEC), the forerunner of the present EU. With a market of 1.6 billion people, a China-led ASEAN will be larger than the EU and perhaps politically stronger within two decades.[12]

China is also developing a network of strategic relationships with other nations and regions, which have important implications for Europe and the United States. These include strengthening political ties and bilateral trade with India, developing a new supplier relationship with Latin America, and cooperating politically with Russia in the Shanghai Cooperation Organization to support authoritarian governments in central Asia. In all these regions, economies are growing, and in any of them a potential superpower may emerge: these are the so-called BRIC nations – Brazil, Russia, India, and China. Between 2000 and 2005 the BRICs contributed 28 percent of the world economic growth in dollar terms and 55 percent when adjusted for purchasing power parity. They currently hold nearly a third of the world foreign exchange reserves, and their share of global foreign direct investment has tripled to 15 percent since 2000.[13]

Each BRIC nation is, of course, quite different and owes its progress to a special set of circumstances. The Russian economy is growing rapidly thanks largely to high energy prices. Brazil now has its first genuinely popular government and, notwithstanding severe draught in the Amazon and a spate of recent scandals, continues to thrive under its experiment in democracy. Benefiting, like Russia, from rising commodity prices, the Brazilian economy is also modernizing rapidly. India, finally, has become the world's second great IT power, and brainworkers are proving to be its greatest natural asset. The "Hindu rate of growth" belongs to the past. The BRICs are expected to be the big markets of the future. One, or all, of them may also – like China and, in part, because of China – become world powers. The results would be a much more complicated international political scene, vast increases in the size and strength of world markets, and the liberation of human potential in many quarters of the globe.[14]

China's moves, in East Asia and elsewhere, represent attempts to counterbalance historic dependence on the United States and Europe – an end that can also be served by setting one against the other. The growing Chinese importance in the world economy should not be confused with a commitment to free trade. The latter is only a means to stabilization. Exports provide employment, produce wealth, generate knowledge, attract foreign capital, and, at the bottom line, strengthen the power of the central state. The opening of the world market at this point goes hand-in-hand with the rise of conservative authoritarianism in Beijing. Mercantilist motives are prominent in policy making. China hoards dollars (today's gold) as a buffer – to protect national security – and for this reason is prepared to pay a price by holding on to a depreciating asset.

Beijing also brings in foreign capital and institutions in order to discipline and eventually displace corrupt regional communist party satraps through whom the central authority must govern today; attracting investment from the West is, in other words, an integral part of the ongoing reconfiguration of the government. Big financial banks and equity funds are more than happy to introduce "best practices" into China, while at the same time making money. They should not labor under the illusion, however, that the Euro-American presence will be permanent, but, like Good Moors, be prepared to do their worthwhile job – and then go. Manufacturers in joint enterprises should also recognize that their stay in China will end once China has learned how to compete. Purveyors and practitioners from the realm of high-tech weaponry must act on the principle that any spear handed over today can be pointed the other way tomorrow.[15]

Today's China is following the growth model of successful Asian modernizers, such as Korea and Japan, as suited to its unique conditions. One of these special circumstances is the legacy of Maoist isolationism and in particular the Cultural Revolution, which wasted a generation of intellectual capital. Managerial infrastructures have had to be stamped out of the ground in post-Mao China and are still very weak by comparison to historical counterparts. Dependence on foreign technology remains overwhelming and will be heavy for some time to come. Yet, the situation is changing rapidly thanks to crash R&D programs and a breakneck expansion of higher education. Because China's extraordinary growth has thus far taken place largely without the benefit of an adequate number of trained professionals, it may even accelerate once this deficit has been overcome. Finally, like Russia or the United States – but unlike either Japan or Korea – China can become self-reliant to a high degree. Where it lacks domestic resources, China invests abroad, scouring the world in search of, for instance, oil. Self-sufficiency is the long-term goal of the same overall economic policy, which today, paradoxically, depends largely on free trade. China's planned modernization, which extends to every sector of national life, aims at strengthening Beijing's power, stabilizing East Asia, and restoring a traditional form of hegemony in the region.[16]

The strong China policy may not be a threat – and indeed has been a boon in many parts of the world up till now – but it will, if successful, reduce European, and US, world power.[17] Europe desperately needs economic growth to maintain its international standing. New markets must be opened, risk aversion decreased, and entrepreneurship rewarded. The now-flagging European liberalization process must be given a push from the bottom up – and once set in motion, it must be sustained through competition. Market-induced change has unexpectedly begun to take on a life of its own in the former accession nations of Eastern Europe – where growth advances at a handsome clip of nearly 5 percent – and in Turkey, the western Balkans, and Ukraine. Europe should think of these fast-moving catch-up economies as comprising a nearby China – with big markets and large pools of accessible, cheap, and highly skilled labor. Their successes can also serve as models for policy making. Western Europe may, for the first time in a millennium, be reformed from the East.

Saving the Euro

Since it was launched in the early 1990s as a political project, many influential economists have warned that the proposed EMU was not an optimal currency area because conditions varied too significantly across the region for a one-size-fits-all monetary policy to work: it would apply at different points in the business cycles of the various member nations, in one place too early and in another too late. Adoption of such a policy was like using a single thermostat to regulate temperatures at the same time in both Lisbon and Helsinki. Adjustment mechanisms for coping with the differential impact of a single European monetary policy do not exist in the EU: labor mobility is restricted, and fiscal transfers ("buffers") are unimportant. Though admitting that these intrinsic problems would slow growth, euro advocates have generally maintained that they would be offset by reduced transactions and borrowing costs and increased market transparency, because goods previously priced in a dozen or so different currencies across the EU would have a single common denominator. Price convergence has not resulted, however, and the euro has increased neither rates of intra-EU trade nor investment.[18]

A euro credit market has, however, sprung into existence. Sovereign debt in Euroland is of course denominated in euros, as is much private debt. Internationally, the euro is second to the dollar and is used widely in both government and international trade finance. The euro provides welcome competition to the dollar and helps reduce overall borrowing costs. The euro is also of particular benefit to ill-managed member economies, whose credit ratings it artificially boosts. The overall consequences of this situation are, however, problematic. Italy has been the main beneficiary of this bootstrap effect. Until recently, Italian sovereign debt traded at rates little higher than, for example, the Netherlands, even though Italy did not and probably cannot limit its budget deficits to 3 percent, as required by the growth and stability pact ("Maastricht Criteria"). Italy has also experienced serious wage inflation and suffers from high costs and unemployment. Although such considerations affect Italian creditworthiness, Italy's government bonds have only recently begun to carry a default premium. The relative lack of one is due partly to the European Central Bank's (ECB) policy of soaking up potentially suspect Italian paper, which comprises a disproportionate share of its reserves. This course may be perilous if the Italian economy continues to lose competitiveness. The ECB has warned that it will refuse to accept Italian paper in the future unless the government puts its house in order.[19]

Apart from strengthening the public finances of the Italians and other southerners, the EMU has not fulfilled the terms of the original bargain on which it was built. The euro has brought the Federal Republic of Germany essentially nothing. Its purpose, as defined by Chancellor Helmut Kohl (1983–1999), was to lower Germany's profile to gain the acquiescence of the rest of Europe to reunification, which, he feared, would revive fears of German domination. He also hoped that the imposition of the stability and growth criteria would force the future ECB to act with *Bundesbank*-like restraint. Not the rise, but the unexpected and abrupt decline of German power would, however, be the rule in the 1990s; the euro pact has been, in other words, superfluous to the problems facing the Federal Republic. Furthermore, the ECB can no longer discipline the German government as the *Bundesbank* did previously, a result partly evident in the huge increase in public borrowing. German credit standing, indisputably at the top of the league in the early 1990s, is now slipping southward. Even though huge one-time cuts in the military budget reduced Germany's borrowing needs, the Federal Republic is saddled with heavy long-term debt, which will provide a drag on the economy over the next decade.[20]

Nor has the euro paid off for France, which arguably has made the greatest sacrifices for it. The French entered the EMU with a "strong franc" (*franc fort*), which was achieved, at the cost of double-digit unemployment, by nearly two decades of shadowing a tight German monetary and fiscal policy. The primary reason for the French entering the EMU was to reduce dependence on Bonn and Frankfurt, the headquarters of the once almighty *Bundesbank*. Today France can no longer get special help from Bonn, as it did in 1992 when the franc came under attack, and it remains dependent on a different Frankfurt institution, the

European Central Bank, the President of which, though French, does not answer to Paris. France has no more influence on the ECB under Jean-Claude Trichet than it did over the *Bundesbank*. The management of the ECB is beholden to no one but its directing board of central bankers, whose overriding concern is with currency stability, not growth. France can no longer, as before, inflate its way out of a recession. Nor can it or any or other EU member state influence ECB policy. The necessary mechanisms for policy coordination simply do not exist: the ECB has no counterpart to the US or British treasury departments, which bring together different strands of economic policy and are subject to democratic supervision. The ECB's counterintuitive decision at the December 2005 meeting to raise rates for the first time in five years met with a chorus of outrage from EU finance ministers.[21]

Nor has the euro fulfilled the hopes of its champions on the political Left. It has disappointed, for instance, many engaged, prominent, but now despairing, progressive-minded theoreticians from the Delors camp, who expected it to provide the elusive breakthrough to a "social Europe." Buoying this hope was the somewhat imaginative idea that such a single, rule-governed currency would provide the cross-continent stability needed to reduce inflationary expectations and, through centralized systems of wage bargaining, facilitate both wage reduction and the workplace rationalization needed for competitiveness; they, in turn, would generate savings for "active labor market policy" – that is, government retraining schemes tailored to the requirements of modernizing economies. Trends in the Eurozone have, however, moved in the opposite direction: declines in overall wage increases have occurred only where centralized wage bargaining has broken down. "Active labor market policy" was at best only partly successful in the Nordic lands, where "wage compression" had diminished and the national union-dominated negotiating apparatus had fallen apart prior to the introduction of the single currency. In any case, neither Denmark nor Sweden – or, for that matter, Norway – uses the euro. In much of the rest of Europe, pernicious high unemployment remains the rule, and weakened national governments are usually quick to capitulate to strikes against labor market reform.[22]

The euro has also disappointed the hopes of those who expected it would result in victory over You-Know-Who – a misconceived notion.

The new currency will not be able to "displace" the dollar, which also enjoys incumbent advantage, until Europe generates single markets for mortgages and pensions; without them, pools of capital will be too small for megascale operations. Nor has adoption of the euro benefited specifically European interests. On the contrary, big banks and financials in the City and on Wall Street are the largest gainers. Frits Bolkestein's Financial Services Action Plan might eventually have made some difference in this respect by creating a single market for financial products. The most one can hope for now is that the big continental financial centers will try to revive elements of the single-market plan informally rather than through the EU mechanism.[23]

Above all, the euro has disserved the cause of the European political federation. Two years of Franco-German fudging on the growth and stability criteria, the flagrant violations of Greece and Portugal, and the inability of Italy to bring its national finances under control have deeply offended the fiscally virtuous Finns, Irish, Austrians, and especially the Dutch – as reflected partly in the June 2005 referendum – thereby adding to the unpopularity of the euro. Rightly or wrongly, 90 percent of the public blames the introduction of the single currency for price gouging. A strong majority of Germans, who were never keen to drop the deutsche mark in the first place, want the old currency back. The Italian Lega, Berlusconi's coalition partner, has called for a return to the lira and has not been disowned by the government. The Swedes, the Danes, and the British overwhelmingly prefer to remain outside the Eurozone. Though committed to entering the EMU by the accession treaties, the eastern Europeans would be ill-advised to do so; as developing countries, they need cheap money and can tolerate higher rates of inflation than advanced industrial states. One by one, the new member states are backing away from their euro commitments. The EMU has not provided, and probably will never provide, a stepping stone to political union.[24]

Germany, France, Greece, and Portugal have, along with Italy, become chronic violators of the stability and growth pact, which is in tatters. By late 2005, twelve of the twenty-five EU member states were in violation of the pact, and substantial improvement is not expected in 2006. Coordination of fiscal policy – viewed as essential to the single currency – is absent. No national government has made adequate provision to deal with increasing pension costs. The enforcement power of the European Commission is nil, and the European Court of Justice refuses to intervene to correct matters. The credibility of the euro depends on little more than the self-restraint of the national governments. In other words, there is good reason to worry about currency instability.[25]

The eminent economist Martin Feldstein, the current director of the National Board of Economic Research, pointed out years ago the danger posed by the euro. Feldstein's argument was that exogenous pressures from an expanding and increasingly competitive world market similar to those that in the 1970s and 1980s had caused governments to devalue in order to gain trade advantage and sop up unemployment – engendering short-term gain at the cost of long-term pain – would have different, but perhaps equally grave, consequences in the Eurozone. The rigid rules governing it create an adverse selection problem, he maintained, which provides incentives to rule breaking. Governments can no longer cause the external value of the currency to depreciate in order to counter a cyclical downturn but can only increase the deficit. This bias is systemic; its effects are difficult to confine to a single country, not least of all because the ECB's implied commitment to bail out an offending nation creates a moral hazard problem. Worse, the ECB has no feedback mechanism to prevent or offset large budget deficits. Inflationary policy, by eroding the real value of obligations, could provide one way out of the dilemma, but it would destroy both the raison d'etre of the ECB and the credibility of the euro.[26] The threat of a financial panic is, in short, real.

One should forget about fixing the EMU by widening allowable deficits, pegging them to cyclical changes, or introducing inflation targeting – all of which are rife with opportunities for fudging and evasion.[27] The euro can only be saved by changing the rules under which the EMU operates. The EMU should be transformed from a single European currency area to a parallel currency area in which the euro's value is determined by competition with reissued national monies. Although the idea may at first seem fantastic, it will be easier to implement a transition *from* the present euro than *to* it; the process should be conducted nationally rather than community-wide because the imposition of a single rule would be asymmetrical in effect.

The euro makes a good *numeraire* or standard of value because, like most US states, the EU cannot run a deficit; there is, in other words, an intrinsic advantage to using it. The euro could also become a "basket" currency – like its forerunner, the ecu – which would reflect aggregate values of national monies. National currencies would not, in such a reformed monetary union, be pegged to the euro but move against it in the market. Nor would money supplies be constrained by a growth and stability pact or similar criteria; instead, their value would be determined by competition. Inflationary policies would drive values down and increase borrowing costs. Virtue would be rewarded by stabilizing parities and reducing risk premiums. Fiscal and monetary policy could, in any case, reconnect to the business cycle. The adoption of the euro as a parallel currency would restore a necessary measure of economic sovereignty to the member states, while keeping alive the idea of monetary union. The authority of national governments would be strengthened, and growth rates would improve.[28]

The parallel currencies proposal is of course open to the objection that it would increase the costs of transactions by making it necessary to change currencies when crossing borders. This problem will not exist in two-currency countries, but where exchange is necessary it can easily be managed if the new monies are issued in the same printed and coded format as the euro. They could then be used interchangeably in automated teller machines (ATMs). Exchange costs are likewise trivial for credit card transactions. Consumer choice in a parallel currencies system would rest with the individual economic actor, who, if so inclined, could become a miniarbitrageur.

The growth and stability pact started to fray badly in fall 2002 and broke down irretrievably in November 2003 even though it wasn't officially declared dead until March 2005. Thanks in part to the immense US payments deficit, the euro has maintained its value remarkably well in 2005, and – declining gradually over the year – it dropped only slightly against the dollar after the two referenda. Inflation is a growing threat in some countries, but not an immediate danger. Complacency, nevertheless, always invites trouble. One cannot, by definition, predict a market panic. Its causes could be economic, but also legal – in the form of a challenge to the European Court of Justice's Supremacy Doctrine – or political – an adverse reaction to leadership failure. In early 2004, financial experts from Goldman Sachs and Morgan Stanley started recommending that buyers take heed of the "country factor" when purchasing Eurobonds. However, there is little evidence yet that discussion of a financial "Plan B" has begun except, as reported but officially denied, at the *Bundesbank*.[29]

It may well be, as Wolfgang Munchau has often argued in the *Financial Times*, that a monetary union requires a high degree of macroeconomic policy coordination; the breakdowns of the nineteenth-century Latin and Nordic unions (and contrariwise the success of the German *Zollverein*) would seem to indicate as much. If the survival of the EMU depends on the existence of sound and binding rules, it is in fact already dead – done in by the chronic violation of the growth and stability pact. The persistence of labor and product market inflexibility – a main source of its problems – eliminates necessary buffers to exogenous shock. A third prerequisite for the rule-based system, central bank autonomy, has also been victim to the machinations of Antonio Fazio, the long-term governor of the Bank of Italy. The rejection of the proposed constitution, moreover, rules out political union as a corrective in the foreseeable future. The Belgian economics professor, Paul de Grauwe is only partly right, however, in contending that "if we want to retain the euro in the long run, we need a political union."[30] The EMU can also be saved at a much lower cost by reintroducing the euro as a parallel and market-responsive currency.

Reform of the EMU must begin before any country becomes terminally ill. Timely action will be needed and may have begun. In late November 2005, Jean-Claude Trichet, the president of the ECB, made it clear that the ECB would no longer accept as collateral the bonds of the Eurozone countries whose credit ratings were slipping. The announcement marked a break with the economic fiction that all such bonds are of equal value and, apparently, was intended as a warning shot that further fiscal slippage would not be tolerated. Market reaction was subdued – an ill omen.[31] No provision was made for exit from the EMU on the theory that it should be more painful to leave than to stay in, even if a bailout of some kind should become necessary. If such a rescue operation should fail, a distressed country could leave the EMU and simply remonetize back into a reissued national currency. This action would almost surely entail a partial de facto default, because the new issue would necessarily be weaker than the euro. Crow would have to be eaten for a fresh growth spurt to take place. Yet, the damage could likely be contained. If several economically ailing countries should have to leave the EMU at the same time, the big G-8 powers would, however, have to rescue and reform or – in a crushing blow to "Europe's great experiment in transnational governance" – liquidate it.

Dismantling the Eurocracy

Europe's economic welfare requires, above all, that the half-finished single market be completed. The EU remains fragmented: while many member states are among the most regulated OECD countries, others are less so. The price dispersion pattern follows the general OECD trend rather than a specific European one, but with levels 25 percent higher across the EU than in the United States. Since exogenous pressure from the world market is chiefly what drives liberalization, Europe needs an open trade policy in both goods and services. Extra-EU trade barriers must be lifted in the pending Doha Round of the World Trade Organization (WTO) negotiations. The further resurrection of 1970s-type nontariff protectionist barriers must also be prevented. These include contingent antidumping measures (which increased by more than 50 percent between 1991 and 2003), such as "safeguards" in steel, and " voluntary export restraints" (VERs), such as those against Chinese textiles. Within the EU, the Services Directive, which in its draft form would extend to 70 percent of the economy, should be revived.[32] Neither this nor any other desirable EU liberalization measure can pass, however, until the present budgetary impasse breaks – and this will require structural reform.

The process must begin by accelerating the phase-out of the Common Agricultural Policy (CAP) – a stumbling block to both the progress of the Doha trade negotiations and the internal development of the EU – and be followed by further institutional changes in Brussels as well as the restoration of sovereign powers to the member states. The two most important recent reports on the EU's dismal economic performance, by the blue-ribbon Sapir Committee and by the House of Lords' European Union Committee, agree on the urgency of these matters. Although these excellent studies pinpoint crucial EU shortcomings, they too readily assume that the Brussels institutions can be repaired by shifting priorities, restructuring existing institutions, and reallocating assets. Neither report calls for new programs or presents any grand reform plan.[33]

The same thing cannot be said about the ambitious report of the " Round Table on a Sustainable Project for Tomorrow's Europe" chaired by Dominique Strauss-Kahn, a Socialist and former French minister of finance. Commissioned by President Prodi and published in May 2004, its analyses and recommendations percolated down after eighteen months of high-level deliberation on the long-term changes facing the EU. The brew has the acidic flavor of the hard Left. Strauss-Kahn and his team nevertheless deserve credit for having recognized that Europe's economic as well as political problems require democracy in addition to institutional tinkering. His recipe for reform is, however, manipulative and authoritarian; its consequences would be dystopian.[34]

Strauss-Kahn looks to a reinforced *dirigisme* and a propagandistic neopolitics to solve the EU's economic and political problems. He bases his case on the disputable philosophical premise that a political Europe is legitimate because, resting on a unique social model deeply rooted in the past, it embodies a distinct set of values, which are threatened from abroad (by You Guessed It!) and from within by the shortcomings of the EU. Well aware that a European *demos* does not yet exist, Strauss-Kahn does not expect a proposal like his to be popular. To change public opinion, he advocates intense application of the "community method." This will entail doubling the European budget, setting up local and regional outposts to monitor and direct a vast program of political education, organizing "pan-European media," introducing compulsory highly slanted Eurocourses into the secondary school curriculum, subsidizing European political parties, and setting aside seats for them in the European Parliament. The process of *demos* creation, which is expected to take about twenty years, should begin, Strauss-Kahn maintains, with the adoption of the European Constitution. The economic component of this policy, which is delineated rather than explained, calls for heavy doses of industrial policy, large social transfer payments, and the leadership of a French-dominated Eurogroup. It would also require increasing expenditures on a European defense force set up, curiously, to enforce a policy shaped by Europe's "soft power" diplomacy. Strauss-Kahn's plans for European reform, in short, propose making tomorrow's coffee with yesterday's used grounds. They are intellectually bankrupt.[35]

How, then, should the EU be repaired? One might start with the big-ticket items – the CAP, the regional funding (so-called structural policy), and the R&D programs – and then turn to its more important rule-making power, which impacts national economies even more seriously than the transfer programs. The EU budget is surprisingly small (about 100 billion euros per year), and in the next cycle it will likely shrink to about 1 percent of the EU GDP. The argument for not raising this figure is only partly economic; it rests chiefly on member state fears of EU misuse – because of fraud – and public resistance to any tax increases. No "net contributor" member state, including the historically generous Germans, will "shell out" more money for Brussels; and their publics all clamor for fair shares of the pie (*juste retour*). Although accession costs will continue to mount more rapidly than officially acknowledged, significant budgetary savings can be made by improving transfer mechanisms – a staggering 6 percent is eaten up in administrative overheads – and still far larger sums can be recovered by winding down defective programs, such as the CAP, which together with regional funding consumes more than two thirds of the budget.[36]

The CAP itself absorbed 45 percent of the 2004 budget and makes up 44 percent of the proposed budget for 2007–2013, even though agriculture (after enlargement) accounts for less than 4 percent of the EU GDP. Although the CAP once consumed nearly three quarters of the EU budget, it presently comprises slightly less than half, and by 2013 it will be reduced to 30 percent. The farm subsidy program is now in the process of being shifted from one of price support to one of income maintenance (tied into land preservation). Although the change has not generated immediate budgetary savings, it is expected to lead eventually to the elimination of the costly scheme. Though applied inequitably to the recent accession nations, the fractional CAP payments received by small eastern European farmers have actually stimulated new production, increasing the overall cost of the program. The trend will continue once Romania and Bulgaria join. The unwelcome prospect of still higher bills may delay the future accession of Turkey and Ukraine. More immediately, the CAP blocks the progress of the Doha Round and thus also stands in the way of the general tariff reduction needed to make

European industry internationally competitive with China and India. Europe pays a heavy indirect as well as direct economic – not to mention the high political – cost for the CAP.[37]

Nobody but Jacques Chirac bothers to defend the CAP as "modern." A reminder of the CAP's worst consequences might nevertheless be a worthwhile discussion backdrop: it raises food costs for everyone, especially low-income groups; beggars third-world producers; inflates farm land values; leaches the soil; and rewards those owning, as opposed to those working, the land. Most farmers draw no benefit whatsoever from it – and all consumers pay heavily for it. The total cost of the CAP to the EU, which includes direct payments from both Brussels and the states and food price increases, was about $150 billion in 2004 or 1.2 percent of GDP. Abolishing the CAP would produce huge welfare benefits for Europe (half of the global gains) and generate roughly $75 billion annually in new revenue for repatriation to the member states. They could then make discretionary use of such funds.[38]

The CAP is – according to the authors of a recent technical study – a relic. It was part of the original political bargain on which the integration project was founded. The initial purpose behind the policy was simply to raise domestic commodity prices in order to offset the purported trade advantages enjoyed by predominantly industrial (read German) economies, as opposed to primarily agricultural (read French) ones. Forget that the theory itself holds little water and that the CAP may have been unnecessary in the first place: it was part of a deal required to bring the French into the European Economic Community (EEC), as the EU was originally called. The consequences of this bad bargain have been momentous as well as unintended. From the trade standpoint, it should have been possible to do away with the CAP, which was conceived neither as a revenue measure (for tariff yield), for which it is unnecessary, nor as a means to gain export advantage (through export subsidies), which has over time become a serious problem for developing economies. The CAP is kept largely out of the fear that the EU will fall apart without it.[39]

The CAP is very resistant to change. It rests on special treaty agreements, which can only be amended by unanimity; its revenues, moreover, are, in EU jargon, "nondiscretionary" and beyond control of the European Parliament. Changes in the program require complicated and increasingly difficult interstate compromises as well as the wherewithal to work side deals. Each new phase in development has added a new level of institutional complexity to the EU and compounded the difficulties of reform. For more than ten years – and until the appearance of Margaret Thatcher on the scene – the only two net contributors to the European Economic Community were the then wealthy and productive West Germany and the then poor and uncompetitive United Kingdom. The famous rebate Mrs. Thatcher clawed back remains a bitter bone of contention even today.

The Mediterranean accession of the once poor Iberians (along with Greece and Ireland) resulted in a second "grand bargain," funded by the wealthy (and the then reunifying) Germans – the regional funding scheme – and created a whole new set of stakeholders. International pressure in the form of the Uruguay Round of the former General Agreement on Tariffs and Trade (GATT), now the WTO, brought the only major alteration – the administrative shift in the program from one of price to one of income supports; yet it hardened organized farmer resistance to change, especially in France.

Finally, the accession of ten new member states from eastern Europe resulted in the issue-begging adoption of a sliding scale to determine eligibility for subsidy payments, which will not bring the new entrants into parity with the "old" member states until 2013. The inclusion of the easterners may create a barrier to future enlargement, bankrupt the EU, or lead to abandoning the CAP altogether. No national "player" can make concessions to the CAP without offsets elsewhere – at a time when resources cannot grow, claims on them increase, and demoralization is rife. The CAP can either break the EU or provide the anvil on which to strike a new EU bargain. The Doha Round could well provide the forum in which the fate of the EU is eventually determined.[40]

The so-called structural (or regional) funds now consume nearly 30 percent of the EU budget and are scheduled to rise to 41 percent in the period from 2007 to 2013. Regional funding is redolent of payoffs: unless deep-seated accountability problems can be corrected, the program should simply be scrapped. The likelihood of any such action is low: for reasons both good and bad, all member states are loath to grant new powers to Brussels. Nor do the regional funds end up in the hands of those who need them. The recipients are not the poorest nations;

the largesse is spread unevenly among all the member states, including Ireland and Luxembourg, the two wealthiest member nations – and, on a per capita basis, among the largest recipients. Spain, now in the economic middle range of the member states (and still growing at a good clip), is the largest single beneficiary country. Italy, Germany, Great Britain, and France all get smaller amounts (though still more per capita than the poorest states), as do even healthy and wealthy Finland and Sweden.[41]

The new accession nations of Eastern Europe get what's left. There are, of course, limits to which weak economies can absorb subsidy infusions without igniting inflation, but they will never be reached. The newcomers are too numerous, and the EU budget is too tight for them to receive – as did Greece and Portugal for many years – handouts from Brussels worth 4 percent annually. Even if future regional funding is specifically targeted at only the poorest new or prospective entrants – as both Sapir and the Lords recommend – they will receive only a small fraction of the largesse, which once flowed to the more fortunate Club Med countries (and Ireland!).[42] The expenditure of regional funds should not be discretionary but should be specified by Brussels and limited to the express purpose of defraying the costs of meeting the *acquis communautaire*. Otherwise, they will continue to corrupt. Regional funding, the chief beneficiary of the shrinking share of the CAP in recent overall budgets, is also likely to increase in the future.

R&D is the third largest budget item, and it is slated to double over the next budget cycle to 70 billion euros. The importance of R&D to economic growth needs no elaboration at this point. The raw data underscore the need for new investment in the field. In 2003 the United States spent nearly $285 billion on R&D, 46 percent of the world's total. As a share of GDP, both Japan (3.2 percent) and the United States (2.6 percent) outpaced the EU (2.3 percent). In 2005 Korea led the world in R&D funding as a percentage of GDP. Whereas, between 2000 and 2003, overall world R&D expenditure declined as a share of GDP, China's increased dramatically and, at the present rate, will outstrip that of the EU by 2010 – a result due in part to new US investment in China. More Chinese scientists and engineers graduate per year (220,000) than European (180,000) or American (60,000). Europe makes exceptionally poor use of its vast brainpower resources, employing annually fewer new technical graduates than the United States. They must be put to use.[43] The current outlook is bleak. Whereas, over the past four years, R&D outlays within the EU have been flat, the United States spent 12 percent more during 2005 than over the average of the period. About two-thirds of the US expenditure was nonpublic as opposed to just more than half in the EU. The EU's R&D problem derives chiefly from the lack of private-sector demand and is due to an inhospitable climate for new investment.

The question of the hour is, Will the rallying cry of "Fewer farmers, more scientists!" be enough to save the EU? The expert drafters of the Sapir Report certainly hope so. The British presidency gave high priority to increasing the R&D budget and the role of scientists in the award of grants and improving the university curriculum. The French are also committed to pro-science policy as a component of a defense buildup. Merely pumping EU money into technology will not, however, solve Europe's R&D problem: past attempts to pick winners have been notably unsuccessful. Results from the EU's six previous framework programs for R&D have been consistently disappointing. Accountability in the R&D program remains so loose that the most recent EU annual audit, the eleventh refusal in a row to approve expenditures, singles it out as a problem area. Often criticized for bureaucratic heavy-handedness, the framework program's primary purpose has been to promote the European agenda rather than to advance scientific inquiry. The successful encouragement of innovation will require the seventh, and still pending, FP to break with the self-serving history of EU research sponsorship.[44]

The EU must, finally, reduce excessive regulation. Its costs are staggering. A recent study by a team of New York Federal Reserve Bank economists headed by Tamim Bayoumi argues that cutting red tape and eliminating excessive taxation would raise investment by 20 percent, hours worked by 10 percent, and EU GDP by 12 percent. Accepting this conclusion "as an important empirical finding," *The 2004 European Competitiveness Report* of the European Commission noted additionally that recent economic research confirms that a stringent regulatory regime is disproportionately costly for small and medium-sized firms; restrictions on entry, often justified in terms of externalities, are (as argued by public choice theory) merely a mechanism for creating rents benefiting politicians and the interests supporting them; and economy-wide product market regulation curbs competition, weakens corporate governance, and reduces productivity by slowing down technological catch-up.[45]

It is hard to know how much of this regulatory burden originates with the EU, to ascertain the comparative costs of different types of regulation, and to measure externalities. A few numbers shed light on the magnitude of the problem. EU legislation now accounts for a minimum of half the laws passed by national legislatures and, at least in Germany, more than 80 percent of them. The European Commission produces more than 3,500 rules every year – only a third of which are subjected to a cost-benefit analysis. In Great Britain alone, there are now more than 80,000 pages of EU regulations. Between 1973, when the United Kingdom joined the EEC, and 2002, Brussels generated 101,811 regulations and directives. The Commission initiates on its own between 3,500 and 4,000 business regulations and directives per year. The British Federation of Small Business estimated that in 2004, compliance with this mass of rulings cost 4 percent of GDP. The pace of regulation has actually slowed down since the early 1990s. Costs, on the other hand, are thought to have increased as a result of the shift in regulatory emphasis legislation from the single market to the environment and workplace safety.

Breaking ranks with his colleagues, the often outspoken Frits Bolkestein recommended in 2003 that the Commission give the member states the power to wave "not only the yellow but also the red card" in order to curb overregulation. In September 2005, President Barroso finally picked up the cue. In a "bonfire of the inanities," he promised to scrap no less than a third of the pending directives, thereby slimming down the EU rulebook from 85,000 to 50,000 pages. Enterprise Commissioner Günter Verheugen has since promised to do better in the effort to slay the public perception that Brussels is a "bureaucratic monster whose tentacles leave no village untouched." In addition to scrapping 70 pending draft laws, Verheugen promises, in a three-year assault, to trim back 222 regulations and 1,400 related enactments (including one from 1968 stipulating the allowable number of knots in wood) as well as to compress no less than 45 cosmetics directives into a single one compact enough to fit on a single piece of paper. George Parker, the wry

Financial Times veteran on the Brussels beat, noted without further comment that "the vast operation of screening the EU's *acquis communautaire* has been criticized by some officials ... who fear that Mr. Verheugen is trying to unravel the European construction."[46]

Needed are not only fewer but better rules. Omnibus approaches like the so-called precautionary principle, originally written into the Maastricht treaty, must be dropped. The attempt to apply it has exacted a staggering toll but, to date, accomplished almost nothing. The precautionary principle goes beyond the preventative principle, which deals with known risks: it attempts to assess all *potential risks* of food, pharmaceuticals, and chemicals. Of particular present concern is the Registration, Evaluation, and Authorization of Chemicals (REACH) program. It would, if enacted in 2007, require vetting not only all future products but the more than 30,000 substances in use prior to 1981. The cumbersome three-stage process will extend not only to manufacturers but up the supply chain to the end user. All products sold in the EU must be lead free, for instance, by July 1, 2006. These products include electronics, whose microboards use lead solders for which no known substitute exists. The amounts involved are tiny, 0.5 percent of world consumption. Replacement costs are unknown. Total costs for REACH have been estimated at up to $5 billion.[47]

In its present form, REACH will violate WTO rules and is protectionist, will discriminate against US exporters to Europe, substantially raise costs within Europe, and eliminate several tens of thousands European jobs. It has already brought about a preemptive shift in product development away from the EU, where bringing a new chemical to market at present takes three times longer and costs ten times as much as in the United States. Chemical producers worldwide vehemently oppose REACH. If history is any guide, they will eventually get their way simply because it is impossible to administer a decree as sweeping as REACH on the basis of something as fathomless as the precautionary principle in a field as complicated as chemicals. As put by the authors of a recent study, "Community assessments of chemicals have been slow, and many chemicals in use lack relevant assessment data. At the same time, many new chemicals are introduced on a regular basis, making it impossible to conduct extensive multi-year assessments for every single chemical."[48] REACH is, in short, a policy of overreach run mad. It not only achieves nothing at great cost, but it undercuts the efforts of the Commission's economic directorates to stimulate growth. REACH has contributed to the decline of the European chemicals industry and the overseas shift of new investment.

Behind the strange story of REACH is the European Parliament's desperate bid for relevance. The Mad Cow Disease panic of the mid-1990s, which caught the EU unprepared, presented a golden opportunity for the European Parliament to develop a new cross-border constituency of the ecologically concerned. Green causes have received plenty of attention ever since. Supported by the commissioner for the environment, the European Parliament has had a decisive influence on policy toward new health, food, and related technologies. It is in fact also the main political force behind the EU's restrictive policy toward the emerging biotech field. The consequences of this opposition reach far beyond REACH. They affect not just a branch of industry but a whole sector of technological innovation. Neither the Commission nor the Council, in their debilitated conditions, can do much about the situation. Brussels is not an engine of progress but merely the name of a station through which the train passes. A new "hands-off" approach is called for. Micromanagement and invasiveness must be brought to an end. "Harmonization" and "convergence" – bywords for the one-size-fits-all approach to rule making – must give way to subsidiarity – the devolution of authority to the lowest feasible level of decision making – and regulatory competition. The latter neither produces a race to the bottom nor dictates outcomes but allows the capture of comparative advantage. Successful welfare states would, in this scenario, be strengthened rather than weakened, and national diversity would increase.

Hard Case: Germany

It would be tempting to write the recent history of the three big continental economies – Germany, France, and Italy – as one of stagnation. Regression, however, better characterizes the past few years: growth has flat-lined, political systems have faltered, and long-term problems have multiplied. Issues that once might easily have been settled have remained unresolved and been aggravated – to a point approaching systemic failure. Something worse – breakdown – is not a hysterical fear but a distinct possibility. Failure to adapt to a rapidly changing world in which Europe's influence is diminishing is the common problem faced by all three countries, where the strength of liberalization has been waning since the 1990s. Its replacement – by whatever name – is patently unsatisfactory. Schröder's meandering Third Way, Chirac's pompous and hollow neo-Gaullism, and Berlusconi's bizarre version of a Roman Carnival have each led down blind alleys. In the rankings of the World Economic Forum's *Global Competitiveness Report*, Germany has slipped from thirteenth to fifteenth place and France from twenty-seventh to thirtieth. Italy has held at a steady forty-seventh, below Greece, Jordan, Latvia, and Lithuania (in ascending order).

The weak performances of the three big nations share a common cause: coalitions of welfare state stakeholders have repeatedly frustrated necessary reforms. As is obvious, Europeans must work longer and harder, the public sector cannot be allowed to grow, and the tax burden on wage earnings must be lightened. Competition will have to be encouraged, and state aid to industry cut back. Chumminess in banking must end, and transparency must be improved. Above all, flexibility has to be introduced into labor markets. Risk taking, innovation, and hard work also deserve to be rewarded even at the cost of greater social inequality for Europe to build a knowledge-based economy.[49]

The need for labor market flexibility is all the greater, according to André Sapir, because the common monetary policy of the Eurozone precludes the use of the exchange rate to influence external competitiveness. (The only other alternative – running budget deficits – Sapir considers too risky.) Because of national diversity – and the existence of at least four distinct welfare state models – the reform of national labor markets cannot, he adds, be undertaken at the EU level, coordinated as part of a broader reform of capital and product markets, or tied into a macroeconomic structural reform policy; rather, it must be conducted individually by member states and "conceived and engineered" by each of them as befits its own distinct "economic, social, and political reality."[50] This will not be easy.

Lack of growth has hardened the attitudes of wary and defensive publics into a mood of embittered hostility, which regard mere change as a threat. Second-rate national leadership deserves part of the blame for allowing such pusillanimous attitudes to spread. Although the EU has tied the hands, and even bound the feet, of national leaders, the last five years have been an era of political midgets. No head of government or state in one of the big three continental nations has had the gumption to reform. Even angry publics grudgingly admit that protectionism is indefensible and that mercantilist economics cannot succeed over the long run.[51] The nature of the challenge facing the coming generation of political leaders is clear. Whether they will have the strength and foresight to tackle it is not.

The overall trend is depressing – or worse. In France, rivals in both parties bid against one another in denouncing Anglo-American liberalism. The Italian government is simply inert. The current incumbents will likely remain in office until April 2007 and April 2006, respectively. A shift to the Left – to Prodi in Italy and whatever second-rater the French Socialists eventually decide on – would be, if anything, even worse. The German elections of September 20, 2005, were a huge disappointment, resulting in a hung parliament and an immobilized grand coalition. SPD Chancellor Gerhard Schröder was out, but Angela Merkel had to forfeit her reform agenda in order to form a government, which she managed only on November 12, at the last possible minute. Had her bid failed, elections would have been called on November 22 and Germany could quite likely have been without an effective government for several additional months.

The stalemate in Germany, the rhetoric in France, and the gridlock in Italy are evidence, according to the business economist Anatole Kaletsky, that "the ambitious market-oriented economic reform program that started in the 1950s, but really accelerated in the 1990s, was brought to a full stop." Thus the main theme in the politics of all three nations is "public rejection of an [EU] economic reform agenda ... demanded by business and the elites [and] supposed to make Europe's economy the most competitive in the world."[52] This agenda has failed, he adds, to provide the promised better life for Europeans, partly because of the rigidity of European monetary policy and partly by having mistakenly given priority to deflationary measures (pension cuts) instead of first liberalizing markets. It follows from this reading of tea leaves that the comeback of economic liberalism requires either a painful divorce from "Europe's great experiment" in economic and political union or a still more still difficult attempt to reform it.

Nowhere has deterioration over the past several years been more marked than in Germany. Chancellor Kohl was, in his day, the dominant figure in Europe. Chancellor Schröder follows Jacques Chirac's lead-strings. The once-mighty Federal Republic is politically immobilized and was economically badly demoralized until fall 2005, when indexes of business confidence began to turn north. A slow-moving and reversible reform process has been under way, however, since the Schröder years. It originated within a business community prepared to break with the "cozy capitalism" associated with the "Rhenish model" vaunted in the 1980s. The Federal Republic's network of cross-holdings has been nearly unwound since 1999. Yet the leaders of German finance and industry are besieged by anticapitalist politicians supported by a risk-wary public. Outside reinforcement may still be needed to end the struggle.[53]

Europe's former locomotive is in the shops. Over the past five years, growth has averaged less than 1.5 percent annually, unemployment has hovered at more than 4 million and been as high as 12 percent, income has stagnated, and housing prices – contrary to the rest of Europe – have actually fallen in real terms. The Federal Republic has declined in both world and European league tables. At the beginning of the decade, and even after reunification, German incomes were 9 percent higher than the Eurozone average; they are now 1 percent below it. The national debt has increased to well above the EU average. The economic problem is domestic. The Federal Republic would have performed even more dismally without buoyant world markets. Stimulated by massive Chinese investment in heavy equipment, machine tools, and precision machinery, German exports have actually increased impressively over the past five years. Even though demand from China seemed to have crested in summer 2005, Germany remains competitive internationally and especially in the EU; it ran a trade surplus with the former of 150 billion euros, and with the latter of nearly 100 billion euros. The problem facing the Federal Republic is lack of new investment in the industries of the future. The New Economy has not yet taken hold in Europe's traditional powerhouse.[54]

Intellectual capital, Germany's greatest long-term asset, has depleted in relative terms. The nation's unreconstructed educational structure is inefficient and produces the wrong skill sets. German universities have lost their edge in many fields of research. The failure in pedagogy belongs to a more general pattern of onsetting institutional paralysis, which extends to an inability to reform the bloated welfare state and thus slice thinner a thick "benefits wedge" (about one-half of wages) that, in turn, raises labor cost and diminishes wage incentives. The tradeoff for low real earnings is guaranteed job security, which makes employers reluctant to hire and stimulates capital investment in labor-saving machinery, both of which raise unemployment. Germans work fewer hours per year than any of their foreign competitors, and adult employment is lower in the Federal Republic than in most other OECD states.[55]

High real labor costs and heavy taxes drive capital abroad, lowering industrial investment in Germany and exporting new jobs overseas. The German rate of return on investment is half that of the United States. In many fields, business methods in the Federal Republic continue to lag further and further behind best practices. Restrictive regulations plague the retail and service sectors in the Federal Republic and impede business startups. The International Monetary Fund (IMF) predicts that Germany will have to endure another five years of economic stagnation, by which time Great Britain's GDP is expected to overtake Germany's. Let's hope that for everyone's sake, the economists can be proven wrong. A healthy Germany – normally the motor for half of Europe's growth – could mean a revived Europe.[56]

The manufacture and delivery of explanations for gridlock may be the one real growth industry in Germany today. The main theme of many of these accounts is the extreme difficulty the nation faces in making the transition from the corporatist " Rhenish Model" with its social counterpart, the Bismarkian welfare state, to the open-market economy. The problem rests less with business than with the government. According to the political scientist Wolfgang Streeck, "The German economy does not suffer from a lack of international competitiveness. In spite of the high euro, the German trade surplus regularly rises to new heights, and the percentage of the population employed in exposed sectors, while declining everywhere, continues to exceed the figures for any comparable country."[57]

According to Stephan Liebfried and Herbert Obinger, the German welfare state – now the world's most expensive – is the real drag on progress. What is the peculiarity – that special variable – which makes reforming it so difficult? The problem, they say, is fundamentally one of design. The German welfare state was created not as a "safety net" but to maintain status by guaranteeing income during retirement and periods of unemployment. Such earnings-related entitlements give the system a bias toward "backward-looking compensatory monetary transfers" – they reward incumbents before meeting new needs, for instance, in education or for day care. For that reason, they make it hard to change. Longer life spans and higher health costs have crowded out new welfare priorities.

German unification placed a heavy burden on this conservative scheme, adding to its expense, while actually shrinking certain benefits and arousing public opposition to further cuts. Although both Chancellor Kohl and Chancellor Schröder managed to reduce medical coverage – chiefly by stealth and obfuscation – neither succeeded in cutting back overall outlays. There is only scant evidence, according to Liebfried and Obinger, that "in scaling back the welfare state [political] parties do matter."[58] It is an open question as to whether this situation can change in the future.

According to Wolfgang Streek and Anke Hassel, rising nonwage labor costs stemming from the welfare state also broke down the tradition of tripartite cooperation among management, unions, and the state that had maintained German labor peace until the 1970s. Unemployment increased as German companies became less competitive, and national wage bargaining broke down as vulnerable firms imposed reductions regionally and locally and union membership dropped. To keep unemployment down, the government lowered the retirement age, thereby increasing benefit costs. This made the government the fulcrum of labor relations, which previously had been handled by organized management and the union. No longer dependent on union cooperation, management pushed forcefully for a break with the tripartite system and the shrinking unions resisted politically by placing heavy pressure on Schröder to resist further concessions to employers. Since about 40 percent of the SPD *Bundestag* delegation consisted of union officers or affiliates, they were in a strong position to make good on electoral threats.[59]

Gerhard Schröder found himself in a tight spot when taking office in 1998 and would never manage to get out of it. His situation went from bad to worse. Initially, Schröder was seriously committed to reform. As political difficulties mounted, however, forward movement stopped. By 2002, he began moving backwards, toward a slightly updated version of the discredited type of traditional industrial policy championed by the French. Though things could have been still worse without him, the net impact of Schröder's policy on the overall German economy was probably nil. The only important interest to have done satisfactorily during the past five years has been German big business, which, thanks to layoffs and profitable foreign operations, is healthy at the bottom line and cash rich. That is why in 2005, many large firms in the Federal Republic became plum takeover targets of US private equity funds. These outsiders should not be viewed as a threat. They can create value by breaking up and reselling ill-managed companies. Infusions of new talent, ideas, and money should help get the German economy rolling.[60]

With better timing, Schröder's first package might have been a breakthrough. It was a tax bill, which, in addition to lowering rates on both corporations and incomes, granted capital gains relief to banks and other financials selling crossholdings of industrial shares. This was a structural as much as a tax measure. The purpose behind it was to dissolve the interlocking relationship between big business and "house banks," which, traditionally, had prevented Germany from shifting from a closed to an open form of capitalism – that is, the kind of system needed over the long run for economic growth and political democracy. The leaders of both German finance and industry recognized this transition as both necessary and desirable.[61]

Schröder's bill was meant to be an opening act. The sales made possible by tax relief (exemption of capital gains) were to have enabled the banks to raise their capital, increase the liquidity of stock markets, and encourage shareholder, as opposed to stakeholder, capitalism. In December 1999, after months of head-butting with the CDU faction controlling the upper house of parliament, the *Bundesrat*, Schröder finally passed the bill. By then, it was too late. Four months later, the dot-com bubble burst. Henceforth, a wary, inexperienced, and badly burned German investing public would be risk-averse. A new constituency of small shareholders, as in Margaret Thatcher's Great Britain, did not develop.[62] "Stealth taxes" levied over the following year to reduce the budget deficit, moreover, finally undid the effects of Schröder's tax cuts.

Agenda 2010, the German chancellor's most ambitious welfare reform package, took a year to negotiate and, when finally signed in December 2003, had been reduced by half. It provided an 8.9-billion-euro tax cut, reduced state aid and other subsidies modestly, levied a new tobacco tax, limited tax write-offs, and provided an amnesty for tax evaders. It also reduced benefits for the long-term unemployed, denied them the right to refuse job offers, and allowed companies with fewer than ten employees to dismiss workers. These modest steps in the right direction met with heavy public criticism. Michael Sommer, the chief of the labor federation, condemned them as "dismantling the welfare state." Schröder consequently stepped down as SPD party chairman in favor of Franz Müntefering, the veteran floor leader of the Bundestag.[63]

The third reform effort, the more modest Hartz IV package of January 2005, reduced the terms and amounts of unemployment relief in order to force jobless workers into low-paying public sector make-work. The modest measure generated intense opposition, particularly in the former DDR, and later triggered the fusion of the old communist party (PDS) of East Germany with the radicals of the West German SPD associated with Oskar Lafontaine, who had resigned in early 1999 after losing a bitter power struggle with Schröder. It would call itself the Party of the Left. Unemployment actually increased to more than 5 million in the first quarter of 2005 to a postwar high of 12.5 percent. In spite of a 10 percent increase in exports in the final three months of 2004 (even with an expensive euro), growth fell to 0.2 percent. Hopes of a recovery have again been disappointed. With the economy creeping along at only a tad more than 1 percent, stagnation was again the story in 2005.[64]

Gerhard Schröder's unsatisfactory chancellorship has been both cause and effect of a serious institutional deterioration, which has now gone too far to overlook. Although Schröder was, and is still, personally well liked, public support for his government slid steadily downhill until bottoming out at a record low of 20 percent in midsummer 2005. For much of the same period, the CDU/CSU did only slightly better in the opinion polls. Still divided over the Kohl succession and lacking in fresh ideas, it at times made anti-Turkish noises to an off-key undertone of patriotic appeals – all of which fell largely on deaf ears. Not until May and June of 2005 did voter sentiment significantly improve, only to deteriorate again over the summer as the September election approached.[65]

The SPD, nonetheless, was driven out of power or suffered heavy losses in a long succession of local, regional, and European elections held in 2003 and 2004. In the crucial statewide election of May 22, 2005, held in Rheinland-Westfalen – the most populous German state and a bastion of social democracy since 1949 – Schröder suffered a defeat so crushing that he decided to move up the general election a year, from September 2006 to September 2005. He clearly needed a fresh electoral mandate to continue. Without one, his best option was to give Merkel, the CDU chancellor candidate, a chance to fail.[66]

The group in which Schröder lost voter support most heavily was organized labor. This is hardly surprising given high unemployment, the breakdown of centralized wage bargaining and the tripartite tradition, the loss of 100,000 union members per year, and the rise of left-wing demagogy. Its loudest voice has been Jürgen Peters, who took over the powerful Metal Workers Union after leading a wave of industrial actions beginning in 2002. They culminated in June 2003 with the collapse of a strike for the thirty-five-hour week. Undeterred by the debacle, Peters's rhetorical militancy reached new extremes. Stridency and weakness have walked hand in hand.[67]

In a desperate bid of his own to arouse SPD support for the May 2005 elections, Franz Müntefering, the new party chief, launched his own demagogic campaign against foreign "locusts" – the US private equity firms active on the German buyout scene. His intervention was a trial balloon for the September 2005 election. The ground for Müntefering's campaign was prepared a year earlier in a politically staged show-trial in Duesseldorf. In the dock was no less a figure than the CEO of Deutsche Bank, Josef Ackermann. His crime? Paying multimillion-dollar bonus packages to the top-level negotiators, who in February 2000 had arranged the Vodafone buyout of Mannesmann, a former pipe producer turned cell phone operator. The first megatakeover in the Federal Republic, the multibillion-dollar deal generated the largest windfall ever to bless German shareholders, which – since the bursting of the bubble came two months later – will likely be the only big one for years to come. Wall Street would have made celebrities, not criminals, of its architects, who, in any case after a few months of harassment, were finally exonerated by the German courts.[68] In December 2005, however, a German appeals court ordered a retrial of Ackermann, who in the meantime had turned the Deutsche Bank around. It was expected to last for months. Rainmaker persecution will lead only to capital flight.

CDU/CSU electoral victories at the state level compounded Schröder's difficulties in trying to run the country. The wins have also brought to the surface a fundamental structural problem, which both main parties agree must be solved if the Federal Republic is to meet future challenges. This is the unique kind of German federalism designed for the special adjustment problems of the postwar period. Today it immobilizes the government. Agenda 2010 took a year to negotiate because the CDU/CSU dominated the upper house or *Bundesrat*, which can block virtually any legislative act. Such elections have therefore often encouraged negativism by eliciting large protest votes. This is, however, only the tip of the iceberg.[69]

The subaquatic mass is far more significant. The Basic Law of the Federal Republic ordains a "uniformity of living standards" among the states. To enforce this rule, the federal government passes tax bills but leaves collection and administration to the individual states, entrenching interests at that level. Equalizing the tax burden requires an intricate system of cross-payments and subventions, which, on the one hand, deprives regions of comparative advantage and misallocates resources and, on the other, complicates decision making and frustrates change. A top-level bipartisan reform commission – formed to circumvent federal obstacles impeding the solution of pressing public policy problems – met over twelve months in 2004. After reaching agreement on a number of important specifics, it broke down with a refusal of two small states to grant the federal government the authority to set up "super universities," something that would presumably have put them at a disadvantage. The "federalism issue" gridlocked progress even on the special blue ribbon committee set up to devise ways of bypassing it.[70]

Within the EU, German influence plummeted. Schröder started out in 1998 as a Third Way socialist allied with Tony Blair and as an advocate of reforming the CAP and a champion of the open economy and enlargement, but he successively abandoned these positions in favor of an alliance with Chirac, based on maintaining the farm subsidy program, pursuing industrial policy, restricting labor mobility, and imposing tax harmonization. The turning point was a Franco-German bargain of October 2002, which preserved the CAP for the fifteen member states (especially benefiting France) but phased in the scheme in the accession countries only after several years. From that point, Schröder was in Chirac's pocket.

Like Chirac, Schröder tried, after 2002, to reconnect business to the state. He fought the EU takeover directive aimed at standardizing rules (and eliminating those that discriminated against non-member nations), dragged his feet on ending state subvention of the *Landesbanken*, objected to Barroso's appointment as Commission president, arranged for the designation of a trusty Commission vice president for economic affairs, who could block single-market initiatives, and lobbied for the creation of European champions. Like Chirac, he took a personal hand in trade missions, curried favor with Putin, and backed lifting the arms embargo on China. His last great act before the September elections was to clinch a deal with Russia for a gas pipeline running offshore along the Baltic coast from Vyborg to Greifswald. His reward was a seat on the board of the new Gazprom-controlled energy supplier. The pipeline deal confirmed the new special relationship developing between Berlin and Moscow. Brussels was not consulted.[71]

Schröder indeed had traveled far from Kohl's independent line and Germany's traditional support for open markets, not to mention from the red-green coalition's original principles. At the top of the list in 1998 were such issues as torture, forced-labor camps, and public executions. These human rights matters were neither raised in Russia, whose bilateral trade with Germany doubled between 1999 and 2003, nor put on the agenda in Beijing. In December 2004, on his sixth state visit to China, Schröder promised to lift the arms embargo in return for billions of dollars of orders for 23 passenger aircraft, 180 locomotives, several power plants, and a sewage treatment plant. Josef ("Joschka") Fischer remained silent about the matter. Michael Rogowski, president of the Association of German Industry, did not "feel well enough to be present at the deal-closing in the Great Hall of the People." After months of intense pressurizing had failed to generate any support in the *Bundestag* for lifting the arms embargo, even within his own party, Schröder curtly announced that "it says in the Constitution that foreign policy is made by the federal government" and asserted that he was ready to lift the embargo whatever the delegates might say about the matter. Desperation had turned Schröder into an arms merchant.[72]

He seemed to do everyone a favor by advancing the election. A CDU/CSU sweep would give Merkel a chance to grapple with German federalism, tackle the welfare state, and open markets. The time is ripe. German corporatism is on its last legs economically, the unions are crumbling, and management is keen to change. The mainsprings of German industrial strength are intact. Only politics stands in the way of necessary reforms. It's obvious what's needed. Half of the United States' growth advantage over Germany in the past five years can be attributed to the rise of Big Box Capitalism – to China-sourced Wal-Mart and its imitators.[73] Restrictive German retail regulation still obstructs this easy path to growth. It should be lifted. Overprotective German labor legislation, which prevents both firing and hiring, is indefensible. Labor market flexibility must be introduced to end unemployment and increase the numbers at work. Reform in these two areas can ignite economic recovery and reduce the burden of the welfare state.

Neither these nor other basic reforms will have a chance in the near future. To form her government, Merkel sacrificed her reform program. Her "flagship measure" is a 3-percentage-point increase in the value-added tax to 19 percent, which will be used to plug the budget deficit, and a scaled-in elevation of the retirement age to sixty-seven. Said one saddened political analyst, "This really gives no hope to anybody in Germany. . . . Germans would like one idea, one phrase, one catchword to encourage them. This is the lowest common denominator." The coalition policy, which burdens a stagnating economy with tax increases against a background of rising interest rates, seems unlikely to spark growth and, if the example of Japan in the 1990s remains relevant, could be seriously deflationary.[74] Merkel's lack of a mandate – which meant that the anti-Blair and lame-duck Schröder represented Germany in EU functions until mid-November – was also a heavy blow to the British EU presidency of late 2005. The electoral deadlock had the same effect on business sentiment, which turned sharply south, threatening what promised to be a budding recovery. In spite of underlying industrial strength, Germany will remain politically weak.[75]

Hard Case: France

Wouldn't it be great if Chirac acted like Schröder – and just stepped down? Chirac's presidential term will not, however, expire until April 2007. Chirac first entered the cabinet in 1967, first became prime minister in 1974, and first became president in 1995. When his present term ends, he will have been at the summit of French politics for nearly forty years. During this seemingly endless career, he has "left no permanent mark" on France, done nothing about unemployment, and has not undertaken any major reform beyond, perhaps, abolishing military service. He has, according to recent biographer Bertrand Delais, "basically done nothing... because he believes in nothing – except perhaps the way we live in this country." Neither the referendum debacle, nor a stroke in September, nor even the rioting immigrant youth, who torched several thousand cars for two consecutive weeks in October and November 2005 – the worst disorders since 1968 – changed the regal way he governed France. Through it all, unlike General De Gaulle, he appears never to have considered resigning.[76]

One should add – lest it not be obvious – that Chirac also believes in holding on to power. Thus, the overriding concern of policy making for him – more important than Europe, more important than the economy, more important even than the loss of French influence in the world – has been to turn back the challenge of the determined and politically savvy forty-six-year-old insurgent, Nicolas Sarkozy, his former finance and present interior minister. Chirac worries little about the official Socialist opposition, a graying, spiritless, spineless, easily divisible, intellectually depleted, and shrinking party. The Socialists tumbled into despair after the defeat in the first round of the 2002 presidential election. Chirac expected them to split on the Euro-constitutional referendum, and they did. The Socialists are following the French Communists through the Way Out of history. Sarkozy, however, is something new on the scene. Young, cocky, a non-Enarch, and independent minded, the challenger threatens the circularity of the French political process. Round, round, and round again – it has the intellectual tension of a Tibetan prayer wheel. Or at least it would if Chirac had his way: wounded by the referendum defeat too severely to win reelection in 2007 and probably too old and feeble as well, Chirac placed his support and the power of the French state behind his alter ego, Dominique de Villepin, and the young, pompadoured aristocrat promptly took up the cudgels against Sarkozy.[77]

In 1995, Chirac promised to "restore the cohesion of France," tackle the unemployment problem head on, and "act with determination for strong and lasting growth." In 1995, unemployment was at 11.2 percent; ten years later, it is at 10 percent; in 1995, growth was at 1.8 percent; ten years later, it runs at an annual rate of 1.9 percent. Public finances remain squeezed, the "social fracture," as demonstrated by the rioting in the *banlieues*, is worse than ever, and the welfare state remains unreformed. The economy has exhibited some signs of life but is now being stuffed back into a *dirigiste* girdle. Fifty-four percent of it remains in the public sector. The tax burden is still crushing. According to World Bank league tables, the cost of hiring an additional worker in France is equal to a staggering 47 percent of salary. Because it is nearly impossible for an employer to fire anyone, the employer has a powerful disincentive to hire anyone; of 154 countries, ranked by ease of firing, France ranks 147. Such excessive employment protection, together with the thirty-five-hour week, keeps the number of hours worked low and unemployment high. The excessive minimum wage (61 percent of the national median as opposed to 36 percent in the United States) provides a special disincentive to taking on unskilled and untrained labor.[78]

The lack of anything solved or changed and the monotonous predictability of nothing ever being accomplished is extremely demoralizing. French public life is morose. The historian Perry Anderson thinks that the fall of communism drained France of the common bond of hope and aspiration needed for the sense of spiritual community on which, since Rousseau, French nationhood has rested. He points out as well that Anglo-Saxon liberalism – with its notions of incremental progress developing from competition within a pluralistic society – has never found a home in France. Indeed, it seems unnatural, or as put by the great historian Francois Furet, "The [present] condition is too austere and contrary to the spirit of modern societies to last."[79]

Neoliberalism, à la française, adds Anderson, has never caught on in France. Since François Mitterrand's famous U-turn, in 1982 from socialism to the market, the French electorate has rejected every attempt at reform. Laurent Fabius, recently head of the Socialist *non* faction, was also the first prime minister on the Left to discover "the culture of the firm." He was turned out in 1986. Chirac, who as prime minister launched the first wave of privatizations on the Right, got the heave-ho two years later. Pierre Beregovoy, pillar of the hard franc, met with same end in 1993. Edouard Balladur, an "Orleanist moderate," went down at the polls in 1995. Alain Juppé, who attacked the pension issue head-on, triggered a huge wave of strikes and was unceremoniously dumped in 1997. The Socialist Lionel Jospin – actually the most active privatizer of the lot – got routed in 2002. Shrewdly calling in the stodgy Jean-Pierre Raffarin to introduce unpopular reforms, Chirac threw him to the wolves after the referendum debacle.[80]

Raffarin was, by all odds, moderately successful. In spite of massive public sector strikes in June 2003, he managed to introduce modest reductions in civil service pensions and copayments for medical treatment. He also introduced primary care "gatekeepers" for referrals to prevent duplication of services and screen out abusive overuse of the system. Needed to stave off financial collapse, these modest measures represented steps in the right direction. They were, however, only stopgaps. The French medical system, though good, is the most expensive in Europe and will become more so with increasing life expectancy and rising healthcare costs. A more complicated matter, the pension system discriminates against employees in the private sphere and provides disproportionate benefits to politically privileged public sector interests such as railroad and electric-power workers.[81]

Threatened cuts to benefits programs can always be counted on to trigger demonstrations in France. In Paris alone, 1,461 demonstrations took place in 2001. Raffarin's pension reform bill set off general strikes in May and June of 2003, which twice brought the country to a halt. The effectiveness of such work stoppages stems not from the size of the labor movement – a mere 8 percent of the employed belong to unions, less actually than in the United States – but for several main reasons: the syndicates (along with employers) control and administer pension and medical funds, public employees represent more than a quarter of the labor force, almost every family in France depends, at least in part, on wages or pension benefits from the sector, and alternative means of expressing political opposition in France are, finally, limited.

France's "republican monarchy" is ill-adapted to modern democracy. One man, placed at the summit of power – with all the levers of state at his disposal and without any real opposition – can only, according to the former socialist minister of culture, Jack Lang, "create confusion, doubt, and finally rejection by the citizens."[82] Unless it begins in the streets, change in this rigid system can only start at the top. The president of the Fifth Republic, whose institutions were designed by and for Charles de Gaulle, has near-dictatorial powers. Mitterrand, an avowed opponent of "presidentialism," succumbed utterly to its temptations during his fourteen years in office. The French presidential system lacks US checks and balances. Judicial appointments are subject to political interference. The legislature remains captive, and the president makes all senior civil service appointments. The media is too weak to expose this system.

There is, first of all, no real French tradition of investigative reporting. Although these matters were well known to insiders, the public did not learn until late in his term that Mitterrand had been a Vichy official and protected war criminals in public positions, or that he had been diagnosed with prostate cancer shortly after taking office, or that he, a married man, had not only kept a mistress – hardly a shock – but had raised their daughter. Surely, some of these issues are more important than others. Still, the press did not see fit to reveal any of them.[83]

Nor did it, until years later, expose the widespread corruption surrounding Chirac in his eighteen years as mayor of Paris. Grafting was hardly confined to the capital. In Europe, France ranks above only Greece and Italy in the league tables of Transparency International. More than 500 politicians have faced charges of one kind or another in the past few years. Chirac's operation involved taking a 2 percent cut on all public contracts, about a quarter of which he diverted to secure the complicity of the Socialists and Communists. Forty-seven of Chirac's closest former associates stand under indictment for embezzling public funds, including his chief of staff and, most embarrassingly, Guy Drut, a gold-medal-winning hurdler and member of the now disbanded French Olympic Committee. In February 2004, Chirac's heir apparent, Alain Juppé, was found guilty of corruption. So long as he remains head of state, Chirac, affectionately known as "The Crook" (*l'escroc*), enjoys immunity from prosecution. He, otherwise, would also face charges of vote rigging.[84]

The mock-democratic institutions of the Fifth Republic enable Chirac to make far-reaching commitments, often in violation of the letter or spirit of the law and without benefit of a genuine public mandate. After Chirac flushed Jospin in 2002, no election was held until March 2003. The results of the presidential election were deceptive. Only 19.9 percent of the electorate voted for Chirac in the first round, the lowest ever, and still fewer for his National Assembly lists. The regional elections of March 2003 were a complete repudiation of the government in power and resurrected the Socialists. The Chirac party lost in nearly every department. Chirac's preferred venue is behind the scenes. France does not like to be bound to the rules it makes for others in the EU, especially those for competition and state aid. It is also the slowest in implementing regulations and directives and among the least reliable in enforcing them. This bad behavior prompted an investigation by the French Socialist deputy, Marcel Floch, who blamed it for the loss of French influence in Brussels. A flurry of commentary ensued, much of it irrelevant. French influence has actually increased over the last three years; the mode of its exercise has merely shifted from official to unofficial terrain – from the drudgery of the Commission and the bickering of the Council to deal making, albeit in the name of the EU, with other, and often foreign, heads of state.[85]

If this policy rests on a design, it was a plan to organize a "core Europe," which, according to the journalist John Rossant, is "a kind of protectionism lite, which promotes national champions and, when necessary, uses market methods to advance *dirigiste* goals. The other traits [are] a determination to keep US influence at bay and bend EU rules to promote the interests of the core, even at the expense of the periphery."[86] In January 2004, to frustrate a bid from the Swiss Novartis, the French treasury organized the takeover of the Franco-German drug maker Aventis, by the much smaller Sanofi-Synthelabo to create a French national champion in pharmaceuticals. In August 2004, the Commission, moreover, capitulated to French demands for an injection of half a billion euros into the chronically ailing Machines Bull in order to prevent France's national IT champion from going under. Earlier it acceded to, and even helped arrange, the Alstom bailout. In the financial sector, in December 2002, the treasury brokered the merger of France's first megabank, when Credit Agricole took over the scandal-ridden state-owned Crédit Lyonnaise.[87]

Privatization has by no means stopped. It continues less from a desire to promote free enterprise than from a need to raise money to reduce the budget deficit and to relieve that state of the subsidy burden. France Télécom, like its German counterpart, wildly overexpanded in the late 1990s; to raise money, the state had to sell a part of its holdings in fall 2004. Electricité de France, an unlisted company, while protecting its domestic monopoly, also went on a foreign acquisition binge. It would also have to issue stock for a third of its capital in late 2004 in order to keep its nose above water. Gaz de France found itself in a similar situation. Air France similarly merged with the Dutch national carrier KLM in order to stay in business. Although right-wing governments are reluctant to sell majority shareholdings, even this can often be done without ceding control. The role of the state in the economy remains huge and continues to grow. Prime Minister Villepin is hard at work crafting legislation to protect ten "strategic industries" from not only foreign but EU buyers. The list of them includes not only biotech and pharmaceuticals but also casinos and yoghurt.[88]

Only Nicolas Sarkozy, it seems, can get France out of its present rut. President Chirac has detested this former protégé since 1995, when he backed Edouard Balladur as the UMP candidate. Sarkozy was out of the picture until 2002, when, to his subsequent regret, the present dauphin, Dominique de Villepin, helped rehabilitate him. Chirac apparently promoted Sarkozy to chief of the Treasury in order to saddle him with responsibility for the intractable budget problem. Sarkozy, nonetheless, put on a public show that kept him in the limelight. Chirac had unwittingly created a rival. Within a few months, "Super Sarko" became the darling of the political Right and the favorite of the UMP party to succeed Chirac. In November 2004, Chirac forced out Sarkozy as finance minister but, to prevent defection, allowed him to remain chairman of the UMP. He was the preferred presidential candidate of 80 percent of the party until summer 2005, when his popularity began to slip. His hard line during the fall rioting would cost him support from the center but win him friends from the extreme right-wing Front Nationale of Jean-Marie Le Pen.[89]

What does Sarkozy really want – other than to replace Chirac? He has spoken boldly about the need for economic reform, but he has also tried to organize Euro-champions. His record at the Treasury is decidedly mixed. He stanched the already excessive French budget and bludgeoned supermarkets to break with retail price maintenance, but he failed to scrap the thirty-five-hour week. Sarkozy arranged the takeover of Aventis by Sanofi-Syntholab and presided over the merger of Air France and KLM. He engineered the bailout of Alstom, preventing its takeover by Siemens. Sarkozy further launched an initial public offering (IPO) for a portion of the aero-engine maker Snecma and sold 10 percent of France Télécom. Additional such deals were in the works when he was forced to step down. Sarkozy may be an official champion of market reform but he has consistently played it safe. Like Tony Blair, the man does not show his hand until forced to. He is, withal, a breath of fresh air. It will be impossible to determine which way the wind will blow until, if and when, he reaches office.[90]

Hard Case: Italy

Italy shares many common problems with Germany and France but by no means all of them. Italy is not, like Germany, burdened with a gridlocked federal system or immobilizing corporatist institutions; indeed, nothing works quite that well there. Nor is the Italian public, like the French, fixated on a widespread and deep-seated hostility to greed-driven, atomistic Anglo-Saxon "ultraliberalism"; Italians tend to be individualistic, undoctrinaire, and admiring of someone able to turn a quick buck. Moreover, the head of government does not have to contend with either a well-organized opposition or rebels in his party. The former is notoriously weak; the latter is his creation. He has no reason to worry excessively about challenges from the judiciary either: Berlusconi knows from experience what can be bought with money (he has been indicted many times but never found guilty). The same holds for much, much more as well: there is always enough cash on hand. Ancient Romans governed by bread and circuses. Silvio Berlusconi owns the circuses – the broadcast and print media, public relations firms and advertising agencies, and prestige athletic teams – as well as much of the bread. He is the richest man in Italy and probably in Europe. It has been said that having Berlusconi at the Viminale is like having an amalgam of Bill Gates, Sam Walton, Warren Buffett, George Soros, Bernard Ebbers, and (if he were still alive) Walt Disney – in the White House. Should one add, perhaps, Jim Carrey? Berlusconi not only owns the circuses: he is the circus.[91]

Yet, he has disappointed both those who expected the worst from him and those who might have hoped for something better. He has been neither tyrant nor reformer, but a fizzle. And as he has fizzled, Rome turned. An odor of decomposition is unmistakable. Once a major export power, Italy has become Europe's sickest economy – with the worst growth record in Europe over the past five years. The OECD expects the country to contract by 0.6 percent in 2005. It may, in other words, be leading Europe into recession.[92] There is no more give in the economy. Inflation has priced Italian goods out of many export markets, particularly those in which they face new competition from China. Italy cannot, because of the rules governing the euro, allow its currency to float downward, nor can it devalue the lira by raising the deficit – it already violates the growth and stability criteria. Nor does the government wield the authority needed to reduce costs by cutting benefits, raising the length of the work day, stripping away excessive labor protection, or breaking up cartels and other market-perverting schemes. Italy is in a box. Since the two referenda, the Eurobond market has placed a one-quarter-point risk premium on Italy's sovereign debt, which will drive up borrowing costs on the country's excessive national debt – at more than 105 percent of GDP, the highest in the EU. The yellow light is already flashing.[93]

Berlusconi came into office with a huge majority, a backlog of goodwill, and a hatful of tricks with which he promised to restore prosperity. Cutting down the welfare state and introducing labor market flexibility are in Italy, as elsewhere, the two essential reforms. Berlusconi made three successive attempts to turn things around – the first (April 2002) was a new law to enable employers to dismiss employees; the second (October 2003) and third (November 2004) were plans for tightening up the pension system. Each of them triggered huge general strikes – three of the six he would face – and Berlusconi capitulated before all of them. Such confrontations might not have been necessary or perhaps could have been turned back if he had been able to count on the political Right and Center to support a strong reform program. He never

devised such a plan, however, because that would have required breaking up the cozy relationships between state and private power, which
existed at every level and in every region of the country.[94]

Berlusconi is, indeed, Italy's most prominent living beneficiary of
this clientage system. He could never have built an empire based on
construction and television in the Italy of the 1980s without a powerful patron. He only entered politics after his *padrone*, the coarse and
venal Milan Socialist Bettino Craxi, fled to Tunisia to avoid imprison-
ment during the corruption scandal, which eventually brought down
the "First Republic" in 1992, and with it, the old parties. This was the
mani pulite or clean-hands campaign led by Milanese prosecutors, which
revealed that Italy was in fact *tangentopoli* – Bribe City. With the old
system in collapse and elections under new rules pending in early 1994,
Berlusconi – or better, the giant public relations firm he controlled –
organized Forza Italia!, a "postpolitical" party of his own, in a matter
of weeks. It took its name from a football cheer and its money from
the many companies the media mogul controlled. Forza is to a political party what Muzak is to music: it provides plenty of reassuring but
meaningless sound.[95]

The coalition Berlusconi headed – which included the Lega, a xenophobic but free-market party, which sought autonomy for the north,
and the neofascists, which aimed at milking the state on behalf of its
constituents in the *Mezzogiorno* – swept the elections against a disorga-
nized Left. Curiously, however, Berlusconi proved to be vacillating and
indecisive, the Lega bolted, and Forza was out within a year. Voted back
into power with a commanding majority in 2001, Berlusconi has acted
true to form as a man of words rather than deeds. One need worry no
longer. Berlusconi is not a proto-Mussolini but merely a populist mutation of the old-fashioned politician from the party, which dominated
every government in the "First Republic," the Democrazia Christiana
(DC).[96]

His nostrums – chiefly tax amnesties and partial privatizations – no
longer work, however, politically or economically. Each of the two electoral tests of the government's popularity – a combination of local and
Euro-parliamentary elections of June 2004 and regional ones of April
2005 – was disastrous. In the latter, of the Right lost six of the thirteen
in which elections were held (of twenty overall). These voters cared

little about Berlusconi's memorable Euro-gaffes (like publicly inviting the handsome Danish prime minister to bed his cheating wife so that she could escape the clutches of her ugly Venetian guru). Nor did they register protest of the magnate's manipulation of the media, his attempt to curb the independence of the judiciary, or his overt encouragement of tax dereliction. Nor did their reaction have much to do with his wildly unpopular pro-American stance on the Iraq war. Even though the two election votes came after successive income tax cuts, which gave Italy the lowest rates in western Europe, they were straight meal-ticket votes. Zero growth, flat wages, inflation, and ballooning home prices are grinding the lower-middle and working classes. Apparently heeding the message, Berlusconi resigned in April 2005 and then arranged to be reappointed. He expects to remain in office until the general election in 2006.[97]

Disgruntlement within the business community is also widespread. Italy's economic problems are well known. It has too few large, internationally competitive firms and is woefully underrepresented in high-technology fields. The comparatively few big companies are inefficient conglomerates dating from the fascist era, and they depend heavily on state aid. The traditional strong point of the Italian economy – a host of family-owned manufacturers of specialized machinery and consumer products – is today besieged by Chinese competition. The banking structure is archaic, and the comparatively few publicly traded firms are subject to manipulation. Italy badly needs structural reform.[98]

Berlusconi has done little beyond the purely rhetorical to restore growth. His gestures include demands for coordinated intervention to lower the euro, the proposal of a European four-year plan for public works, and a plea for protection against Chinese imports. Italy lacks the financial and educational infrastructures needed to adapt this family-based economy of small producers to the new challenge. The government has barely addressed this problem. The university system remains the worst in Europe; Berlusconi's only attempt to rectify the situation was to pass a law granting promotions (unaccompanied by salary increases!) to junior faculty.[99]

Under pressure from Brussels, and thanks to a handful of successful financial entrepreneurs, the world of banking has slowly begun to move. In October 2005, Unicredito took over the German HVB Bank in a 15-billion-euro deal to produce the fifth-largest banking group in Europe and a market leader in eastern Europe. Missing from the picture, however, is still any indication that the structure of the Italian economy has begun to shift toward IT or any other new innovation-based branch of production; Italy remains chronically underrepresented in them. Berlusconi has done nothing to loosen the clientage bonds that link business and the state at every level of operation in every corner of the peninsula.[100]

The horrific Parmalat scandal exemplifies many of these problems. When news began to surface that the giant dairy company from the city of fine dried ham had been cooking its books for more than a decade, one place you could not read about the breaking story was in *La Gazzetta di Parma*, which, as it happens, is owned by the company's president and CEO. Such coziness was apparently a way of life in Parma, according to testimony by Parmalat's founder, Callisto Tanzi, whose gargantuan debt – $17.5 billion – originated partly in bailouts of projects favored by local politicians. Berlusconi tried to dismiss the mess as something inherited from the bad old days but gave little support to the efforts of his finance minister, Giulio Tremonti, to replace Italy's mishmash of regulatory agencies with an equivalent along the lines of Great Britain's powerful Financial Services Authority. He preferred to put the lid on the issue. After the banks, which had sold Parmalat's spurious paper, refused (with one exception) to indemnify investors they had misled, claiming lack of liability, the government decided to bail out those with burned fingers to the tune of about $15 billion – or approximately the amount of sacrifices made to contain the budget deficit of the previous year.[101]

Opaque reporting, poor governance, weak regulation, and toleration of corruption all contribute to the "Italy risk," which increases borrowing costs, deters foreign investment, and infects the euro. A "moral hazard" problem is indeed present. The Commission has warned Italy about the widening deficit but deferred doing anything about it. With high unemployment and stalled growth, it makes economic sense for Italy to increase the money supply so long as it can count on a bailout from its Eurozone partners. If one, or one of sufficient size, is not forthcoming, Italy could drop the euro and reissue the lira – as the Lega now demands – at 20 percent below par. Bondholders would be defrauded, and the national credit would be weak for years, but growth would take hold over the short term. Italy would return to the pre-euro era – and so might the rest of Europe as well. With an economy nearly the size of France's but with little apparent power in Brussels, Italy – as has often been said – "underpunches" in the EU. Berlusconi's gauche theatrics may provide a form of light relief, but they have hardly changed this fact. Not by strength but by weakness, Italy might finally exercise the influence it has previously lacked in European affairs.[102]

As 2005 drew to a close, the Italian picture darkened. A strange sense of foreboding overhung the country. Italians were convinced after the London bombing outrages of July that they would be next; a wave of anxiety swept the country. Evidence also mounted of growing Mafia infiltration of the banking system: a wiretap of a small bank in Gelà, on the southern coast of Sicily, for instance, revealed that it was run as a joint venture by the Cosa Nostra and a local mob, the "Stidda." In casual conversation, employees frequently referred to it as a "Mafia bank." Then there was a second event – a trial in Rome of four men accused of murdering Roberto Calvi, the Mafia-linked financier known as "God's banker," whose body was found swinging some twenty-five years ago – as his Banco Ambrosiano collapsed – under the scaffolding of Blackfriars Bridge in London. The trial unearthed compelling evidence that Calvi had in fact first been strangled to death, then stuffed in the back of a car, and finally shoved off the bridge at the end of a rope. The story seemed to corroborate the accusation of the victim's wife and son (both now living in Canada) that he had been killed by mobsters at the instigation of the powerful and mysterious P-2 Masonic Lodge "to cover up the extent to which the Vatican Bank, which funded anti-communist causes in Eastern Europe and Latin America, was entangled with organized crime."[103]

There was the further strange matter of the Fiat heir, one of two, who, had he not been rushed to the hospital thanks to a timely call from his partner for the night, a transsexual called both Patrizia and Leno, would likely have died from a "lethal cocktail" of cocaine, heroin, and alcohol. Little more than a week later, in an entirely separate matter at the opposite end of the country, the deputy governor of Calabria and left-center politician, Francesco Fortugno, was brazenly shot four times in bright daylight, while voting at a polling station. Although Fortugno was the highest ranking assassination victim in thirteen years, Berlusconi did not so much as send his widow a letter of condolence – for whatever reason, a very bad sign. Some commentators interpreted it as a warning of the fierceness of the government's determination to win the next election, be it by foul means or fair.[104]

To this end, Berlusconi has become the engineer of a "putinesque" restructuring of the Italian electoral system. Included are a measure, now passed, to strengthen the powers of the prime minister, who will no longer require the assent of the president to appoint or dismiss the cabinet; a devolution measure, which would assign the regions new powers in the fields of education, police, and healthcare – a concession needed to hold together his coalition with the Lega – and finally, a law to introduce strict proportional representation by party list – a measure designed to give the Forza bloc an advantage over the more diffuse formations of the Left, which would also exclude from parliament parties receiving less than 2 percent of the vote, a measure also intended to cut down the size of the opposition.[105]

The ploy will fail, however, if the popularity of the government continues to erode and the leftist bloc forming around Signor Prodi holds together. The results of the primary were, in this respect, almost suspiciously auspicious: in a turnout twice as large as expected, which was organized by the well-disciplined ex-communists, Prodi received more than three quarters of the vote. Accusations of fraud and "fixing" came from both Left and Right. To prevent further erosion of Forza electoral support, Berlusconi has two powerful weapons at his disposal. One is the media, which he, of course, controls – and to this end, he is pressing hard for a bill to lift the remaining limits on political advertising. The other is to introduce into the campaign that symbol of Italy's economic woes, which, according to the polls, 80 percent of Italians profess to hate – the euro or, as it is referred to on the hustings, the Prodi euro. Although as president of the Commission, Prodi seemed, at times, to turn against the single currency, he was, as Italian prime minister, the architect of the austerity policy of the late 1990s, which Italy had to follow in order to meet the entry criteria for the EMU. The tough approach ended a five-year period of expansion and brought growth to a halt, which, accompanied by persistent double-digit unemployment, has never resumed.

The state of the Italian financial system makes it highly risky to raise the euro as a campaign issue. The sources of Italy's vulnerability – the

gaping budget deficits, the dishonest bookkeeping, the endemic chumminess and lack of transparency, the overvaluation of the euro, and the
declining competitiveness of the economy – are nothing really new. The
discrediting of the one institution with the power and moral authority to manage the difficult situation, the Banca d'Italia, is. The Italian
Central Bank has been, until recently, the one official institution above
reproach. As a result of the "Fazio crisis," this can be said no longer.
The bank's charter, which derives from the fascist era, provides for the
lifetime appointment of the governor, who can be dismissed only by its
board or by the president of Italy. The president lost this power when
Italy entered the ECB, but the ECB did not gain it. The sole power to
dismiss Fazio thus rests with the bank's governing board, but the governor of the bank can determine who gets appointed to it. Antonio Fazio
cannot be dismissed but, at the most, only be "asked to resign."[106]

Fazio is another case of someone who carelessly forgot about the
"wire." He was overheard, on an obviously leaked telephone tap, giving
advice and promising to help an Italian bank (Banca Antonveneta) trying to resist takeover by a Dutch bank, ABN-Amro, and subsequently
aiding a much smaller Italian bank, Banca Populare Italiana (BPI) to
buy the, in fact, larger Banca Antonveneta. He did this contrary to
the recommendations of staff and even though BPI faced indictment
for various violations of the law. Fazio's backroom dealing represented
an outrageous violation of EU rules, his bank's own charter, and recognized best practice; it was, at the same time, "business as usual" in Italian
finance or, as expressed by two Italian economists, "The real reason for
Mr. Fazio's resilience is a textbook case of 'regulatory capture,' in which
the regulator internalizes the benefits of the regulated, rather than those
of the nation."[107]

The government was divided about what to do. The finance minister, the highly respected Domenico Siniscalco, demanded Fazio's resignation, refused to allow him to represent Italy at an important meeting of the World Bank, and even mocked his mannerisms, once he
arrived. Berlusconi hesitated to fire the central bank governor knowing
that his Lega partner backed him, whereupon Siniscalco quit in disgust.
Although Berlusconi later half-heartedly suggested that it might be wise
for Signor Fazio to consider an honorable retirement, Fazio remained on
the job until December, when a Parmelat-type scandal broke out around

BPI, whose president was put under arrest. Fazio then finally stepped down. ABN-Amro had won its battle and got its bank, but Fazio won the war. In a November 8 survey of Italian banking, the *Financial Times* reported that "for foreign banks, it is a tough question to ask whether the ABN deal is a precursor to the snapping up of a raft of Italian institutions. Such deals are demonstrably difficult."[108]

The Fazio crisis played out in late September concurrent with difficult negotiations over the annual budget and how, specifically, to cut the massive 21-billion-euro deficit by 11 billion euros to 13 billion euros in order to keep Italy's huge national debt − 120 percent of GDP − from ballooning any further. This problem would have to be faced by Siniscalco's successor, Giulio Tremonti, who had already served twice as finance minister but resigned a year earlier after Fazio had sabotaged his attempt to enforce new corporate governance legislation passed in the aftermath of the Parmalat scandal. Well regarded, though also known for his expertise in "creative financing," Tremonti managed in November to secure passage of a bill that lopped off 6 billion euros in expenditure and increased privatization in order to bring in the budget at a targeted 3.8 percent deficit, within hailing distance of the much-violated stability and growth criteria. Whether, as previously, the gap will later be revised upward cannot be predicted.

The markets, however, are acting as if it will, and the European Central Bank is taking whatever action it can to prevent it from doing so. On November 10, 2005, the ECB announced that it would accept as collateral only bonds rated single A. Although the ranking allowed even the lowest-rated countries, Greece and Italy, three notches of downgrading, it was meant as a stern warning. It was also a risky one. Spreads widened a single basing point, or 0.01 percent − small numbers except in large amounts. Italy's debt amounts to 1.5 trillion euros. Unprofitable German savings and loans have, according to Anatole Kaletsky, invested "hundreds of billion of euros" in arbitrage operations by buying Italian bonds and going short on their German equivalents. If the spread grows "in the event that Italian withdrawal [was] taken seriously by the markets," they would be highly vulnerable.[109] Such a shift in sentiment, as reported by the *Guardian* on November 10, had already begun: "In short, billions upon billions of hedge fund Euros have quietly been placed on a bet that the German-Italian spread will at some stage explode. . . . They are speculating that Italy will eventually be forced out of the euro so that it can devalue the currency and re-inflate its economy."[110]

Kaletsky predicts that "some time between now and the...general election...the country's continuing membership in the Eurozone will become politically incompatible with present monetary conditions."[111] The two antidotes would be a highly unlikely ECB shift toward a loosening of the stability and growth criteria or a more probable continued decline in the external value of the euro, even against modest rate increases. While it would be rash to predict future market sentiment, three facts are indisputable, according to the lawyer's bible of central banking, *Mann on the Legal Aspect of Money*. Despite the prohibitions in EU treaties, the Italian government would, first, "have the legal authority to re-create its own currency" and, second, also "be entitled to rewrite financial contracts, including its own bond obligations into the national currency." Investors who claimed to be "defrauded by such a redenomination could not," finally, "expect support from British or American courts."[112]

Steps in the Right Direction

Can the wasteful and immobile institutions of Brussels be reformed and the big member states of the EU revive, as previously in the history of integration, by means of institutional accommodation to market-based change? An ultimate answer will have to depend, in large part, on politics. Economically, the necessary process has already begun. Its importance has been unappreciated because it has started in an unexpected place – the region of the former Soviet bloc. With growth currently running at more than 5 percent, the eight accession nations from the bloc are Europe's economic pacemakers. More importantly, most of them have – or soon will have – embarked on the kind of structural reforms the rest of Europe needs to thrive in the emerging world of global competition. They have pared down the state, simplified taxation and economic regulations, attracted high levels of foreign investment, and rewarded enterprise.[113]

The adoption of such policies has less to do with ideological conversion to competitive capitalism than post-Soviet realities. In places like the former bloc, where the state ran the economy, there is no available alternative to open-market policies other than corruption and thuggery. Although success is never assured, this fundamental truth – which holds equally for China – impels the forward development in ex-communist states of free-enterprise economies framed on the classical liberal model – resting institutionally on the rights of property and contract. It also frustrates *dirigiste* programs, such as the often unworkable accession plans drafted in Brussels, which will eventually have to be simplified and reduced in scope. The present weakness of the EU is a boon to sound development because it rules out policies such as tax harmonization – a favorite of both Schröder and Chirac – which would deprive the emerging eastern European economies of comparative advantage and restore the parasitical bureaucracies of the not-so-distant past.[114]

The recent changes in the region were largely unforeseen because the accession states got a lousy deal – one acquiesced out of weakness and vulnerability. The new nations were not taken in as equal members but as junior partners in a European *Doppelstaat*. There were plenty of grounds for pessimism concerning their fate. The easterners were to receive only a fraction of CAP subsidies; their labor mobility would be restricted for years; and regional payments were to favor the near-rich southerners at their expense. The costs of taking over the *acquis communautaire* – the corpus of EU regulations – were, in addition, heavy, and the expense of implementing them, prohibitive. According to most calculations, even if such laws were never fully enforced, entrance into the EU would drain resources from the new entrants. The political liabilities of membership were, if anything, even greater. The accession process was imposed from above, from one executive authority to another, without either the participation of, or any consultation with, political parties and in the absence of any serious public debate. Prior to accession, the EU had made itself unpopular in many parts of eastern Europe. Most citizens in the new member states viewed Brussels as a cloak for traditional western European domination. Yet, accession can be made to work if, as one high-ranking Estonian commented, the Commission "stops treating us like mice in laboratories."[115]

The EU's conduct of accession policy, according to Alina Munghiu-Pippidi, is woefully deficient. Adoption of the *acquis communautaire* should not, she argues, be confused with progress toward democracy; the

enlargement negotiations have amounted only to "a process of check-
ing off a massive and...non-negotiable list of EU laws and regulations, chapter by chapter." The reforms necessary for stable systems of
self-government are, she adds, by comparison, "not part of the main-
stream process...but remain minor in the business of enlargement."
The mass of EU legislation has, therefore, "failed to affect the substance of the governance process at the domestic level. Nor has it, being
unsupported by bottoms-up developments [changed] existing patterns
of behavior."[116]

Concerning the corruption endemic in post-Soviet states, the EU's
"name and shame" approach (part of the celebrated "open method of
coordination") was worse than useless. Televising news clips, as directed
by the enlargement authorities, of police officials making arrests of
local mafiosi up for prosecution in special anticorruption courts simply increased public cynicism: the crooks' sneers at the cameras made
it all too obvious that they expected to be let off the next day. In fact,
anticorruption policy has only been effective when designed and put
into force locally. Regional policy provides another instance of EU ham-
handedness: "Devolution of power from the center to newly invented
meso-governments, with no tradition and no relation to existing territorial units," was bound to be complicated, according to Munghiu-
Pippidi, and "it was also not popular," because "voters were displeased to
be saddled with still another costly layer of government." More embarrassing yet, according to Ms. Munghiu, regional funding often ended
up in the pockets of politicians: the government party used "infrastruc-
tural funds to lure over 50 percent of Romanian mayors to move over to
their party between 2001 and 2004 [thus overturning] the results of local
elections."

Driving EU policy was the one-size-fits-all mentality of Brussels
officialdom – as Minghiu puts it, "the need of the Commission to
impose a model they thought would facilitate the effective absorp-
tion of regional funds, with no thought given to how this will
impact...national political systems." Once Poland and Hungary had
managed to get the new regional agencies operating, the EU switched
course, abolished them, and restored power to the central authorities.
The "regional model" was not dropped, she adds, because EU enlargement experts realized that "state building from the top down [would

fail]," but because "it had become clear that ... artificial creations could not be entrusted to meet the pressing deadlines on spending structural funding." In other words, they were too inefficient to give money away. This very persistent and serious problem is a guaranteed waste maker and corruptor. Eliminating the cooked-up regional authorities did not solve the inefficiency problem but merely centralized it.[117]

Post-Soviet governments in power everywhere use "administrative resources" to remain in office. They campaign with government vehicles, control the public media, and, when possible, exclude minorities (e.g., the Russians in Latvia and Estonia). EU funding encourages such tendencies. The new EU response to such things is to obfuscate, in Minghiu-Pippidi's words, "to underestimate all election problems." But "denial" only begins at this point. With few exceptions, accession nations cannot afford the high costs of the *acquis communautaire*. Nor can, or should, they try to meet the growth and stability criteria of the EMU, a condition of accession, which Brussels uses as a cudgel, even though half the countries of the Eurozone are themselves now out of compliance. Neither the accession nations, nor the Commission, nor even the old member states want to disclose to the public that in eastern Europe, implementation of the *acquis* and membership in the EMU are unrealistic; it would be tantamount to admitting that the accession process cannot work as officially constituted. This would horrify the French and Germans, who fear less tax-burdened and bureaucratic competitors; it would also embarrass and likely force out of office the politicians who committed their countries to such impossible conditions.[118] Hypocrisy is the optimal solution: pretend that things are okay; otherwise, they will get worse. For the rest, let new members, and those who might follow them, paddle their own canoes. When given the chance to do so, they have done surprisingly well.

Within six months of accession, by early 2005, the beginnings of prosperity, underpinned by institutional reform, had brought about a tidal shift in sentiment in the accession countries toward the EU. Foreign investment was the key to growth, and free-market reform the magnet that drew it. There are a few milestones. Estonia provided the model, Slovakia copied it first, and while Poland sways back and forth, the Czech Republic will probably follow suit in March 2006 if the ODS party replaces the unpopular social democrats. In Hungary, the former traditional-authoritarian Fidesz party of the Right has taken a free-market turn; it, too, promises reform.[119]

This growing, if still patchy, commitment to classical liberal ideas is, in turn, creating a new mood in eastern Europe, whose statesmen now view themselves less as spokesmen for threatened national interests than as representatives of a regional association of like-minded peoples whose authority is on the rise. Within a year of entering the EU, the nations of eastern Europe have ceased to be passive recipients of *Diktats* from the powerful West and are becoming active agents of change. They fully expect the EU of tomorrow to give weight to their views concerning the internal structure and external dimensions of the association. On the whole, they favor enlargement, competition, and diversity – a broader, looser union along the lines traditionally advocated by Great Britain. This is the constituency that Tony Blair would need as president of the European Council in the second semester of 2005 to put Europe on the course its future welfare requires.

THREE

Innovation

Do science and technology hold the keys to the future of the European Union (EU)? The notion reflects the conventional wisdom that research and development (R&D) drives growth in the knowledge economy through change brought about by the interaction of intellectual breakthrough and marketplace discovery. The result of this process, innovation, is an often-heard but much-abused word in Eurocratic Brussels, which, while advocating progress through R&D, stifles it. The gap between European promise and performance has widened since 2000 and is likely to grow in the future even with more active EU sponsorship of R&D. Europe will therefore not only fall further behind the United States but also lose ground to the emergent superpowers of China and India, which are expected to advance more rapidly than either the EU or the United States.[1]

The broad contours of the scientific innovation process – which the futurist RAND Corporation terms the global technology revolution – are evident even now as it unfolds. The global technology revolution advances in three overlapping waves: the familiar one of information technology (IT), the controversial one of genomics, and the arcane one of nanotechnology. Each dates from a path-breaking invention: the microprocessor, genetic engineering (recombinant DNA) in 1971, and the atomic force microscope (AFM) in 1986. The three waves interact in complicated ways. The latter two presuppose the development of IT; they require computational modeling tools demanding "petaflops" (thousands of trillions of floating-point operations per second) of computing power as well as terabytes (trillions of bytes) of storage. These requirements have given rise to a whole new branch of the hardware and software industry called bioinformatics and have also spurred on the search for ever-smaller and more powerful engines of knowledge transmission and diffusion, thereby stimulating the development of nanotechnology.[2]

Nanotechnology is defined as the science of substances measuring less than 100 nanometers (one ten-millionth of a meter) in at least one dimension. Such substances are generally submolecular; in biology, nanoscience deals with the scale at which biochemical processes take place within cells. Nanosubstances are so small that gravity affects their movement less than viscosity; they thus have different properties than larger microsubstances and act more like a wave than a particle. Nanoscience rests on developing the use of such tiny units as building blocks of a new type. An obvious application is to consumer items, where nanomaterials have superior properties such as water repellence; a less obvious one is biomimetics in which artificial materials, operating through a DNA template, imitate cells performing (or failing to perform) biological functions. In addition to such medical applications, nanoscience opens the gates to the continued operation of Moore's law, the doubling of microchip capacity every eighteen months.[3]

Whereas the IT wave has long since begun to break and the nanowave is just beginning to form, the genomic wave is still rising and likely will not peak for years, even decades, to come. Mapping the human genome can be compared to the development of the periodic table in the 1880s. It may well be that whereas chemistry and physics defined the science of the twentieth century, biotechnology will shape that of the twenty-first century. "We appear," according a team of RAND futurologists, "to be on the verge of understanding, reading, and controlling the genetic coding of living things, affording us revolutionary control of biological organisms and their deficiencies."[4] The result may be lives made longer, and arguably richer, by genetic targeting of drugs, by the repair and replacement of body parts either biologically or biomimetically, or through genetic engineering. The prospect raises the most searching ethical, not to mention scientific, questions of the age.

In Europe, the debate has been technological-parochial – focused, often obsessively, on the gastronomical tract and, more specifically, on the genetically modified (GM) food that passes through it. Edibles are in fact only one of three product applications of GM technology. Call it the green one. The others are red (medical) and white (industrial). All three colors are functionally interrelated. One cannot, in other words, have one without the other; each of them – as well as the broader implications of the revolution of which they are a part – should be considered together in overall policy making. The debate has also been skewed by the sowing of politically inspired confusion and disinformation at the expense of sound analysis, scientific knowledge, and economic growth. The costs have been heavy. Having been largely bypassed in the IT revolution, Europe has also been sidelined for the past five years as biotechnology has advanced in the United States and elsewhere. Although the antiscience tide turned in mid-2005 – when a backhanded agreement was reached that enabled the individual member state to determine whether or not to plant GM crops – the decision came five years too late; Europe lags far behind. The same is true for nanotechnology. The high-tech setbacks of the past several years will take at least a decade to overcome. The EU can only be part of the catch-up process. Member states must take a more active hand in policy making. Within them, universities must be revived as research institutions and new relationships struck with both business and the world of finance.

Any discussion of even the immediate scientific future must proceed with caution. A couple of preliminary points should nonetheless be borne in mind. Demand – in this case, fundamental human needs – drives the genomic revolution more forcefully than its IT predecessor; it also raises much more profound ethical problems, which require non-market solutions and prefigure a need for large-scale political engagement. At the same time, innovation will be no less critical to the biotech revolution than it was to IT. No one can predict precisely how, when, or where innovation will occur. It is, however, possible to ascertain how the process takes hold in the new economy.

Scientific breakthroughs initially yield lab-bench knowledge that is tacit rather than codified; a few key researchers (or their students) are normally responsible for the big ones. The cooperation of the scientist-inventor is thus required for successful commercialization of a product. Such figures are in fact the main resource around which firms are built or transformed in IT, biotechnology, and (according to preliminary data compiled by the Nanobank Project) nanotechnology; technological change is correspondingly concentrated in relatively few firms, industries, and places. Such change, at this early stage, does not occur evenly or incrementally but at the "exceptional firm" able to make "metamorphic progress."[5]

Comparison of publishing and patenting data across the biotech and nanotech fields makes it possible to determine, measure, and assess developmental probabilities once the stage of codification has been reached. Such data (using baselines of 1986 and 1973, respectively) suggest that nanotechnology has reached a state of development comparable to that reached by biotechnology in the mid-1980s and that knowledge is no longer only "tacit," because diffusion is now taking place. This diffusion is highly concentrated by location and follows a predictable path from a university or research center to commercial application. "Star scientist authorship of articles as, or with, employees of a firm," is therefore "a potent predictor of eventual success in [the] biotech [field]."[6] The same assumption can be made regarding nanotechnology in the near future. The implications of this fact should be sobering for Europe, according to the authors of an important recent paper. In nanotechnology, as in biotechnology, "the strength and depth of the American science base points to the US being the dominant player . . .for some time to come."[7] The authors also conclude that the United States will face increased international competition in the future, especially from China and India. Having fallen behind in research and being pressed hard from the rear, Europe will have to surge forward in product development in order to maintain its position over the coming decade.

The EU must share responsibility for Europe's sluggishness in the new technologies. In a bid to court popularity with a science-skeptical and increasingly anti-US public, acquire an important new "competence" in the field of food safety, and keep Common Agricultural Policy (CAP) subsidies from getting out of control, Brussels has tried for nearly a decade to block, by hook or by crook, both the importation of GM crops (from the United States) and the cultivation of them in Europe.[8] It thereby set in motion a runaway train of antiscientism, the stench of whose burning brakes is now overpowering. To stop its momentum will, however, require more than a new Commission directive or regulation: the raison d'etre behind EU obstructionism – the precautionary principle – will have to be junked for pro-innovation policy to take hold.[9] This will require an embarrassing and unprecedented climb-down.

The anti-GM policy has had several dire consequences. It has, as intended, hurt the United States, particularly the farmers of the Midwest, but at the same time inflicted far greater damage on Europe itself – virtually destroyed the field of molecular biology, not to mention much of the agbio and biopharma industries. The technologies now bypassing Europe are not only critical to growth of the new economy but environmentally friendly and humanitarian. GM crops are needed to raise living standards worldwide. Indeed, without them it will be impossible to feed a growing world population by 2030.

Food Fights and Their Consequences

The fate of European biotechnology as well as Europe's economic growth over the next decades requires repudiation of Brussels' attempt to block GM food by neoprotectionism disguised by the rhetoric of health and environment. It has not only fouled the US-EU relationship but set back the creation of a sound and sensible international regulatory regime for biotechnology. In the future, the unfolding genomic revolution will – for better or worse – have to be dealt with piecemeal. Europe's hand in it will be much smaller than before the food fight. A transatlantic partnership will no longer be strong enough to shape the global framework for biotech policy. Other powerful, and quite different, interests will also have to be included in top-level decision making.[10]

Europe has also been willfully blind to the apothegm of the four Ps – protectionist policy punishes its perpetrators – and thus has fallen victim to it. The rescue of European biotechnology calls for more than merely pouring money into R&D, as the EU now intends to do: decision-making authority will have to be restored to the member states – as Brussels now grudgingly recognizes – and they must introduce the necessary reforms. Only after each member state has come to its own terms with biotechnology – and science-driven change more generally – will it be possible to develop a sound framework for policy making at the European and international levels.

The food fight started with the fear of poisoning. Yet GM food and food-processing materials have been consumed not only in the United

States but, albeit less wittingly, in Europe over the past ten years, without having had any detectable adverse medical consequences.[11] No reputable authority disputes this fact. In 2001, as the agricultural political economist Robert Paarlberg points out, "the EU Commission for Health and Consumer Affairs released a summary of 81 scientific studies of GM foods conducted over a fifteen year period. None of the studies – all of them financed by the EU, not private industry – found any scientific evidence of added harm to humans or the environment."[12]

In recent years, the focus of antibiotech activism has gradually shifted from consumption to production – to the purported threat posed by biotech crops to biodiversity. This is, to be sure, a more complicated issue than the open-and-shut case of food safety. Although when left untended biocrops tend to die out more often than strains developed in the wild, it is impossible to exclude all possibility, be it natural or human, of seed or pollen migration. Although a major recent study of the contamination scare in Oaxaca, Mexico, proves conclusively that fears that GM corn (maize) will take over native strains are unfounded, crop introductions must clearly be examined carefully on an individual basis. The precautionary principle makes this impossible; it rules out accepting all risk of any kind whatsoever. Like cultivation, importation of GM crops remains highly restricted. Consequently, Europeans will not only face high food prices but experience the genomic revolution largely second-hand.[13]

Public opposition in Europe to GM foods is a deep-seated and pervasive reality. Comparison with the United States is illuminating. Americans are in fact little less wary of GM foods than Europeans; about half the public "opposes their introduction," while a quarter favors it. According to a poll conducted by the Pew Initiative on Food and Biotechnology, Americans are also less averse than Europeans to plant than animal modification. The US public is divided on stem cell research and opposed strongly to cloning, yet generally favorable to medical applications of all the various procedures. The greater US acceptance, or lack of resistance to, GM food, according to pollsters, is due chiefly to a greater voter trust in regulatory and political institutions.[14]

The Brussels authorities have tried to build new structures at the European level by capitalizing on fear. The demagogic approach has taken a heavy toll. The public has been aroused and misled. Junk science has replaced informed inquiry. Cost-benefit analysis has dropped by the wayside. The EU itself operates at sixes and sevens. Sound policy making has become all but impossible. Uncertainty and confusion pervade and undermine it, exact further economic costs, and weaken Brussels' writ.[15] Recently, the EU commissioners concerned primarily with economic growth have belatedly started back-peddling in a vain effort to reverse the antibiotech policy pursued since the mid-1990s. The tide has also turned globally. The EU's attempt to promote international protectionism in the name of food safety and environmentalism delayed but could not prevent impressive GM crop acreage increases, especially in the past few years. The restrictive policy has not stopped research but merely increased Europe's brain drain. What caused the food fight, and how did it get out of hand?

The European side of the story begins with Mad Cow Disease. The frightening outbreak of bovine spongiform encephalitis (BSE) in Britain in the mid-1990s caught European food regulators flat-footed, convinced the public (in the United Kingdom and elsewhere) that the opinions of experts were unreliable, and, as deaths mounted into the hundreds, fanned fears of contagion into a mass hysteria readily exploitable for political gain. The result was a campaign against so-called Frankenfoods, waged locally by ecological and environmental activists, championed nationally by green political parties, and sponsored by Brussels as part of an anti-American broadside supported by farm protectionists and motivated in part by fears, seldom expressed in public, that the introduction of productive GM food technologies would increase output and drive up the costs of the CAP to unacceptable levels. Biotechnology, it need hardly be emphasized, had nothing whatsoever to do with the outbreak of BSE.[16]

On the US side, the explanation for the food fight begins with the heavy-handedness of Monsanto, the dominant force in the biotech field. A chemical company turned artificial seed producer, the firm's product introductions represent a public relations disaster of historic proportions. They have had the effect of mentally associating biotechnology with big US agro-multis, an obsession with "profit at any cost," and superpower bullying; the anger it aroused has, at the same time, blinded the public to the immense potential benefits of the new crop technology.[17] General skepticism concerning the merits of biotechnology may persist for years to come. Monsanto made a classical marketing error: it forgot, in introducing its breakthrough products, that the ultimate market for seeds was the food-eating public rather than the farmers who bought and planted them. The St. Louis–based company made little effort to address consumer concerns before, or while, developing the product. Monsanto invented each of the two strains that today dominate the markets for GM foodstuffs and other crops. One of them, glyphosate, is resistant to a patented and still-proprietary herbicide (Roundup Ready) and marketed for corn (maize), soybeans, and canola (rapeseed). The other, chiefly for cotton, *Bacillus thurengiensis* or Bt, eliminates the need for pesticide.[18]

Both varieties raise output per acre significantly, reduce consumption of chemicals impressively, and have substantial collateral environmental benefits. They do not require tilling and leave the subsoil ecostructure intact, reduce chemical spill-off and also the pollution of water and streams, increase habitat, and eliminate threats to endangered species by improving acreage output. New strains are being developed for plants that are salt- or drought-resistant as well as for crops that grow more rapidly – thus increasing wood supply and freeing up land for alternative uses – have special medicinal properties, or are suitable to high latitudes. Biotechnology is still at an early stage of development, and its broad implications are only beginning to be realized. Clearly, however, the future cultivation of GM crops will substantially increase the provision of world foodstuffs, lead to meaningful improvement in the quality of edibles, and have numerous important nonfood applications.[19]

Monsanto's critics have accused it of developing Frankenfoods in order to monopolize the seed business, a charge given credence because the glyphosate-resistant variety was engineered specifically for its in-house herbicide – whose patent will, however, soon expire. The company is additionally suspect for prohibiting reuse of its seed corn and requiring users to repurchase it annually. The procedure seems, but is not, wanton, wasteful, and costly. The biotech seeds (F1 hybrids), produced from pure parental strains, do not breed true; therefore farmers must go back to the seed merchants after every planting.[20]

This practice *does* involve an undesirable degree of single-source dependence, but it is contractual, legal, enforceable, and arguably necessary to contain externalities – such as the spread either by natural or human agents of seed pollen. This threat is, however, diminishing. The development of so-called "terminator technology," which kills a seed after a single planting season, sounds cruel but may provide the ultimate solution to the contamination threat. A "blocking gene" for corn, which prevents GM contamination, is also now on the market. It is also possible to determine by satellite whether contamination is occurring. Nonetheless, the need to monitor seed use does raise serious antitrust issues, which must be dealt with in the public forum.[21]

Although Monsanto might have done a better job of merchandising, the firm had little choice to recover the heavy investment required by GM technology (about $200 million to patent a biological trait) other than to sell a product that created cost savings in the big cash crops. Price competition would then, it was hoped, spur demand – as in fact has happened in much of the producing world. As R&D costs decline, attention can be redirected to improving quality, creating a "second generation" of specialized products, and serving humanitarian objectives – that is, effort can be devoted to making food better and healthier as well as cheaper, developing medicinal (e.g., nonallergenic) edibles, and improving strains of staple crops (e.g., yams and cassava) consumed by the world's poor. As in the IT industry, spread of the new technology can also eventually be counted on to reduce the power of dominant producers. Barriers to entry are low in biotechnology compared, for instance, with the nuclear power industry. There should be ample opportunity for niche and specialized producers.[22]

Capitalizing in October 1998 on a concocted crisis in which an experimental field seeded with Bt-based corn was wrongly accused of threatening the habitat of monarch butterflies, the EU Commission imposed a moratorium on new approvals of genetically engineered commodities, only nine of which had by then been introduced as opposed to some fifty in the United States. By this time, one out of every three acres in the United States was being planted for export, and three-quarters of soybeans as well as a third of all US corn were genetically modified. The ban was highly protectionist. House Speaker Dennis Hastert got it right in stating that "devoid of scientific or health concerns, the [Italian] government wants to protect their markets, and they don't have a more productive product. Basically, they don't want their farmers to be more productive because they'd have to subsidize them more." The restrictive measure would shut down some $300 million worth of US corn shipments per year until, in response to a World Trade Organization (WTO) complaint from the United States and other major exporters, the EU eventually lifted it in May 2004.[23]

Its replacement was not, however, free trade but a noxious new labeling regime. A law was in fact already in effect, which enabled producers of organic food to so indicate in their packaging. The new law required reams of new paperwork. Required was the "farm to fork" labeling of all foods, processing agents, and food stocks – including animal feed – containing GM products, except for bioenzymes. In Europe as well as in the United States, such enzymes are used in the making of most cheese and the brewing of nearly all beer. The new law also contained a particularly onerous tracking stipulation – extending even to derivatives of GM plants, such as corn oil or beet sugar, which leave no chemical traces. It "obliges every operator in the food chain to maintain a legal audit trail for all GM products, recording where they came from and where they went."[24] The detailed requirements could only have the effect of stigmatizing biofoods, such as tobacco or liquor, as hazardous.

The traceability rule is flat out discriminatory. In Europe, where GM crops are not grown, the regulation presents few problems. It overwhelms US exporters, however, who will be required to segregate GM and non-GM produce throughout the food chain at the very low threshold of 99.1 percent nonbio. All of which may be moot: "The traceability requirements are so complex and detailed," complained the president of the US food processors association, "that they equate to the [methods] for handling nuclear waste. What perception will such a [procedure], applied to food, bring about in the minds of European consumers?"[25]

There is no serious rationale for any of these safeguards and plenty of doubt concerning their feasibility. A spokesperson for Britain's Food Standards Agency called them a "cheat's charter," because the labeled product being devoid of any detectable material, inspectors would have to rely on "paper trails," and the success of the procedure depended on the "honesty of a producer in a third country."[26] The content requirements stipulated for the labeling have no scientific basis whatsoever but are the result of political compromises. The exclusion of bioenzymes from the disclosure requirement has no explanation other than to protect European producers. The official political rationale that they will, as put by Health and Consumer Affairs Commissioner David Byrne, "help in building public confidence in new technologies" is disingenuous; the primary purpose of the policy is to delay, even prevent, their introduction.[27] The only certain outcome of the new labeling law is the entrenchment of a costly new bureaucracy, the European Food Safety Authority (EFSA). Although the EFSA was authorized in 1999 – after a pseudo-crisis concerning the dioxin contamination of Belgian chickens – it could not be set up until 2003 because of a running battle over where to locate operations. Notwithstanding a stream of Berlusconi's insults to Finnish cuisine, the food authority's offices were, as planned, eventually divided between Helsinki and Parma, Italy.[28] The four idle years caused by the delay in inspections witnessed no outbreaks of food-related illness.

The EFSA is, however, only the tip of the food-safety iceberg. The European Commission's Joint Research Center in Ispra, Italy, supports its activity scientifically by developing new systems for monitoring and detecting GM foodstuffs. For this purpose, the Sixth Framework Program (FP6) for research, moreover, also set aside funding of 685 million euros. What did it matter that Geoffrey Podger, on his first visit to Washington as executive director of the EFSA, freely admitted that there is "no new scientific evidence" to suggest that French housewives, Italian schoolchildren, or serious British trenchermen face any threat from Frankenfoods? The issue, he insisted, was about the need to change perceptions.[29]

In April 2004 the EU's health commissioner, David Byrne, proudly announced, to that end, the activation of a largely redundant new food control system, which, among other things, includes the setup of thirty-seven new Border Inspection Posts to screen incoming products from non-EU countries, the creation of "national surveillance networks on food and food safety that will link in with the EU's early warning system," the introduction of "food and feed control systems" as well as "control of GM food," and the placement of restrictions on EU sales of products from the accession countries.[30]

Like other byproducts of "beneficial crises," such as the duplicative European Air Safety Authority (created in 2002 after the crash of a Swiss jet) and the European Center for Disease Prevention and Control (organized after the 2004 SARS scare in China), Byrnes's outfit spreads its influence by mission creep. The recent Nutrition and Health Claims Directive (NHCD) calls for the introduction of "nutritional profiling." The NHCD would ban the use of all unproven health claims ("Guinness is good for your health!"), require labeling of any potentially adverse medical consequences of product consumption, and disallow even verifiable claims to the contrary. The potentially harmful effects of olive oil (fat content) would, under this system, be listed but not its beneficial ones (source of "good" cholesterol). Member of European Parliament (MEP) Martin Callanan regards the directive as evidence of the nanny-state gone mad.[31]

Although vehemently opposed to the complicated new requirements, hard-hit US cultivators of corn and soybeans still do not know how they will be implemented or how to react to them. A US complaint filed in late 2003 with the WTO remains unresolved because the WTO lacks specific authority to modify regulations adopted to protect public health. Complicating matters still further, the European Court of Justice ruled that the EU was not legally responsible for the enforcement of GM bans adopted by individual member states, including those unsupported by scientific evidence of any kind. The EU is not expected to admit more GM imports until at least 2006.[32]

The United States filed suit only after it became evident that EU resistance to GM foods was increasingly influencing the policies of other nations, threatening US interests worldwide, and complicating attempts to negotiate constructive solutions in the biotech field. In August 2002, with his country facing famine, the president of Zambia refused GM-based US emergency food relief because he had been told that it was "poison" and that by cultivating it his country would also fall afoul of EU import regulations. According to Norman Borlaug, the Nobel Prize-winning father of the Green Revolution, concerns of African corn contamination are groundless because neither natural nor GM temperate-zone corn will grow well in African ecologies, and "even if some curious farmer were to plant some GM grain received as food aid, its continued presence in the field would be unlikely.... In Zambia, a land-locked country with poor transportation and low agricultural productivity, [moreover] the prospects for exporting corn to Europe in the foreseeable future are almost zero."[33]

After Zimbabwe, Mozambique, and Malawi echoed Zambia's complaints, US trade officials decided to act. By then the EU had made considerable headway in influencing intergovernmental organizations (IGOs), nongovernmental organizations (NGOs), and even the development of markets. As the world's leading food importer – including 75 percent more than the United States from the "third world" – the EU could count on a serious hearing from that quarter; then too, the United States unwisely cut development assistance to poor countries by half in the 1990s, while European donors remained very much on the scene.[34]

Generally, protechnology and humanitarian organizations have therefore not promoted GM foods. The Food and Agriculture Organization (FAO) of the United Nations now mostly gives advice on how to regulate biotechnologies, which their director general has declared unnecessary to alleviate world hunger by 2015. The largely European-funded Consultative Group on International Agricultural Research (CGIAR), whose stated goal is to promote "cutting edge science to reduce poverty and hunger," has stopped field testing "golden rice" at its facility in the Philippines for fear of antagonizing local NGOs. The World Bank has backed off from endorsing GM in the face of EU opposition. The United Nations Environment Program has set up a special program to help developing countries draft precautionary biosafety regulations, which, it insists, must be in place before any GM planting begins.[35]

The EU-sponsored Cartegena Protocol concluded in 2000, finally, explicitly endorses the precautionary principle and allows governments to restrict GM imports even of seeds – one stage before the farm – without any scientific demonstration of risk. Real regulatory clarity in the biotech field, concludes an expert from the Brookings Institution, "is many years away. Following the trail of responsibility for managing . . .risk is like playing an annoying game of 'whack a mole.' Every time one looks to a national, regional, or international institution for guidance, another one pops up with its own inconsistent standards."[36] Plantings have, in short, been delayed not only in Europe but precisely in those countries most in need that are also now committed to introducing EU-designed regulatory systems they are ill-equipped to manage and cannot afford.

In the meantime, alarm bells began to clang at the Commission, once the directorates for science (which earlier had turned its back on European biotechnology) and agriculture at last recognized that a sharp decline in private investment was wrecking the industry. By 2003, field trials had virtually ended in Europe, "small and medium-sized enterprises had stopped participating in innovative plant biotechnology research," and large biotech companies had "relocated research . . .and commercialization of new GMOs outside the EU."[37] Agriculture Commissioner Franz Fischler, a determined advocate of biotech development, spent the better part of the year trying to straighten out the mess.[38]

"Coexistence" – the idea that as a matter of "free choice," both GM and non-GM plants should be cultivated once "noncontamination" was assured – was his mantra. The emotional though nonsubstantive matter of food safety was downplayed in the "coexistence" campaign on the spurious grounds that because only EU-authorized crops could be planted, it was a nonissue. Six months of roundtable discussions with environmental groups (Friends of the Earth, Greenpeace, etc.) on the one hand and agrobusiness representatives on the other led only to the underwhelming "key scientific finding that co-existence must be addressed on a crop-specific basis, because the extent of the gene flow and movement of materials between crops are highly dependent on the biological characteristics of the crop in question and on agricultural practices."[39] Any farmer could have told the expert parties as much.

The discussions otherwise got nowhere: the organic/environmentalist lobby, strongly backed by the pro-Green faction in the European Parliament, demanded complete indemnification from biotech growers for contamination under the precautionary principle – a deterrent sufficient to discourage the increased GM plantings sought by the agricultural commissioner. As with the even more divisive stem cell issue, such technical problems paled beside unresolved political ones. Member states split in unusual ways not only on allowable GM contamination thresholds but on the role of subsidiarity in the regulatory process. The Commission, along with the odd couple of France and Great Britain, favored repatriating to national authorities the power to set up "GM-free zones"; at the same time, small nations, such as Austria and Luxembourg, pressed hard for a policy of community-wide regulation.

The Commission, later upheld by the European Court of Justice, rejected an Austrian attempt to restrict GM plantings in certain regions on the grounds that it had no scientific justification for doing so – apparently in violation of its own stated policy of "coexistence." As matters now stand, countries whose elected officials have decided to adopt such bans face being directed by the Commission, acting under order of the European Court of Justice, to overrule their own laws and allow GM plantings. One could not, according to one disgusted commentator, have made up such an absurdity.[40]

The issue of biotech cultivation still remains a muddle, but at least a glimmer of hope is in sight. As of mid-2005, the EU had approved the introduction of two new GM products, the Anglo-Swiss company Syngenta's Bt11 maize (corn) and Monsanto's almost identical NK603 maize, both for human consumption, but could still, to be sure, not make up its mind on the animal feed, 1507 seed maize produced jointly by DuPont's Pioneer Hi-Bred and Dow's Mycogen, even though the EFSA had concluded that it is "no less safe than its non-GM comparators."[41] In April 2005, moreover, because of the mistaken release in the United States of 700 tons of Bt10 corn – which resists the antibody of the antibiotic ampicillin – by Syngenta, the EU slapped on a requirement that *all* imports of US corn will require an accredited lab report. The (unconfirmed) fear is that humans eating cattle fed with Bt10 feed could develop immunity to antibiotics. According to the company, however, the Bt10 antibiotic-resistant marker gene "has been approved and widely used around the world for many years, including within the EU, and is not active in the plant and therefore has no impact on the safety profile of the maize."[42] Stuck with a product sold under contract, which cannot be delivered, US exporters fume.

The US industry could, however, take at least some consolation in the publication of the EU's new register of authorized GM imports, which, for the first time, has introduced an element of predictability into the grain trade. The situation was less promising for the European bioindustry, which continues to shrink, because, according to a director of its professional association, "the regulatory machine in the EU isn't running consistently yet. If you're using this technology to bring a product to market in ten years, [one] would perhaps move one's research somewhere else, where there's consistent application of the [rules]."[43]

This inconsistency will exact a high price. Monsanto's decision to pull up GM stakes in Europe, to mention only a single upshot, was a huge blow to Europe's wheat farmers. Wheat must be bred in the place it is grown. The new markets opening in the Far East will have to be supplied by US growers.

EU farmers will pay a heavy price as trade protectionism is reduced and GM crop harvests increase within the community and flow in from overseas. Farmers will not, however, bear the brunt of the burden; the greatest costs of EU's misconceived biotech policy will fall to others. As a result, in Europe the agbio tail wags the biopharma dog. Biopharma is a $100 billion business, or a twelfth of the worldwide medicaments and vaccine industry. The European biotech industry, by sector composition similar to the American, is just more than half in healthcare but between only 5 percent and 7 percent in agbio. The food fight may doom it. European biotechnology is in even worse shape than it appears to be at first glance. The entire industry, which is smaller than a single US firm, Amgen, contains about as many companies (nearly 2000) but employs half as many, spends less than 40 percent as much on research (6 billion euros), and has annual revenues of only 50 percent as large. The Europeans also face capital shortages (raise less than 20 percent as much as in the United States), and suffer from an especially acute lack of access to critical venture capital, where it raises less than a third as much. The hostile environment bio-Europeans face has made it difficult to attract investors and impeded recovery from the burst bubble of 2000.[44] Unwisely subsidized by privatization proceeds and for years having to contend with a hostile minister of environment from the Green Party, German firms appear to be especially wobbly.[45]

According to a recent study sponsored by EuropaBio, the trade association for the industry, the inability to raise venture capital will seal the fate of most innovation-critical fledgling companies in the field – those six to ten years old. The more successful of them will likely be swallowed up by the 4 percent of companies that account for 60 percent of the industry's revenues. Only one of these mature market leaders, the Swiss firm Serona, has the bulk of its operations and does most of its research in Europe.

Most product development will have to take place elsewhere.[46] The shortage of funding in the EU is due less to the cost of money, which is actually quite low, than to the risk of uncertainty and the lack of supportive infrastructure. Successful venture capitalists – a rare breed, even in the field – are not just lenders but must also be supervising managers who operate on the cutting edge of technology and hold participations in, as well as advise, start-ups. Networks of such critical figures normally form around major research institutions and the localities housing them.[47] The product pipeline of European biotechnology is also thin. According to the Commission, 39 percent of respondents cancelled research projects on GMOs between 1999 and 2003, and the number of field trials in the EU declined by 61 percent. Key European players, such as Bayer and Syngenta, have moved their laboratories overseas, as has the sector giant, Monsanto.[48]

The British situation is particularly worrisome. Forty percent of funding by UK companies in the register of the top 700 international firms is in the "biotechnology and pharmaceutical sector," which comprises about a third of the total European industry by numbers employed and half by revenue and market capitalization. In 2003, capital spending fell by nearly a fifth to about $1.5 billion, and research spending dropped, for the first time since 1990, as opposed to an 11 percent US increase. Britain – birthplace of the double helix and one-third participant in the Human Genome Project – no longer vies with the United States for world biotech leadership. The number of crop-protection research centers dropped from six in 1996 to zero last year when Syngenta moved operations to North Carolina. The three biggest UK biotech companies – Amersham, Celltech, and Powderject – are all foreign-owned. As for research, according to the head of Oxford University's plant science department, it is "withering on the vine" – demoralizing the profession, and making it difficult to recruit high-quality graduates. In November 2004, after years of appeasing biotech Luddites, Trade and Industry Secretary Patricia Hewitt finally pledged to the passage of a new law to end biovandalism and to raise the R&D budget from 1.9 to 2.5 percent of national income.[49]

Policy Cleanup

In July 2003 the Commission issued guidelines for the "coexistence" of GM and non-GM crops, which, though vehemently opposed by eco-NGOs, represent the beginning of wisdom in Brussels regarding the food fight. They recognize that "a single approach for the entire EU would be unrealistic"; measures must be crop-specific, and "regional and local aspects should be fully taken into account"; farmer choice should be respected and planting requirements not be imposed; and best practices should be promoted. The guidelines further recommended on-site regulation of isolation, barriers, buffer zones, pollen barriers, and reliance on traditions of farmer cooperation and national liability laws. In September, the Council of Ministers endorsed the Commission's emphasis on restoring the competitiveness of European biotechnology.[50]

Two years later, on June 27, 2005, the Commission brokered a compromise that enabled five member states (Austria, Germany, France, Belgium, and Luxembourg) to maintain bans on the importation of EU-authorized GM products and directed the remaining ones to develop satisfactory plans for "coexistence" of non-GM and GM cultivation. In July, Spain – which prior to the ban had begun GM planting and been "grandfathered" – presented an elaborate plan, which at least on paper offered the necessary guarantees against contamination. The Spanish plan, in turn, derogated policy responsibility to regional authorities, which will determine, within general guidelines, whether and how to plant transgenic crops.[51]

The new EU policy has broad implications and is tantamount to an admission – something virtually unprecedented – that Brussels is ill-equipped to make GM policy. It also sets the stage for increases in cultivation within existing EU boundaries; removes the GM issue from future accession negotiations with other "breadbaskets" like Romania (where GM crop is already planted), Turkey, and Ukraine; will weigh heavily on the CAP; and will place French commodity producers (as well as their minor counterparts in other anti-GM member states) at a serious competitive disadvantage.[52] Whether, finally, the Commission's decision to respect de facto the subsidiarity principle will set a precedent for further reform in other fields remains to be seen. It could be a first step in an orderly devolution of authority to the member states.

A single extraordinary report – Genomics and Crop Plant Science in Europe – drafted by Professor Edoardo Vesentini under the auspices of the European Academies Advisory Council lays out the essentials of a serious EU biotech recovery strategy. The report calls for the development of a coherent, and quite different, EU innovation policy to rescue European plant genomics and biotechnology, the two being scientifically inseparable. Such a strategy requires eliminating "inadvertent restraints on research activities" caused by other EU legislation (e.g., energy, chemical, and recycling policies) and providing "cohesion in public funding for the priorities in plant science and the linkage to plant breeding."[53] The strategy must also be governed by cost-benefit analysis, extend from genomics research to plant breeding, and be oriented both to process (genome sequencing) and product (specific applications).

The problem facing European biotechnology, according to the report, begins with money. Comparison to the United States is instructive: in addition to substantial support from private foundations and various government agencies, the National Science Foundation (NSF) – as part of the National Plant Genome Initiative – runs a $1.3 billion program aimed at understanding the "structure and function of all plant genes at levels from molecular to the organismal and interactions within ecosystems."[54] The United States thus holds a commanding lead in plant genomics. Like Australian research, which focuses on drought resistance, Vesentini recommends that European scientists should marshal their energies around the study of genomic issues relating to local climates and soil conditions. Such a program should, he adds, emphasize many GM-relevant points: knowledge-based crop breeding; toxic waste reduction; study of the genetics of pest and pathogen resistance, symbiosis, nutritional use efficiency, and tolerance to drought, salt, and other minerals; the reduction of chemical fertilizer inputs; and the design of forest trees specialized in the sequestration of carbon dioxide (CO_2). The research effort should cut across the new fields of genome sequencing, proteomics (the systematic analysis and documentation of proteins), metabolomics (a new science driven by advances in mass spectrometry coupled with chromatographic separation procedures), and bioinformatics. It should, finally, be oriented to the discovery of new nonfood applications, sustaining the environment and securing the world supply of food and minerals.[55]

The laundry list of tasks set out in the report requires leadership at the EU level, according to Vesintini, partly because of its public-goods character but for other more pressing reasons as well. Private investors, the main and growing source of R&D funding, are "reducing their in-house research in the EU because [they are] pessimistic about the future of plant genomics." A similar worry is behind reduced university budgets and a decline in cooperation between research institutes and the private economy.[56] Adoption of the OECD's positive reform agenda of 2003 will be needed, the report adds, to change this situation. The agenda calls for reducing "forms of agricultural support that distort markets or require trade protection" like the CAP, overcoming the obsession with food safety, and amending "energy, chemicals and recycling polices," which inhibit "novel applications for non-food crops."[57]

This is a tall order indeed. It would mean breaking with food and environmental protectionism, jeopardizing the support of eco-NGOs now reveling in their new-found prominence, pulling the EU's CAP lynchpin, and restoring power to the member states. It would also have to rest on a new growth consensus within the public. More immediately, it would require reforming the Framework Programs (FPs) for R&D. None of these things is likely to take place. The revival of the Lisbon Agenda of 2000 attaches a new importance to these programs. They have, however, done little to promote European science or close the widening "innovation gap" between the EU and the United States.

In official parlance, this spread is invariably expressed in terms of R&D funding as a percentage of the GDP – 2.8 percent as opposed to 1.9 percent in Europe – as if comparable outlays would produce identical results. This overlooks a lot. Europe already trains far more scientists than the United States, and they publish more academic papers. Yet overall employment of them is much lower, especially in industry. A higher rate of private investment in research accounts for most of the US lead. About 25,000 European science and technology graduates per year leave to work or study in the United States, three quarters of whom remain there. Europeans account for about 4 percent of the total US R&D pool. The US manpower advantage owes primarily to the US ability to attract huge numbers of foreign graduates from outside of the West to jobs or advanced training.[58] The discrepancy in Euro-American outputs, as measured by quality as well as quantity of research, stems more from the level of scientific inquiry and the relationship between business and the academy than it does from overall investment rates. To produce a research product of equal value to that of the United States, Europe will need, in the words of *The Lancet*, a "comparable number of excellent research centers with flexible and open career structures and a strong entrepreneurial culture." This would, if anything, require getting the EU out of R&D and, as Vesintini emphasized, economic regulation as well.[59]

The FP6 (2002–2006) does little more than its predecessors to reduce technological lag. It has been a huge disappointment from the standpoint of plant science – worse than the two previous ones and without "specific plant thematic priorities"; if anything, it impedes progress on the biotech front. The FP6 also skirts the issue of basic research. It consists, like its predecessors, of a hotchpotch of conflicting priorities, seven in all, which are held only together by the common purpose of strengthening the EU. The priorities are life sciences, information society technologies, nanotechnology, aeronautics and space, food safety, sustainable development, and citizens and governance – which between them will eventually piece out a 20-billion-euro budget. Seventy percent of the sum will be allocated with a view to building permanent institutions ("excellence networks" and "integrated projects"), and 15 percent will be set aside for small and medium-sized enterprises.[60]

Who knows how all the money will be spent? The aeronautics and space portion has murky, half-classified quasi-military applications in the fields of nuclear physics, rocketry, and outer space. The "soft science" projects provide a window into academic obscurantism. They bear such titles as "Improvement of Sustainability Strategy: Elaboration for Economic, Environmental and Social Policy Integration in Europe," "A Framework for Socio-Economic Development in Europe? The Consensual Political Cultures of the Small West European States in Comparative and Historical Perspective," and "A Better Understanding of Progress and Challenges" – to mention only a few of the less-unwieldy descriptors.[61] The current FP is also weighted down by the *juste retour* expectation, watered down by the preference given to international cooperation, bogged down by asphyxiating application procedures, and "dumbed down" by the EU agenda.

The policy-driven character of the research program is evident in the wordy official announcement of first-year awards (166 million euros) in the field of food safety: "The project and networks, some of which will receive up to euro 17 million each, will tackle consumer-oriented issues such as food-related disease and allergies, the impact of food [sic] on health, environmentally-friendly production-methods, and environmental health risks, making use of the new approaches offered by FP6 Most of these major new research initiatives will contribute to the implementation of relevant EU policies with solid proposals and recommendations."[62] The primacy of such political priorities left little money in FP6 for basic research.

In 2003, the Science Commission addressed this problem by characteristically first inventing – and later trying to fill with content – new acronym programs, such as New and Emerging Science and Technology (NEST), supported by projects such as ADVENTURE for "new avenues in science" and INSIGHT for "discoveries that might entail risks of problems for society." Seeded with a budget of 28 million euros but with promises of substantially more to come in the future, Science Commissioner Philippe Busquin promised that NEST would "tackle the need for more flexible and responsive funding of cutting-edge interdisciplinary research at the European level."[63] His verbiage meant that, for the first time, albeit in only a small way, actual scientists would have the final word in making R&D decisions instead of having to operate within the dictates of EU policy. This first small step toward the creation of a mechanism for evaluation along the lines of the US National Science Foundation, NEST would be followed at the end of the year by a proposal for a more permanent European Research Council (ERC) funded by 2 billion euros. It was set up to address "concerns that framework research programs are heavily bureaucratized, put excessive emphasis on applied projects, and have unclear peer review."[64]

If money alone could do the trick, the forthcoming FP7 (2007–2113) should have provided the necessary impetus to change. The program called for a huge – more than threefold – increase in overall European R&D expenditures, to $87 billion, ranging from 12 to 15 percent by 2013. This amount might have been to make a real difference in the rate of innovation. Warning of the widening gap with the United States in the GM field, Commissioner Verheugen promised in April 2005 to put "biotech back on top of the EU's investment agenda." As things now stand, however, only $15 billion of the total funding is earmarked for basic science. The rest will go into "research . . .relevant to the needs of industry" or be channeled into "cooperation programs" aimed primarily at strengthening the "collab-oration between researchers in different member states."[65] The main purpose of the plan is obviously not to encourage pure scientific inquiry but to build a major new EU research constituency, similar to those con-structed around the CAP and regional funding but heavily weighted toward security issues. Busquin was quite unambiguous about this mat-ter. "Europe," he declared, "is paying a very high price for the artificial and uniquely European separation between civil and military research." European aerospace and defense industry groups welcomed the project. They would find out by the year's end, "how the security research activ-ities will interface with the European Defense Agency."[66]

The FP7 will focus on five "major themes' and two "research prior-ities." The themes include "taking a cue from the US National Sci-ence Foundation . . .in the field of fundamental research . . .involving advanced mathematics or quantum physics with an eye to new elec-tronic and IT breakthroughs"; building a "European research infrastruc-ture" in key fields such as biotechnology and providing scholarships in them; promoting private-public partnerships to create "common research agendas" in areas of special EU interest; creating "European nodes of excellence"; and coordinating EU and national research pol-icy. The two research-related priorities are space and security – Galileo and high-tech policing – and call for "a massive program of military research."[67] It remains unclear how the flat research budget adopted in December 2005 for the 2009–2013 budgetory cycle can accommodate these many priorities.

University reform holds the key to improving European research: it will, according to the French experts Philippe Aghion and Elie Cohen, in the end distinguish *innovating* from *imitating* nations – the leaders from the followers. European higher education is in bad shape – how bad remains open to debate. A recent and respected Chinese annual survey of world universities reported disturbingly that all of the top fifty were American except Oxford, Cambridge, and the University of Utrecht, which came in thirty-ninth. To change this situation, one must move mountains. Internal reform will be needed to turn the European uni-versity into a growth engine. This calls for a new relationship between higher education and the rest of society. Two less desirable alternatives remain open for promoting growth through innovation: either industry or the state could take responsibility for directing research. Power would then devolve to one or the other. The universities would be reduced to vestiges of authority and responsibility.[68]

The EU has tried hard to assert leadership in reforming higher education but has few tools at its disposal and so far has made little progress. The purpose behind this effort is to "challenge US domination of global education" – as if this were somehow intrinsically worthwhile. Is the advancement of human knowledge not a sufficiently worthy purpose? Launched in 1999, its main project is the so-called "Bologna Process" aimed at creating a European Higher Education Area (EHEA) by 2010. Ongoing discussions – punctuated by meetings of national education ministers and university association presidents – have taken place over the past several years. As matters now stand, the EHEA will eventually turn into a European accreditation agency. The long list of objectives written into its founding treaty also leaves plenty of openings down well-trodden paths of mission creep, which could eventually lead to a European ministry of education.[69]

The main goal of the Bologna Process is to standardize the European university curriculum along the lines of the US model. Existing degrees would be replaced with three-year Bachelor's and two-year Master's degree programs, the shorter period of the former being because of the extra one year required in Europe to qualify for the secondary school–leaving certificate. US-style course credits and major requirements will also be introduced in keeping with the design. The reform serves a number of different ends, some official, others implicit. It is expected to make European degrees internationally comparable, facilitate university transfer within the EU, reduce the length of degree programs and therefore costs, increase faculty accountability, and, in general, weaken the guildlike character of the European academic profession. A challenge to entrenched interests, the Bologna Process has met with varied, and often hostile, receptions. University administrators have praised it as rational and farsighted, but faculty often damned it as an expensive way of "dumbing down" curricula. Students have been generally outraged by it as a plot to globalize through the back door.[70]

There may be less to the Bologna Process than meets the eye. The importance of what it is trying to accomplish is easy to exaggerate. The US method of accreditation is little more than a means to provide a convenient basis of comparison across a large, diverse, and dynamic field; it provides a common framework but no single yardstick and is not a guarantee of equal outcomes: a degree from Harvard will always count for more than a comparable one from the hypothetical Podunk State or the mythological School of Hard-Knocks – although how much more depends on a number of specifics. Nor is a US degree, as sometimes in Europe, a license to enter a profession; responsibility for maintaining standards normally rests with private state or (depending on the specific field) national professional associations, which also serve as accreditation agencies. The academic accreditation process, in other words, plays only a secondary role in maintaining standards. Unlike the general situation in Europe, a US university degree is never a legal entitlement.[71]

Flexibility is what in the end makes the US system of credit evaluation effective; it could not otherwise adjust to changing demands, requirements, and levels of achievement. Whether in the more bureaucratized context of European institutions a similar system would work in whole or in part is unknown. Not included as participants or consultants in the Bologna Process, US universities and accrediting agencies remain wary and confused about it, do not yet recognize its equivalencies, and seem troubled by the rigidity apparently being built into the scheme.[72]

If at this point, the Bologna Process is more a matter of form than substance, the Process *can* serve as a catalyst to critical change at the national level if it recognizes diversity, respects accomplishment, and allows participating nations to advance at their own pace. The United Kingdom has turned its back on the EU-sponsored scheme because it has already gone at least partway toward introducing reform along US lines. Among the large countries, moreover, the British have the best-existing university system. Why saddle it with changes needed elsewhere? In France, Prime Minister Raffarin introduced a reform bill in October 2004 for convergence with the Bologna Process, without, however, publicizing the fact that it was part of an EU scheme. The ploy failed miserably: the proposed bill triggered a huge national wave of student-led strikes, and the government capitulated. In Italy, there is much talk about the Bologna Process but only bureaucratic action; the university system is immobile. Among the big countries, only in

Germany has the Bologna Process really taken hold.[73] Introduction of the new degree system began in 2004, with completion planned by the end of 2006.

In the Federal Republic as elsewhere, significant change will require giving, or restoring, to universities the authority to compete for students, faculty, and money.[74] Whether and how this can be done without sacrificing freedom of inquiry is at this point less important than that it must be done. Universities are today drifting off into irrelevance as state bureaucracies like any other.[75] In Europe, unlike the United States, the real work of educating men and women is done at the secondary level; the result is a highly qualified pool of native brainworkers substantially larger than in the United States. If properly mobilized, it can provide the critical source of Europe's future comparative advantage.

Only in Britain has the government taken the first necessarily hard and unpopular steps needed for university reform: increased tuition and the number of foreign students in order to provide additional funding, cut scholarships in favor of loans, encouraged the raising of private money, and induced competition for resources across the board. The London School of Economics tops the adaptability list: it has maintained its standing by maintaining a fifty-fifty balance between British and foreign students, who pay three times as high tuition.[76] Although Sciences Po has picked up the cue from its British counterpart, reform in France is otherwise at an impasse. Two huge issues must be dealt with before progress can resume – the special role of the elite schools, which produce the handful of men and women who run the country, and the tradition of centralizing research in state-directed national institutions, which diverts intellectual resources from the university system and creates a separate bureaucratic hierarchy.

Germany is at the moment the most interesting laboratory for university reform. Perhaps it has always been the idea of the university as a temple of knowledge and graduate studies as the driver of research and, as recently as the 1960s, as model incubator of self-regulating corporatist democracy (*Gruppenuniversität*). This most recent experiment – one, incidentally, coupled to a vast expansion of the university system – has, however, failed, according to the editors of a recent journal devoted to the reform of German higher education. The *Gruppenuniversität* fostered rigid obstructionist bureaucracies at the state level, which have reduced university autonomy vis-à-vis the individual states (*Länder*) and impeded reform. Reunification brought no change in this respect; the West German system was simply transplanted. Budget constraints have for years governed policy making, as evident in the deterioration of facilities, overcrowding, and lack of course offerings. The universities have thus become a vast parking lot for idled students who have no serious intention of completing their studies.[77]

Reform in the Federal Republic faces a number of large obstacles. Germany has no real tradition of private universities and a weak one of public-private cooperation in higher education; new ones must be created in a nation of few independent foundations. University enrollment has always, moreover, been open to holders of the secondary school–leaving certificate (*Abitur*), and enrollment fees are nominal; threats to these obsolete privileges will be resisted by students. As in France, research is split between the universities and special, often highly distinguished, academic institutes; their roles must also be redefined.[78]

The situation is, however, beginning to change. Private universities have been founded recently in Bremen and Baden-Württemberg. Chancellor Schröder has made at least a start by championing a, to be sure, somewhat utopian proposal to create ten Harvard-like superuniversities with public monies. It ran afoul, however, of opposition at the state level.[79] Germany nonetheless remains committed to the Bologna Process and is the place that will either make or break it. If the Process fails to trigger overdue change, it will become meaningless, or worse, and count as merely the most recent of many failed EU attempts to overreach.

The food fight was the wrong battle for the EU to wage, because biotechnology is a complicated field with far-reaching and diverse ramifications. The hysteria fanned over nutritional safety cannot easily be put to rest. The bad climate for biotech policy will hinder European research for years to come. FP7 represents a bid to turn the situation around and at the same time supply a new rationale for the EU. The promotion of R&D can hardly justify the Commission's existence. FP7 serves the following priorities listed in order of importance: strengthening the authority of Brussels, increasing Europe's potential military power, contributing to economic growth, and advancing science. It will require something more than a bigger and better FP to overcome the legacy of the past decade. While the EU stalled, the genomic revolution – indeed the global technology revolution – spread geographically and advanced scientifically. Impetus to change now comes from abroad. Europe will remain an imitator rather than an innovator in the foreseeable future.

Dr. Frankenfood Goes Global

Strong and surging worldwide demand fuels the biotech revolution. It has no close parallel in the earlier IT revolution in which innovation took place at the laboratory as a generation of visionary scientist-innovators invented new products for markets that did not yet exist except in their own well-developed imaginations. The revolution in biotechnology is not only driven by the basic human desire for a longer and better life but is essential to this goal. The demand for GM derives from the need to raise yields from the shrinking supply of arable land. The need for increasing yields results from urbanization, world population growth, and shifts in consumption patterns – which accompany rising living standards – from traditional high-carbohydrate foods to meat. There is no alternative to the spread of biotechnology but the threat of famine by 2030. Pressure on land and on natural resources also dictates development of substitute fuels and materials, many of which the dynamic science will provide. Such requirements are rapidly extending the area under GM cultivation. Acreage increased by more than 20 percent last year, has grown at sustained double-digit rates for more than nine years, now totals more than 80 million hectares or 200 million acres, and is expected to double by the end of the decade.

Yields are increasing dramatically – those for corn, for instance, by 72 percent since 1995. After the driest growing season in seventeen years, 2005 Midwestern corn yields, predicted at 120–130 bushels an acre, came in at 175 bushels – thanks to new drought-resistant GM strains that iron out weather-related hazards and smooth out the crop cycle. The silo-bursting harvest drove prices to the lowest levels in nearly a decade – a bounty for mankind, a headache for Brussels. But the new abundance is merely the tip of the iceberg. Biotechnology has given rise to a vast array of new products and even opened up new prospects and possibilities for human life itself. Eurocrats would do well – when tempted by further protectionism – to bear these facts in mind.[80]

Understanding why individual nations adopt biotechnology is surely not as simple as looking at A,B, and C – in this case, by examining snapshots of Australia, Brazil, and China (and India as well) as they try to unlock the benefits of the new technology. Yet these examples underscore a couple of basic points. Biotech development meets a variety of needs and is under way in many different places; the result is technology diffusion and the development of research along many trajectories as knowledge spreads, old markets expand, and new ones take shape. In the future, there will be no single, or concentric, world center of biotech research, production, and distribution – but many different ones. Both prospects and perils will correspondingly multiply. Europe's voice will count for less in the future than it might have in the recent past.

For Australia, the main issue is environmental – to preserve a unique and diverse bioculture and make better use of its vast, arid, and largely unpopulated hinterland. The paramount concern in Brazil is economic and political modernization. With the first-ever popularly elected government now in office, Brazil is – thanks in great measure to the increased cultivation of soybeans, especially GM beans, for export – enjoying an unprecedented boom. It is turning the nation into an agricultural superpower, improving land use, and developing the interior. At stake in China and India, where 1.2 billion persons (taken together) still live on the land, is something even greater – the elimination of famine. Other crucial matters at hand are improving the diet, reducing disease, increasing agricultural productivity, and providing long-term political stability. These concerns are also of immense importance in Africa, the one continent in which (with the prominent exception of South Africa) the biotech revolution is only beginning to take hold. The polycentric worldwide pattern of biotech development is also becoming evident within the United States, where several different centers of excellence are forming. In such a fast-breaking field, tight control from the center – such as the EU would like to exercise – is a crippling handicap.

The biotech revolution has a vertical as well as a horizontal axis. The genomic revolution has only yet begun. In August 2005, the sequencing of the first plant genome, rice, was completed and placed for free access in databanks around the world; the breakthrough will, by facilitating comparison with grasses such as wheat and corn, accelerate the discovery process in these crops as well. In the meantime, research continues into the development of new biofoods, materials, energy sources, and medical applications. Within this broad sector, the locus of activity is gradually shifting from crop science to stem cell research and cloning. A new generation of products is also arising from the fusion of biotechnology with processes deriving from IT and nanotechnology. Now recognizing that the momentous changes taking place outside of Europe, together with the operation of powerful forces of scientific progress, are too strong to be resisted, Brussels is determined to avoid a nanotech sequel to the destructive food fight. The EU is indeed committed to taking the lead in a research field whose immense implications are touted as being as broad as those of electricity.

Australia would normally be only a footnote in a short book about Europe. In biotechnology, however, it has its own very strong reasons for promoting development and is becoming a niche power in the field. The island-continent provides a good example of how sound policy influences science-paced development. In an age of globalization, which purportedly favors the big battalions, Australia has enjoyed thirteen years of uninterrupted growth at 3.8 percent, half a point higher than the United States, in part by becoming an effective niche player in many specialized subfields of biotechnology. The "tyranny of distance" combined with dire shortages of rainfall in much of the country limits the population to about 20 million and makes it heavily import-dependent. As a major exporter of minerals and animal products, Australia has, to be sure, over the past few years benefited disproportionately from the rise of China as well as from a big improvement in the traditionally unfavorable terms of trade. It has also managed to make good use of its special natural and rich human asset base.[81]

Australia is expanding its excellent university system by increasing the foreign student population and encouraging research by means, for example, of a $40 million Biotechnology Investment Fund designed to commercialize the intellectual property held in educational and research institutions. It can take credit in this respect for at least one major breakthrough, the invention of proteomics by the Sydney biology professor Keith Williams. The new platform technology "allows the hundreds of thousands of proteins in human cells and tissues to be analyzed" not one by one "but in a high throughput automated way." Biochemists are also analyzing the continent's unique flora and fauna for special useful gene properties such as from the Great Barrier Reef coral for sunscreen.[82]

In response to a national emergency, a critical shortage of water, Australia is also pioneering in the development of drought- and saline-resistant crop strains. The crisis stems from agricultural overuse of the Murray-Darling river system, which covers an area as large as western Europe. Fifty to eighty percent of it has been severely damaged. To save the system, the government has shifted from ruinous subsidized water entitlements to an auction process. The cultivation and development of biotech crops may, however, be needed to salvage the farm economy of the area. Fifty-nine percent of Australian cotton is genetically modified, and approvals are in for several lines of soybean and corn as well as for six additional crops. Research is in high gear in a long line of specific fruit crops, grain, oilseeds, barleys, and canola (rapeseed). Australia is indeed the sixth-largest biotech nation as well as the first in the Asia Pacific region.[83]

One of the last places on earth where large tracts of arable land are still available for agriculture – another one million hectares, without encroaching on the fragile Amazon rain forests – Brazil is poised to become the dominant power in world soybean production within the next few years. As in neighboring Argentina and Paraguay, the past half decade has witnessed explosive annual output increases of 14 percent since 2001. Low land and labor prices combined with a growing season long enough for two and often three annual crops make Brazil's challenge virtually unstoppable. Agriculture now accounts for 40 percent of the country's exports, half of which by value is soy. Benefiting from a world commodities boom and with a government in office, for once both popular and opposed to economic experimentation, Brazil "could [soon] emerge as one of the world's top developed nations."[84]

The recent discovery that modest applications of lime and phosphorous could triple and even quadruple yield in savannah soils triggered the soy boom; the increased use of GM seeds continues to boost productivity. Growth has heretofore taken place not by putting new land into cultivation but by planting in former pasture land, much of it degraded by overgrazing. The shift from range to farm enriches the soil, increases employment, and, in the case of the Matto Grosso, is beginning to open vast new areas to sound economic development. Much recently cultivated land, as well as most old soy acreage, is being seeded in GM. The trend is expected to continue with anticipated future diversification into corn, cotton, and canola and the planned increased consumption of biofuel. The no-tilling feature of GM is also attractive in light of the chronic shortage of tractors in Brazil, especially in the Matto Grosso, where cultivation is expected to increase in the future.[85]

The use of GM seeds is a sensitive matter. Succumbing to EU pressure, Brazil maintained an official ban on the use of the "magic beans" until President Luiz Inacio "Lula" da Silva – contrary to campaign promises and in the face of heated protests from former ecosupporters – lifted it in September 2003. The ban, which cut down US sales in Europe drastically, had been a boon for the Brazilians. By no means, however, did all South American soybean exports to Europe prior to 2004 arrive uncontaminated. Most Brazilian soy exported in recent years has originated in Rio Grande do Sul, a state bordering Argentina, whence, in violation of its contracts, many Argentines sold Monsanto seeds, which were then smuggled into Brazil. Brazilians did not have to pay royalties to Monsanto, and Argentines refused to do so – with the result that the St. Louis seed vendors officially stopped doing business in the southern region for a year. The prevalence of cheating makes it hard to determine how the boycott affected Argentine plantings; it meant little in Brazil, however, where GM crops amounted to about 20 percent of the yield by 2002. Since the largest acreage increases of the past five years have been in the South and Southeast, this figure has continued to rise. Much incorrectly labeled GM produce, often in the form of chemically undetectable glucose, can be assumed to have made its way into Europe's harbors – and digestive tracts.[86]

China will be the world's largest producer and consumer of GM products by 2015 – not only because of the number of mouths that must be fed. From 1958 to 1961, more than 30 million Chinese starved to death in a famine caused by Mao's insane Great Leap Forward. China's food security requires not only high output but capture of technological advantage. Development of GM technology is a commanding necessity – notwithstanding past official policy to the contrary. Fearing that the EU would block its entrance into the WTO, China stopped reporting on its biotech research in 1999 and, officially, banned the importation and cultivation of GM seeds as well as the marketing of its own GM rice. The policy was unsustainable.

Over the next five years, immense shifts of labor from the country-side to the dynamic coastal export zones resulted in a 20 percent fall in grain and rice outputs (90 percent of the total), triggered sharp price increases (of 27 percent, e.g., in the first quarter of 2004), and turned China's previously self-sufficient (albeit at a low level of consumption) food economy into the world's largest soy importer. The United States exported much of the new product. As put by one Chinese scientist, "China's delay in issuing safety certificates did not prevent a flood of crops from entering the country. China has been the largest importer of soybean for the past three years . . .more than 90 percent of it GM." It amounted to more than one-half of world exports. The Chinese could not, in other words, have imported and consumed anything other than transgenic varieties of the product; non-GM reserves were simply not available.[87] Demand for soy is rising with improvements in living stan-dards and increased per capita consumption of meat and bean cakes. Labeling a processed product as GM-derived is not a sales deterrent. Chinese dependence on soy imports is, however, expected to decline over the next five years, in compliance with the WTO, as increased exposure to world markets forces farmers to shift to more productive GM seeds. The new competition will hurt US farmers but benefit US seed producers.

In February 2004, China's Ministry of Agriculture, "impressed by the EU's more flexible attitude towards plant biotechnologies," authorized the issuance of "safety certificates" for five GM varieties – one strain of soybean, two strains of corn, and two varieties of cotton – all produced by Monsanto. The decision marks a turning point. In July 2004 the State Council, China's central cabinet, announced the formation of a special top-level leadership committee for biotech development supported by a national industrial association and guided by a national development plan. Such a committee is one of only four, the others being for econ-omy, law, and Taiwan. Concern that India – which had passed a law making it the first nation to establish a special ministry for biotechnol-ogy – would, as in IT, trump China, triggered the decision to establish the new leadership committee. Its job is to launch a crash program of basic research involving fourfold or greater increases in the budget for biotechnology over the next five years.[88]

During the period of the official ban, China made major progress in the GM field. The world's largest producer of cotton, it commercialized the GM product in 1996. Five million farmers today grow the "miracle crop," nearly all of them on tiny plots. The improved strain has not, in other words, displaced traditional smallholders but increased their chances for survival and is evidence that GM can be introduced into traditional agriculture without causing disruptions and upheaval. About 60 percent of China's cotton is genetically modified, half the seed being provided by Monsanto. The GM seed has cut production costs by 30 percent and sharply reduced farmer exposure to pesticides. Farms planting Bt cotton earned $500 more per hectare than those not using GM seeds. Late-ripening tomatoes, virus-resistant sweet-peppers, and color-altered petunias have been approved for commercial cultivation in China, and 60 other GM plants are at various stages of development.[89]

The most important of them by far is rice. GM rice is not yet officially cultivated, but Bt-produced varieties, one of several strains being produced at an agricultural college in Hubei, began to appear in markets in early 2005. Bt encodes a gene, harmless to humans, which paralyzes insect digestive systems and thus cuts pesticide consumption by eight to ten times, reducing farmer exposure correspondingly and yielding huge environmental benefits. It also saves farmers $25 per hectare while raising yields by 9 percent. Chinese scientists estimate that these benefits will far surpass those of Bt cotton and, if introduced (when essentially developed) in 2002, could have generated $4.2 billion in savings by 2010.[90]

The benefits of "golden rice" promise to be even greater. The first of a new generation of transgenic foods created to improve health (as opposed to lower cost or increase yield), golden rice has been engineered to contain high levels of vitamin A, the lack of which produces night blindness, weakens the immune system, and increases child mortality. The welfare gains from the use of such a strain in Asia (where 90 percent of the world's rice is consumed) would, according to a recent World Bank study, outstrip even those of cost reduction and productivity increases like those of Bt rice and would be even greater, of course, if the new product were adopted in Africa.[91] Golden rice is ready for market and will be distributed to farmers earning less than $10,000 per year, free of cost, by its producer, Syngenta.

Starting from a low base, Chinese biotech research continues to advance rapidly. The cultural revolution retarded the progress of science by a generation. China lacks in particular the special breed of scientific entrepreneurs who elsewhere provide the leaven needed for innovation. Venture capital is still nonexistent, and research is largely state-sponsored. The extent of it is difficult to determine because, according to Boston Consulting, local governments have plowed several times more money into research than Beijing. China is estimated to have about 300 publicly funded laboratories, most of them housed in universities or research institutes in Beijing, Shanghai, and Shenzehn. The provincial government of Hainan has, in addition, announced plans to create a "biopharmaceutical valley" with annual outputs of $1.5 billion. China is also moving rapidly into stem cell research, has built thirty state-of-the-art facilities, and can conduct experiments and tests in an advantageous economic and ethical environment.[92]

Chinese biotech research is not yet up to European speed. US companies have set up labs in China for political as well as cost reasons. As in other industries, these will provide settings for future technology transfers. At this point, however, they do little independent research. China's GM-based generics (insulin for diabetes and interferon alpha for cancer) are, like most pharmaceuticals, still based on ripped-off foreign patents. Although Chinese science has also not yet made a major biotech breakthrough, it has produced an artificial vaccine for SARS and is developing others for liver diseases, in keeping with a policy of promoting research into ailments that especially afflict the Chinese.[93]

Agriculture, and especially rice, is the field in which China has made the most progress. Ten field trials are now under way, the most anywhere. Only the United States spends more on food research. Although with only 20,000 researchers (as opposed to nearly 200,000 in the United States), China's biotechnology is still small potatoes; it now stands to benefit from a reverse brain drain. With university expansion expected to produce as many scientists and engineers as the United States by 2010 and the government having tripled research funding since 1998, China's "biotech engine is revving loudly," and many consultants believe that it is ready "to surpass competitors in Europe and challenge the United States for global dominance over the next decade."[94]

Today viewed as a competitor by the Chinese, India has hopes of repeating the IT revolution in the biotech field. In the space of five years, it is worth remembering, the IT industry of the subcontinent burst seemingly out of nowhere into world prominence. India's importance continues to mount to the point at which it now vies in many fields with the United States for leadership as innovator. The transition in biotechnology will take longer. Although brainwork is India's most important export product, the nation's semiliterate rural poor, 60 percent of the population, produce less than a quarter of the GDP; the monsoon season is still the main determinant of economic growth; and more food is spoiled in India annually than Australia produces. The fate of Indian biotechnology will necessarily have less to do with developments in the laboratory than with solving the immense social problems of adjustment to genetic technology.

India is too big to be bullied out of GM by the EU or into GM by the United States: it will have to adopt the new technology at its own pace and in its own way. Turning the subsistence farmers of India's villages into producers for the market will require improving rural education, developing infrastructure in the countryside, encouraging capital formation, and breaking down a cartelized food distribution system. Although the number of Indians living on less than a dollar per day has been reduced by a third over the past decade, in order to spread the benefits of the gene revolution, India will need to revise laws restricting foreign investment, establish a legal framework for patent protection, promote the creation of enterprise zones, and lower tariffs.[95]

In respect to both crop introduction and industrial development, India has made good starts. To provide overall guidance in the field, it set up a National Biotechnology Regulatory Authority (NBRA) headed by M. S. Swaminathan, the nation's leading plant geneticist, and along with Norman Borlaug, the "father" of the earlier Green Revolution. Prevention of a Frankenfood scare motivated the decision to create the NBRA. The research center, which Swaminathan heads in Chennai, is devoted to the development of "second-generation" crops, which are either of high nutritional value or especially suited to local conditions. The only GM crop planted thus far in India, the so-called Bollgard cotton (produced by Monsanto in a joint venture with a local partner), has yielded beneficial results similar to those in China. Farmers towing with oxen thus now use "the most highly advanced seed technology" available. In India, as in China, seed piracy is a major problem and will remain one until liability laws become enforceable. Five times more GM cotton acreage is in fact planted illegally than legally. Until this situation changes, India will not meet the product traceability requirements of the EU.[96]

In India as elsewhere, agbio is only about 15 percent of the overall biotech sector. In biotechnology, as in the pharmaceutical industry generally, India occupies a large niche as producer of generic medicines but lacks the capital to develop and market blockbuster drugs. Needed are partnerships with big US and European firms (which control 72 percent and 22 percent of the world market, respectively), and they will not act without stronger guarantees for the protection of intellectual property. Product approval, which must be done at the state level, also entails unnecessary expense and delays.[97]

The autonomy of local government in India also has its advantages: the state of Maharashtra, with a population of 90 million and the base for 15 percent of the country's manufacturing, is aggressively promoting the Mumbai-Pune corridor as a biotech center – providing tax breaks, encouraging joint ventures, and investing massively in modern industrial parks. The withdrawal of biotechnology from Europe and the availability of low-priced intellectual Indian talent are expected to draw investment into the Southeast Asia region. High tariff barriers have thus far limited India's success in exporting to its neighbors. If the giant nation hopes to become a regional great power, like China, they will have to be lowered.[98]

No region of the world has a greater stake in biotechnology than Africa, where hunger and chronic illness have bred endemic warfare, political instability, and threats of pandemic and famine. In the judgment of World Bank economists, the welfare gains of GM food technology could help change this dire situation by alleviating "poverty directly and perhaps substantially in those countries willing and able to adopt [it]."[99] In their verdict, the EU ban deserves censure for depriving Africa of these potential welfare gains. Africa's nutritional deficit could be alleviated, first of all, by encouraging the cultivation of "golden rice," which in addition to its health benefits, is easier to prepare than traditional African staples. Genetically hardened strains of these staples – sorghum, cassava, and millet – can, moreover, raise output by 10 to 15 percent simply by creating resistance to traditional viruses. New drought-resistant strains could further raise outputs. Poor farmers from developing countries now plant no less than a quarter of GM acreage; traditional agriculture can be strengthened in Africa and the food supply improved as well if public attitudes there toward biotechnology can be changed in anti-GM places, such as Zambia, and cooperation improved between research, government, and producers in places such as Kenya, which are strongly pro-GM. Europe will have to refocus its food policy to take better account of Africa's needs, and "major players" will have to work jointly to bring new seed to market.[100]

Syngenta's policy of providing free seed to poor farmers set a sound precedent, not least of all because, by changing food tastes, diffusing knowledge concerning the new technology, and improving profitability, it will create an eventual market for its product. The same holds for Monsanto's decision to license technology for a sweet potato, which resists the feathery mottle virus, to a Kenyan research institute free of charge. Provision of a $25 million project by the Bill and Melinda Gates Foundation for vitamin and protein enrichment of traditional food is another small example of what is needed. Since, however, selling food to the world's poor – the supply of a necessary public good – cannot easily be made profitable, both government and business should promote efforts to bring GM strains of African staples to market by supporting institutions, such as the Donald Danforth Plant Center of St. Louis, where such research is being conducted.[101]

Within the United States, the race is on to be the next Silicon Valley. Whether in biotechnology there will be a single regional victor, as in IT, or several – or even none – cannot be determined. There is no particular reason to conclude that history will repeat itself. The contestants in biotechnology are not, as in IT, similarly equipped but represent both public and private sponsorship in various forms. The competition between them is in this respect like the earlier one to map the human genome. It pitted an international consortium led by the National Institute of Health (NIH), which methodically mapped genes one at a time, against Celera Genomics, a start-up headed by the maverick scientist Craig Venter who "appeared on the scene and boldly claimed that [his] revolutionary new technique, whole-genome shot-gun sequencing could do the job in less than half the time."[102] Reviled and ridiculed by the research establishment, Venter prodded the NIH to speed up its program by two years. The race to map the genome ended amicably in 2003 in a tie.

US biotechnology has benefited from the inability of the national leadership to impose an EU-type, *dirigiste* top-down one-size-fits-all biotech policy. Indeed, when President Bush vetoed federal funding for stem cell research, California passed a $3 billion initiative to support it. When the governor of Massachusetts threatened to impose a sim-ilar ban in his state, the powerful local private universities went on a money-raising binge. The diffusion of biotechnology in the United States has been favored by the existence of well-established research centers, a tradition of states' rights, a proscience outlook, and a cul-ture of competition. The Boston-Cambridge-Worcester belt is a major force, as is the Bay Area–Silicon Valley complex in California and the New York–northern New Jersey–eastern Pennsylvania triangle – each of which has traditionally close associations with major universities and research institutions. Other centers have developed in San Diego, California; the North Carolina Research Triangle; and Houston, Texas – all of them, once again, affiliated with major institutions of higher education. To this list must be added more specialized centers such as St. Louis for agbio and Phoenix, Arizona, for biopharma, to men-tion only two of a dozen aspiring new research complexes. The relation-ships that develop between them, the corporate world, and the public sphere will be varied and complex and will depend on the economics and uses of a product developed as well as the laws and regulations in effect. They cannot be guided by any single formula.[103]

Dr. Frankenfood's Lab

A few words must suffice to indicate the range and amplitude of prod-uct development in the three different biotech sectors – the green, the red, and the white. In agriculture, the "first generation" emphasis on cost reduction is far from played out. Indeed, GM strains have still only been marketed in four main crops – soy, corn (maize), cotton, and canola (rapeseed) – though two others, rice and wheat, are market-ready, and still others – potatoes, sugar beets, peanuts, and tomatoes – are close behind. In the final stages of preparation are seeds that convert annual plants to perennials (which reduces plantings and lowers seed costs) as well as others that accelerate growth, bring earlier maturity (for fruit bearing), double yields (canola), and produce harder and sturdier wood. "Second-generation" crop development, emphasizing quality improvement, is also well under way. It includes the production of foods that are more nutritious (golden rice), nonallergenic (nuts), and healthier (low levels of linolenic acid or "bad cholesterol") and taste better (new decaffeinated coffee). Increased use of computer-driven bioinformatics and breakthroughs like the recent sequencing of the rice genome will lower costs and step up the pace of the discovery process. Indeed, "over the next two decades, it is predicted that gene technology will reach every type of agricultural crop in the world."[104]

Medical applications of biotechnology are even more far reaching. Put very simply, knowledge of the human genome makes it possible to isolate a single mutation responsible for causing a disease and treat it directly by introducing antigens that destroy "bad" cells at the molecular level. Cures can, in other words, be personalized instead of being administered generically. The broad implications of this breakthrough are staggering. A mere secondary one is the alteration of the approval process for biopharmaceuticals, which – given correct profiling – can be granted on a selective basis and prescribed only to patients with a specific genetic makeup for which they are suited. Here a precedent has already been set: conditional approval was recently granted for a drug remarkably effective in preventing heart attacks in African Americans. Because it is ineffective in other patients, it could not have been prescribed under existing rules for nonbiomedicines. The new more discriminating approach to approval, which normally comprises half the cost of product development, means that drugs that are now "on the shelf" can be brought to market and that new "niche drugs" can be produced to treat rare diseases or for specific genetic populations. The new selectivity may well revolutionize the economics of the pharmaceutical industry – not to mention medical treatment itself.[105]

Industrial biotechnology ("white") is less visible than either the red or green subfields but potentially no less important. At stake is nothing less than a transition from a petro- to a cellulose-based economy. Cellulose-based compounds can substitute for oil-based in many applications, including automotive fuel and artificial materials such as plastics. The key to their success will be the development of a low-cost glucose to replace crude oil as a feedstock; this in turn will require improving GM enzymes, which break down "biowaste" (nonusable crop leftovers), or increasing yield from new GM grasses. Some 5 percent of bulk chemicals are already biotech, a figure that is expected to double over the next six years. Among the more important applications are amino acid and vitamin supplements, antibiotics, anti-influenza drugs, foundation creams, and rocket fuel. The really serious money is expected to be made in bulk chemicals and fuels.[106]

Biofuel is already on the march. Brazil, the world leader, produces it from sugarcane raised specifically for ethanol. Most Brazilian automobiles are now being equipped to consume either gasoline or ethanol or a combination of the two. Ethanol costs half as much as gasoline in Brazil. Consumption is expected to increase by 50 percent over the next five years. At $50 per barrel, Brazil's cellulose-based fuel is also competitive with petroleum in the European market. Though now generally distilled from corn and 50 percent more expensive than Brazilian fuel, the locally distributed US product is competitive in the US market at about $40 per barrel, even without the existing subsidy of $10 per barrel. Although "grass guzzlers" *can* in part eventually replace gas guzzlers in the United States, the use of ethanol is best envisaged as a component of a diversified national multisourced and networked energy policy.[107]

If today ethanol supplies less than 5 percent of US automotive fuel requirements, this can soon change unless oil prices unexpectedly plunge. Sixteen US plants are presently under construction, which will raise capacity by about 17 percent; add to this a continuation of improved processing efficiency (35 percent in four years) due to better GM enzymes, and the stage will be set for substantial increases. Additional consumption of biodiesel produced from waste products, which now amounts to 2 percent of overall European consumption and is competitive with the petroleum-based product, would reduce US energy dependence still further. Field tests of a hearty, fast-growing high-cellulose GM saw grass for ethanol conversion, which is suitable for planting in otherwise hostile northern latitudes, are now under way. Next year, Ford Motor Company plans to bring out "flex-fuel" models like those in Brazil, which can run on ethanol as well as gasoline.[108]

"Nano" is a technology that converges with biotechnology and IT at the point of application. It can in some cases substitute for either one or both; in other cases, it supplements them or is supplemented by them. If this sounds confusing, it is because units at the nanoscale (one-billionth of a meter) have unique properties, adding "surface . . .to the existing list of solid, liquid, gas, and plasma." Nano is another state of matter. Nanoparticles are not subject to the laws of gravity but behave more like colloids. Thus they can be thought of as subatomic building blocks for structures of a new type. Materials can be made from them with special properties of strength and lightness, interaction with the environment, and resistance to chemical or bacterial agents. Nanoparticles can shrink electronic circuits (thus prolonging Moore's Law) as well as perform logical "and," as opposed to the "either-or," operations of the micro-processor; they can therefore also be built into an eventual molecular scale computer. Nanoscale objects or systems can also be developed with "biomimetic functionality but without fragility," meaning that they can, with the use of genetically engineered templates, replace viruses, pro-teins, DNA, and other biological components to regulate physiological or neurological functions – in short, treat diseases by molecular target-ing. Finally, nanoparticles have been assembled into crystallike "nan-oclusters" with self-replicating and self-assembling properties.[109]

Nanomaterial may have found its way into face creams, special-purpose textiles, and the bumpers of the Chevrolet Impala, but potential strategic significance rather than value to the consumer puts nanotech-nology at the top of the research agenda. Nanotechnologies have mil-itary (and security) applications as sensors, for body and other armor and "stealthy" as well as light-weapons platforms (and in fire control and detection systems), and for healing wounds (indeed for supplying artificial body parts) – to mention only the most obvious ones. Like electricity, nanotechnology is expected to provide a continuous stream of change as opposed to the one-time shock effect of, for instance, the construction of the modern railway system. Governments have gotten into the act early and are committed to the long haul. Reported public sector nanotechnology investment increased sevenfold between 1997 and 2003, and last year amounted to more than $4 billion. In antic-ipation of a trillion-dollar market in ten-to-fifteen-years' time, Pres-ident Bush committed $3.7 billion to the National Nanotechnology Initiative for the period 2005–2008, and the NSF set up a national infrastructure network, integrating the facilities of the thirteen lead-ing research institutions. FP7 plans to spend $4.8 billion on nanotech-nology between 2007–2113. This time, however, every attempt will be made to prevent the spread of antiscience hysteria and in particular to suppress fears fanned by the recent bestselling sci-fi thriller, *Prey*, by Michael Crichton, in which zillions of tiny "nanobots" turn Earth into a mass of "grey goo." Groups like the ecoradical ETC from Canada, once prominent in the food fight, are no longer welcomed by the Commission.[110]

Nanotechnology is just out of the "workbench" stage in which crit-ical knowledge is "tacit" and "localized." Based on a survey of "high-impact articles" compiled by the US "Nanobank," the United States heads the pack. The leading national nanotech regions are the same as for biotechnology, with research centers in Boston, New York, and northern and southern California. The developmental trajectory of nanotechnology may, however, diverge from this pattern, depending on the role of governments, the costs of product development, capi-tal requirements, and numerous other variables, not the least of which are rates of progress in biotechnology and IT. To close the gap with the United States, Europe will have to anticipate as well as adapt to dynamic changes of not one but three ongoing technological revolutions occur-ring in many different parts of the world.

The EU has been completely out of its depth as a formulator of biotech policy. No one in a position of responsibility, at the Commission or elsewhere, understood until far too late the vast, unfolding scientific and economic implications of the genomic revolution – not to men-tion the even greater ones stemming from the three-pronged interac-tive global technology revolution of which it is a part. Change on such a scale can be compared to the great breakthroughs of the industrial rev-olution and has immense implications for human welfare, philosophy, and ethics: it blurs the very distinctions between plants and animals, the animate and the inanimate, and even life and death. The global technological revolution will be a driver of change for decades to come.

The shortsighted men and women of the Euro-*apparat* cared little about what the global technology revolution might have meant elsewhere: in developing superpowers like India or China, in huge nations like Brazil in the throes of modernization, or in advanced societies like Australia, whose policy options are closely circumscribed by distance and nature. In the same years in which the EU imposed a ban on the importation and cultivation of GM crops, each such nation, for reasons of its own, proceeded either openly or covertly to advance biotech research and increased the importation, cultivation, and exportation of GM products. Significant amounts of this output, though none of the parties openly admitted the fact, entered the European food chain. The new GM powers qualify for, and will demand, a prominent role in future policy making. They will no longer kowtow to Europe.

The Brussels authorities also lack the tools needed to make and enforce policy domestically in the vast new "competences" they claim. The Brussels authorities are short on expertise, legitimacy, and mechanisms for coordination. The comprehensive approach advocated by Professor Vesintini in *Genomics and Crop Plant Science* is simply beyond their reach – and even that deals only with a segment of the biotech issue. The "coexistence" GM settlement is tantamount to admitting that in biotechnology, authority should be best relinquished to the member states, and the same is true in the related fields of R&D, university reform, and industrial standard setting. In research and development, the EU should think of itself as (in the Bologna Process) a catalyst to change.

To build a constituency for its broader populist appeal to anti-Americanism, the EU fanned a food scare, which drove Europe's biotech policy. It has been not only negative in character but parochial, unscientific, demagogic, dishonest, and counterproductive. It has damaged US-EU relations (as intended), sabotaged international regulation in a fast-breaking field where the need for supervision is exploding, and set Europe back economically and scientifically. Years will be needed to repair the damage. Such facts are now widely recognized. The Euro-*apparat* is intent on reversing course. Europe's failure to meet the targets set in 2000 by the Lisbon Agenda, along with the loss of competitiveness over the past several years, is causing near-panic at the summits of European statesmanship. This is, however, only one reason why research and development is at the top of the reform agenda. The other is that agreement on the importance of R&D has become the lowest common denominator in a politically divided Europe still reeling from the shock of the two constitutional referenda.

Dismal is the single word that best describes the EU's record in the field of research and development. The evident absurdity of promoting a specific European approach to scientific inquiry – which knows no borders other than the untrammeled pursuit of knowledge – is reflected in past FP performance. Europe has little to show for its money. What else can be expected when strengthening Brussels drives the R&D program? The EU need not, however, seek a new raison d'etre in the promotion of science and technology. The great challenge it faces – and perhaps eventually its greatest accomplishment – will be to strengthen democracy within and along Europe's borders. That should be its purpose and justification as well as the source of a new legitimacy.

FOUR

Democracy

The public repudiation of the proposed European Constitution, a gut reaction felt far more widely and deeply than registered in the famous French and Dutch referenda, was a good thing – but might not remain one if the wrong lessons are drawn from it. In addition to the unpopularity of the document itself, one should consider what its adoption would have erected: a flimsy, oversized superstructure anchored to a sagging foundation. Something so claptrap would soon have collapsed, scattered debris across a continent, and brought to an end the fifty-year history of European integration. The project may yet fall apart, but should not be allowed simply to disintegrate. It should be revived. Although an unreformed Europe will not likely to revert to the chronic internecine warfare that made a nightmare of the first half of the century, it will be enfeebled, demoralized, and at the mercy of giant non-European superpowers. This is nothing to wish for: decline is not desirable, and decadence anything but a happy ending.

Before giving up on the European Union (EU), the citizens of the member states should try to reconfigure it. The responsibility is theirs and inescapable. Structural breakdown is a harsh reality: the Brussels institutions no longer work and, in their present form, cannot be made to work. No member state or group of member states, moreover, has both the strength and the desire to lead, nor is this possible in the teeth of public opposition. The next great step in the integration process must grow out of, and rest on, the consent of the governed. A democratic consensus can only be built one step at a time. The day of grand designs is over. None worth having is, in any case, on hand. Bold reform programs are, except in Germany, an anathema to political conservatives everywhere. The plans of the intellectual Left suggest the wisdom of putting itself into receivership. The fix-up schemes of well-intentioned centrist reformers are little better. Science and technology cannot become the EU's salvation. Europe's peoples must determine the design for a new Europe.

Their voices must first be heard at the national level. Reform of the economy and the welfare state must – with two important exceptions – begin there. One need not worry about the disruptive effect of new EU initiatives: ambitious Europe-wide schemes for the makeover of financial markets, pension and mortgage markets, healthcare, and, above all, labor markets are no longer in the cards. As for the welfare state, a subject of endless discussion in Brussels, the EU lacks the tools to either "Europeanize" or otherwise reform public services, which are diverse, deeply anchored in national tradition, and politically almost untouchable.[1] Only responsible, elected national governments have the potential strength to make the tough tradeoffs between growth and stability needed to restore economic competitiveness.

The European Monetary Union (EMU) is the most important exception to the rule that reform must begin from the bottom up. A brake on growth, the EMU is also vulnerable to attack from several quarters – law, markets, and politics. Confidence in it is being sapped by the failure of official Monnetist integration teleology. It could collapse. As an antecedent to macroeconomic reform, moreover, the EMU must restore monetary and fiscal sovereignty to the member states.

EU-level reform of the Common Agricultural Policy (CAP) is also urgently needed. The agreement reached at the December 2005 summit to leave the CAP untouched until 2013 will paralyze the EU. Only a last-minute miracle can, moreover, prevent the European refusal to curtail the farm subsidy program from derailing the Doha negotiations and thereby halting in its tracks a fifty-year trend toward trade liberalization. This runs contrary to the interests of Europe itself. A strong World Trade Organization (WTO) is not only crucial for world economic growth but necessary for an international framework of commercial regulation in a world where power is shifting away from the transatlantic powers. A breakdown of the WTO would also have severe and far-reaching adverse consequences for the EU: it would lose one of its three still-viable functions – representing Europe in trade negotiations.

With the CAP now safeguarded for another seven years, it will be hard for the EU to demonstrate by improved performance that it is still worth saving, The Commission could help matters by putting its own house in order, and the EMU can be reconfigured to operate more soundly, but without a new rationale, the EU will wither on the vine. National governments must seek popular mandates to reclaim power from the Brussels institutions to make democracy work properly and lay the foundations for a future European *demos*. Such a thing must grow from the ground up, through confidence building. Patience will be required. After ten years of accumulated failure, public mistrust is both wide and deep. Beyond that, the EU must find a new mission rather than persist in the present, blind course of anti-US policy.

The historian Tony Judt views integration as the happy outcome of unintended consequences. There *is* something to this serendipitous notion. The EU, and its predecessor organizations, came into being to promote economic growth and eventually provide a framework for political and economic union. Little thought was ever given to integration as an engine of democracy. The Brussels institutions were therefore not set up to promote it, made little accommodation to it, and made little use of it. The democratic issue first arose with the "Iberian" enlargement of countries, which had been subject to right-wing authoritarian governments since before World War II, and later – with much greater urgency – in connection with the accession of new member states formerly ruled by Soviet masters. With very little forethought, the EU soon found itself somewhat reluctantly engaged in the business of democracy building. Escape from this responsibility was not then, nor is it now, possible. Europe dare not turn its back on its deepest political values. Real credit for the generally successful introduction of representative government under law in eastern Europe belongs, however, to the peoples of the formerly oppressed nations, whom the EU has never treated even-handedly. Their sacrifices attest to the strength of the market and the power of the democratic ideal.

The promotion of economic growth is, even by critics, often cited as the EU's greatest contribution to European welfare. It may have been so in the past but probably will not be in a future globalized world economy. Spreading democracy will more likely prove to be the EU's most enduring accomplishment, remain its biggest challenge, and become, with any luck, its crowning glory. The stakes are only partly a matter of doing what's right; they are also practical. Europe will in fact only be really secure if ringed by healthy democracies; instability, and worse, will result from the absence of such a strong surrounding belt of friendly allied nations in the post-Soviet space. The power vacuum, which now exists, will be left for others to fill.

Enlargement will not only expand Europe but shift its locus south-eastward, bringing in new blood, challenges, and ideas; it will catalyze change in the EU. Europe can indeed be rejuvenated from the east. The EU of the future will break the bonds that constrain its present development: it will no longer be hostage to a Franco-German deal to protect the status quo, which was cut in the name of the "European social and economic model" and is enforced by a rigid and politically irresponsible bureaucracy in Brussels. If it is to survive, the EU of tomorrow will have to complement the polycentric and multilateral international order now emerging. It will have many capitals: not only Brussels, Paris, and Berlin, but Helsinki and Lisbon, Athens and Stockholm, and London and probably Kyiv. It will be home not only to Roman Catholicism and Protestantism, but Eastern Orthodoxy and Islam, as well as many peoples bound by common principle and mutual trust. Such a Europe will be far richer intellectually, aesthetically, and spiritually than anything imaginable by the great men who founded the EU – survivors of a broken world. The Europe of tomorrow will restore continuity with a more distant past: it will be the old Europe, restored, revived, and improved.

The British Nonpresidency

It all started out quite well. The constitutional rejection humiliated Chirac, weakened the hobbling Schröder (who had already advanced the election a year and seemed clearly on the way out), and removed from the table any real prospect that Europe would develop into a political federation. The bitterly divisive issues of representation and voting rules, which had wrecked Nice and divided the Convention for the Future of Europe, therefore suddenly became irrelevant in the future accession of Turkey as well as other candidate-nations. The conduct of the French referendum campaign also strengthened Blair's hand. The public manifestation of contempt for the scapegoated Polish plumber, a symbol of the poor and ambitious job seeker, discredited France throughout eastern Europe. Blair, in short, had handed to him on a plate an opportunity to launch the EU on a bold course of long-overdue reform.

Blair tried to seize the chance on June 24 in his inaugural address to the European Parliament (EP) – one of the best he has ever given. The prime minister wrote the text himself. It was a "fighting speech using biblical language" and meant to be understood as a wake-up call for Europe to engage with the challenge of China and India, reconnect to its peoples, and introduce long-overdue economic reforms. Blair started out to a chorus of catcalls by proclaiming himself a "passionate pro-European" but concluded his remarks to the skulking of the pro-Chirac faction at the rear of the vast hall. Europe, Blair declared, had begun a "profound debate about its future," which he wanted to see conducted frankly, openly, critically, and without the use of intimidation to shut off debate by misrepresenting "the desire for change as betrayal of the European ideal." He warned pointedly that Europe would risk failure by "huddling together [and] hoping to avoid globalization" and painfully reminded his hecklers that the EU had failed to deliver on the promise to improve the lives of Europeans. The proposed constitution had thus become "merely a vehicle for the people to register a wider and deeper discontent with the state of affairs in Europe."[2]

The speech resonated with audiences throughout Europe. It was perhaps predictable that the Polish foreign minister liked "Blair's vision, because Europe today needs to take a fresh look at itself"; came as a pleasant surprise to find an Italian Member of European Parliament (MEP) from the left-center opposition conceding that Blair was "possibly though not probably a great leader, albeit a 'Europeanist'." It was an outright triumph to learn that Le Monde found words of praise for the "Anglo-Saxon model" and for the first time ever demanded reform of the CAP. Blair surely must have been astonished to discover that the bitterly Euro-hostile United Kingdom Independence Party (UKIP) spokesman in the EP, Nigel Farage, backhandedly felt obliged to praise him as "a Europhile who has been mugged by reality. If you can reform the EU, Mr. Blair," admitted a begrudging Farage, "then

I may even change my mind. I may even think it's worth us staying a member."[3]

But what did the memorable words of the persuasive Blair actually mean? It was, commented one reporter, "a classic New Labor, even a third way speech, [which] appeared to offer some comfort to both enthusiastic and skeptical Europeans with a talk of a flexible, liberal economy combined with a strong social framework." The bottom line was that nothing fundamental needed to be changed. The problem, said Blair, "is not a crisis of political institutions, it is a crisis of political leadership." It can easily be fixed up, he added, because "the Kok report ... shows the way" by pointing to the abuses of the CAP and calling for the EU to lead in research and development (R & D). The rest of the speech makes vague appeals for economic liberalization (Lisbon Agenda), better control of terrorism and immigration, and the strengthening of a European security policy. "The broad sweep of history," he concluded," is on the side of the EU."[4]

Blair wobbled over the summer during the "period of reflection" called for by Barroso after the double whammy of the referenda rejections: Europe had ceased to be at the head of the agenda. The extent to which he might have been influenced by the well-formulated views of his chancellor of the Exchequer and designated successor, can only be surmised. Gordon Brown had, in any case, argued that in an age of globalization, a regional trade bloc like the EU is an anachronism whose importance will decline over time. He consequently called for a reordering of priorities, with international trade liberalization at the top, the transatlantic economic relationship coming in second place, and the EU finishing a distant third. Blair's attitude toward Brussels is at least not inconsistent with the views of his chancellor of the Exchequer.[5] The prime minister was nevertheless keen on making a success of his presidency. Few could have imagined during the "period of reflection" the depth of this determination.

Blair's next noteworthy address, a blast of triumphalism delivered on September 27 at the Labour Party conference in Brighton, set the agenda for the unprecedented third four-year term. It spelled out a program of relentless change: for reform of pensions, in energy transport and the local government, and in the criminal justice and national health systems. The speech made only two scant glancing references to Europe, one to decry "the malaise of France and the angst of Germany" and the other to remain "at the forefront of events where decisions are made and not at the back where they're handed down." Britain's interest in Europe, as Blair represented it, was apparently to be limited to market access; no mention was made of anything else. Concerning the importance of the transatlantic connection, by contrast, he left no doubt that "Britain should... remain the strongest ally of the United States." Remaining globally competitive was, in this speech as well as most others, the overarching policy aim.[6]

The postreferenda weakening of Brussels removed a highly divisive issue from British politics. Britain's third-term prime minister apparently intended to keep it that way. As European Council president, Blair would not be an activist. He tried, to be sure, to guide the EU in the right direction – toward economic liberalization and territorial expansion – but neither took any noteworthy initiatives nor made any sacrifices. The Hampton Court EU minisummit of October 27 – a special meeting convoked by Blair as Council president to discuss the challenges of globalization – turned out to be a nonevent. The venue was, according to Timothy Garton Ash, quite appropriate. Hampton Court, a palace built by Henry VIII housed a remarkable Great House of Easement, a lavatory that could handle twenty-eight distinguished guests at a sitting – more than enough to accommodate the twenty-five EU heads of state and government, which, he notes, "needs a good session of Easement." It is unknown whether the guests departed any lighter than they entered. Let's hope so. The summit would then reckon as a success. As it was, Hampton Court gave Blair an opportunity to present his agenda for the remaining two months of the presidency, but it featured only squishy-soft "feel-good" topics: a common energy policy, cooperation between universities, R & D, migration, work and leisure, and aid to Africa. Nothing whatsoever was said at the meeting about the budget dispute, which could make or break the EU; discussion was deferred to the final summit in December. Until then, a cease-fire was to be observed by all parties. The photo ops show Blair and Chirac beaming at one other.[7]

Blair's inaction led to criticism from all sides. Yet little in truth could have been accomplished under the circumstances of fall 2005.

The deadlock resulting from the September 18 German elections produced an impasse that left the country without an effective government. Schröder remained in office, while Merkel desperately tried to put together a grand coalition. The vote, according to Wolfgang Munchau, signified a turning away from reform before it had even started. Merkel's introduction of the flat tax into the campaign accounted, in his view, for the extraordinary deterioration of support for the CDU over the summer. The result was a hung parliament, with an upper house still dominated by the right-center party and the lower one split down the middle between Right and Left. Even before coalition negotiations began, Merkel relinquished her two main economic pledges, to reduce the power of the unions and to cut taxes. This, too, was for the moment a secondary matter: thanks to the unexpected resignation of the two purported flywheels in the cabinet, Frank Müntefering (SPD) and Edmund Stoiber (CSU/CDU), Germany remained leaderless until November 22, when Merkel finally formed her government. By then, it had become too late for Germany to put its weight behind any British reform agenda.[8]

Events nevertheless seemed to be moving in Britain's direction. Rudderless, drifting, and generally morose, for months France witnessed the spectacle of a Balinese shadow-play, in which one-dimensional hand puppets held up on sticks frantically chase each other back and forth in front of a screen, flapping their floppy hinged arms defiantly, while jabbering and screaming in a language the viewer need not understand. The Sarkozy–de Villepin drama rolled on, in other words, with all its characteristically meaningless intensity, indeed with a new ferocity due to the "small vascular incident," which apparently afflicted Chirac in a manner experienced by lesser mortals as a mild stroke. For the rest, it was politics almost as usual. A forward-looking minister of finance proposed a moderately tightened budget and marginally cut taxes. Long-standing scandals (the "Chirac 47") competed for the front page with new ones (payoffs of French diplomats by Saddam Hussein, bribing by the aerospace company Thales, etc.) Of course, striking, or the threat of it, broke out after every attempt at even partially privatizing public corporations (Electricité de France) or at cutting pensions, increasing statutory working periods, and improving labor market flexibility.[9]

Such tedium was only occasionally punctuated by the fall of an icon. The plummet at hand resulted from the disclosure in a recent biography that the inspiration of the French postwar Left, and for decades France's most famous literary couple, Jean-Paul Sartre and Simone de Beauvoir, though sexually distant from one another, "bonded" by playing exploitation games over many years with numerous vulnerable third parties, normally teenage girls living under conditions of great duress (Jewish refugees, penniless White Russians, miscellaneous ex-countryside waifs, etc.), whom Sartre enjoyed seducing and de Beauvoir liked to dominate through her overbearing, steamy, and distinctly kinky sexuality. What they shared emotionally – as indicated in an extensive exchange of nasty letters mocking the physical and mental deficiencies of their unwitting victims – was a perverse pleasure in reinforcing their feelings of mutual superiority.[10] The disclosure that the great philosopher and his sometime amanuensis were, in fact, ordinary low-lifers rattled the imperturbable self-confidence of the French elites, but it was nothing like what was yet to come. It will be a problem for years.

The orgy of rioting and firebombing that broke out in the Arab and African suburbs of northeastern Paris in late October discredited what little remained of the Chirac presidency, tarnished the reputations of his two would-be successors, and set France on a course of introspection and self-doubt. The outbreak made a mockery of the French head of state's hollow pretensions to world leadership, proved irrefutably that the government in Paris is out of touch with reality, and indicated that the vaunted French social model needs a facelift.[11] In the two weeks following the initial disorders, a couple of dozen public buildings were set ablaze, and 10,000 cars eventually got torched – a few of them (gasp!) in central Paris.

Resentment had been festering for years in "the powder-keg towns, [which] poor housing, mediocre education, rampant crime, drugs, crumbling family structures [and] joblessness had turned into pits of boredom and despair."[12] Preferring to bestride the high stage of world diplomacy, Chirac paid little attention to the escalating crisis. Nor did either of the two challengers manage to get a handle on the situation. De Villepin preferred habitual posturing to problem solving and, like Sarkozy, remained obsessed with the forthcoming presidential election, even though they were still some seventeen months away.

The disorder did not result from a violent, hate-driven US-style ghetto uprising of young blacks, the descendants of slaves, out to get The Man; things were not yet quite that bad. The French immigrant rioters committed crimes almost entirely against property and rarely against persons. The rampages were spontaneous, coordinated only by blog and cell phone, selectively destructive, and leaderless. They were a violent, yet measured protest of young Arab and African and second-generation immigrants against The System. The rioters were not religiously fanatical Islamists ready to die in the name of Allah but local representatives – and copycats – of an international have-not hip-hop youth subculture born in the U.S.A. that celebrates violence, glorifies machismo, and worships easy money. The young men had become not thugs – they are still too soft for that – but what Sarkozy impoliticly called them: street punks.

The mayhem says less about the clash of culture than of the imitation of culture. It represents the underside of globalization and can be counted on to strengthen French opposition to it. The riots are a reminder, according to David Brooks, that "for all the talk about American hegemony, American countercultural hegemony has always been more powerful.... This is our final insult to the anti-Americans; we define how to be anti-American, and the foreigners who attack us are reduced to borrowing our own clichés." That is precisely the problem: there is no real defense against transmission of the universal subculture of the wretched urbanites of the earth.

Eleven days passed before the remote and magisterial Chirac deigned to issue a press release on events in the "sensitive urban zones" of high-rise concrete ghettoes that ring most French cities. His statement was followed by the worst rioting thus far. By then, in any case, the disorders had spread throughout France and, indeed, soon to nearly every city in France. The rioting arsonists would leave unforgettable images of the problem facing the French nation. Decades of horrendous unemployment, political underrepresentation, and social exclusion have punctured the legal fiction that an Arab is like any other Frenchman. Odds are that things will only worsen. Given France's suboptimal demographics and the French refusal to admit Polish plumbers into the solid-waste disposal community, surplus North African labor will likely be called on to empty the bedpans of the future.

Business as usual resumed even before the coals went out. On Monday, November 21, travelers faced the sixth strike of the year by railway men protesting the partial privatization of the state-owned SNCF, even after having been guaranteed that only 17 percent of the company would be sold. It was brought to an end by the promises of $140 annual bonuses and more featherbedding jobs as well as Chirac's reassurance that "whatever happens, [SNCF] is a brilliant French enterprise, essential to France." The Paris Metro workers went on strike on Wednesday, and the secondary teachers the following day. In the same week, the Socialists lurched to the Left. Their Le Mans Party conference adopted a platform with commitments to renationalizing Electricité de France, raising the minimum wage, abolishing flexible two-year wage contracts, and boosting pay for working more than thirty-five hours per week. The party also wants the EU to be more federal and "more political, and more social" – whatever that should mean. Did any of this matter? Sixty percent of the French public agrees that the Socialists have "no chance" of winning the 2007 presidential election.[13]

While the riots plunged the country into a collective depression, the government remained in a state of incomprehension. The employment minister, Gérard Larcher, blamed the disorders on polygamy. A raft of inchoate and adequate policies was soon drawn up, including tough controls on welfare chiseling, more apprenticeships, a crackdown on drug dealers, tax breaks for businesses setting up in the ghettoes, and extra money for neighborhood associations. The future will be a bit different. The television news will feature the occasional black anchorperson. Some 50,000 make-work jobs will be promised minorities. Polygamists will be cut off from family support. Nothing essential, however, will change. "The prejudice is," according to Brooks, "impermeable and the labor markets are more rigid. There really is no escape."[14]

The riots provided a rare opportunity for political profiling. The somewhat exotic and raffish Nicolas Sarkozy played the tough cop – the hard man – role to the hilt, even though he, oddly enough, had been the one senior figure on the French political scene to recognize the plight of France's ethnic 6 million Arabs and Africans, admit that it represented a real danger, and try to do something about it. When interior minister, what he actually did about it was put the *banlieues* under a regime of proactive policing – install what amounted an occupation force in all but name. After the rioting broke out, he "dissed" (made disrespectful comments about) the young fire bombers, thereby, perhaps not actually adding fuel to the flames but setting himself up as a scapegoat for the disorders. Although Sarkozy was rebuked by the commentariat for his harsh words, a November 10 poll by *Le Figaro* indicated that 56 percent of the respondents approved of his tough language. His reputation, at least with the voters, apparently did not go up in smoke along with the automobile tires and what remained of Chirac's tattered authority. He in any case felt sufficiently confident to chime in to the Gaullist chorus with the refrain, "Shame! Shame! Shame! Po-ly-gamy is to Blame."[15]

That silver-maned Enarch with a particulate and son of a diplomat, poet-philosopher and Napoleonic wannabe – the preposterous Dominique de Villipin – sought a different role and made himself a fool playing it. He would be Mr. Nice Guy. The heir-apparent to Chirac's mantel rediscovered his (accidental) North African roots, got outfitted in hip-hugging bags, and for several days apparently practiced the ghetto slo-shuffle. Effective reform will, however, require more than turning in pinstripes for gangsta threads. The vain de Villepin appears belatedly to have realized as much. On November 7 the high-toned prime minister delivered a twenty-minute address promising scholarships and apprenticeships to slum dwellers, but to a bemused London journalist, "it was unclear whether the elegant and patrician Prime Minister would greatly influence the rioters, who M. de Villepin [described as] a mixture of youngsters 'competing with each other as a game' and criminals who were benefiting from their rampages."[16]

De Villepin's honeyed words meant little. A day later – in the face of public objections from Sarkozy – he invoked a state of emergency dating from the Algerian war and imposed a curfew in thirty-eight suburbs. The rampage raged on. In his only public comment since the crisis, which broke out two weeks earlier, the lofty Chirac refused to comment beyond fatuously stating, "When the time comes, I will share with you my reflections on the entirety of the problem."[17] By November 14 he had apparently sorted it all out. Extending the curfew for three months, threatening to prosecute the parents of rioters as well as the rioters themselves, making token gestures in the direction of "diversity," Chirac finally reminded his listeners that "it's a good thing to belong to the French community." That was the sum total of the political wisdom he could distill from forty years in public life.[18]

Once the smoldering has died down in the *banlieueues*, pressure will mount to adopt improved French versions of the US-type affirmative action programs, which, after nearly a generation, can be declared an overall success, at least in heading off ghetto uprisings like the ones that destroyed whole sections of US cities in the 1960s and early 1970s and which brought the country to the brink of a race war. Affirmative action means giving blacks and other designated "minorities" preference in employment (especially in the public sector), government-related contracting, university and school admissions, higher education, and government loans. It is very expensive and requires public acceptance of reverse discrimination. Affirmative action has brought about neither quick results nor ultimate solutions, and it has aggravated nearly as many problems as it solved. To make it work will require deep commitment, far-reaching social change, and recognition that without reform France will be even weaker than the immigrant disturbances have revealed it to be. France can no longer afford to indulge in Chirac's, or the imaginative de Villepin's, superpower fantasies. The public will refuse to tolerate such nonsense any longer.

In the United States, the tragic aftermath of the September 2005 flooding of New Orleans awakened the unspoken, and best unvoiced, fears of White America that the historic problem of race had not been solved but only papered over. Affirmative action did not strengthen a parallel subculture, as often mistakenly believed, but truncated the existing one: the strong, the well-born, and the able of Black America have drifted off to Mc Mansions and shopping malls, leaving the others behind in the inner cities and surrounding suburbs both leaderless and losing ground. The social and educational gap between the black urban masses and the rest of society is greater then ever before and widening ominously. The downside to affirmative action has one final dimension: the well-intentioned attempt to nurture a new black leadership class in the US ghetto took a cruel twist. It turned punks into thugs, strengthened gangs, and caused warfare between them – often over the drug traffic – to become endemic. The crime rate rose alarmingly, and the violence and lawlessness percolated upward and reinforced corrupt political machines in many US cities, few of which have ever recovered.

Damage limitation, the French should realize, involves four key things in addition to affirmative action: the warehousing of the better part of a generation of young men in the nation's prisons; the tightening up of the welfare system; the provision of low-paying minimum-wage jobs – for which literacy skills are not necessarily needed – by big box retailers as well as fast-food and other franchisers; and the influx of millions of new immigrants, most of them illegal, dirt-poor, and willing to work cheap – with a strong claim to victimization but a manifest willingness to advance through the system the hard way.

To prevent the smoldering immigrant suburbs of France from becoming authentic, vicious US-type urban ghettoes will require increasing opportunities for employment, improving economic growth, and removing the straitjacket called the French model of society. It will entail reducing the public employment of non-Arab and non-African men and women, weakening job protection, and stepping up competition between wage earners and within business. It will oblige the public to accept, in other words, precisely those things that most French men and women do not want and will result in either a sharp turn to an insular, bigoted, and nationalistic Right or a lazy drift to the feeble, fudging, and nondescript Left. The discrediting of the Gaullists has left least tainted – except for the Le Pen know-nothings – only the bedraggled and struggling Socialists, the party of protected public employees (the portion of the electorate least inclined to make sacrifices) and the inventors of the European social model, which, having flopped in Mitterrand's France, was exported to Brussels, with similar consequences, for transplantation at the European level.

An opinion poll taken in late August and early September indicated that in the months between the referendum and the fiery protests, France had already turned inward. Conducted in five European countries (France, Germany, Poland, Spain, and Great Britain), it disclosed that the French had become the most Euro-skeptical nation of the lot.[19] No one has, in other words, wrested leadership of the EU from France. The French have lost it by default. The suburban mayhem merely confirms the result. This, as it turned out, would be bad news. Chirac became utterly uncompromising. Rather than call for restructuring the EU, Blair abjectly capitulated to the physically weak and politically reeling French president.

The Budget Debacle

Public debate over the 2007–2013 EU budget began in June, the last month of the Luxembourg presidency, in the aftermath of the resounding double "NO" to the proposed constitution. What began as a surrogate struggle over the larger issues of which "vision" would guide the EU's future and who would run, it soon got so far out of hand that it began to threaten the futures of not only the EU but the world trading system. In June, Mr. Blair looked like a sure winner, with his position in line with public sentiment and justice on his side. Because, however, Blair failed to recognize that victory on the budget would require a general overhaul of the Brussels institutions, he eventually got snookered by M. Chirac. It was a repetition of the famous "stitch-up" of October 2002, when, against long odds, Chirac for the first time rescued the EU's giant welfare program for French prosperous farmers. By bringing Herr Schröder to heel and threatening to wreck enlargement unless he got his way, he isolated Britain and the ten eastern European candidate nations, managed to deprive the latter of a fair share of CAP money, and saved the bulk of it for the for the landholding French gentry.[20] Schröder would be Chirac's poodle for the rest of his chancellorship. Three years later, in 2005, and with Schröder still firmly on the leash, Chirac turned the Poles, leaving Blair isolated. "Stitch up II" will have more far-reaching consequences than its predecessor. It will increase the existing inequities generated by the farm subsidies, crowd reform off the agenda for years to come, and gridlock, perhaps even bankrupt, the EU. Europe has dug itself even deeper into the hole. Greater statesmen will be needed to dig it out than the midgets running its affairs today.

The budgetary dispute was less about money than an institutionally inextricable combination of money and power. At stake was the future direction of the EU. The issue it centered on, the Common Agricultural Policy, is often grotesquely misrepresented. The idea, which to some makes the CAP sacrosanct – that it acts as guardian of an Arcadian Europe – is sentimental rubbish. The CAP encourages the output of cash crops requiring heavy doses of mechanization, tillage, fertilization, and pesticide. Then, too, there is the fiction that the money benefits primarily those who cultivate the land as opposed to those who own it. The recent passage of blue-sky disclosure laws in several member states leaves no doubt that the CAP overwhelmingly favors super-rich large property owners like Albert II of Monaco (in northern France) and HRM Prince Charles and the Duke of Bedford in the United Kingdom at the expense of small farmers. Some 70 percent of the CAP funds go to the top 20 percent of large farmers, while nearly three-quarters of those who work the land in the EU have incomes of less than about 10,000 euros per year. Small producers, 20 percent of the total, receive only 8 percent of the overall subsidy payments, and farm incomes community-wide are 50 percent below their peak in 1995. According to a recent study by Groupe Mondiale de Sciences Po, less than 1 percent of French farmers receive more in subsidies than the bottom 40 percent."[21]

The CAP will be even less equitable in the future. It is gradually being switched from subsidizing production to "income maintenance" (bounties for nonuse of agricultural land). The purpose of the reform is not budgetary – it actually raises costs – but partly economic and political. To be sure, it makes sense not to encourage production by supporting artificially high prices, which intensifies cultivation. Yet the main argument for the shift is that the absurdity of paying rich and idle landowners for working less – or less than nothing – will become so readily apparent that the program will die of inanition. In the meantime, however, income maintenance will not preserve the bucolic character of the countryside but, by limiting plantings, turn it back to a wilderness. It will, of course, also reduce employment. Since the citizens of the new member states spend relatively more on food than those of the old ones, the future CAP will transfer even more wealth from the working poor to the idle rich.

The CAP is truly, as the economist Richard Baldwin calls it, a "dooH niboR" scheme – a reverse Robin Hood policy.[22] This is what he means. Gigantic farms (0.2 percent of the total) receive payments on the average of 780,000 euros per year; the 1.5 percent of the largest farms get 27 percent of the money (averaging 70,000 per year); the top 6 percent of all farms by size soak up 53 percent of total funding; and the smallest farms share only 4 percent of total CAP money and receive an average of only 425 euros a year. France receives about half the total, twice as much as any other country. Increasing amounts will be provided for income maintenance for landowners such as the Queen of England, who received 231,559 euros in 2003–2004. Her wealth is estimated at 368 million euros. The Duke of Westminster, who at 7.1 billion euros is far richer even than the Queen, receives 259,710 euros.

The overall amounts involved in the CAP are, as compared to GDP, quite modest and, if subject to rigorous annual review (like national budgets), could be adjusted without inflicting much pain. The seven-year funding cycle normally rules this out: once agreed upon the budget can only be renegotiated with great difficulty. Thus nontrivial sums (when adjusted for interest and inflation), amounting to roughly 10 percent of annual GDP, were at stake. The rigid rules were a veritable invitation to the entrenchment of bureaucracy and thus also a formula for compounding the EUs problems.

The budget (2007–2013) was a knotty issue – though not a pressing one. The EU had until the end of the year to work out the problems and in the past two cycles had failed to meet the deadline, in which cases financing proceeded on the same basis as the last year of the previous one. The Luxembourg Council president was intent, however, upon sewing up a deal in June, before his British successor had a whack at reform. The budget problem arose because all present net contributors (including the Germans) refused to increase their deficits to the EU but agreed at the same time to limit their overall level to 1.1 percent of gross national income; no new revenue (in real terms) would therefore be forthcoming to meet the increased responsibilities the EU faced as a result of further planned enlargement. Savings had to come out of existing lines to balance the budget.[23]

Even after stepping into the Council presidency, Britain preferred not to force the issue. With Merkel waiting in the wings, things looked almost rosy. She had let be known that if Britain were willing to reconsider the rebate, Germany would consider cutting the CAP as well. There was thus no need to rush things prior to the election in September: with Merkel in office, the British felt confident that there would be enough time to get the ball rolling. The rhetorical phase began in June. With his star ascending as a result of the negative referenda outcomes, Blair proclaimed to any and all who would listen that "Europe must reform or crumble." A majority of member states – Sweden, Denmark, the Netherlands, Ireland, and Portugal as well as most of the ten new member states – seemed well disposed to the message. Chirac, however, soon forced Blair's hand. Reeling from the referendum defeat and desperately clinging to the levers of political control, the French president launched a "June offensive," an angry and inflammatory propaganda campaign against Britain as saboteur of the referenda and Blair personally, whom he blamed for the loss of the French referendum. This was a smokescreen.[24]

His real target was the British rebate (clawback), secured by Margaret Thatcher in the early 1980s, which the president of the European Council, Jean-Claude Juncker, eagerly put upfront on the final Luxembourg summit agenda. Happy to sandbag Blair, Juncker proposed that the rebate be frozen – that is, reduced over time in real terms – in order to cover most of the anticipated deficit. Schröder chimed in that the CAP should be "ring-fenced." The Commission declared the British clawback "outdated," suggested that other contributor countries had sounder claims for rebates than Britain, and alleged that the United Kingdom, when striking the original deal, agreed that the others could benefit from similar arrangements "at the right time." Barroso also came out with a proposal for a generalized "clawback clause" for a two-third refund, which would kick in whenever a country's net contribution exceeded 0.35 percent of its GDP – a level so high, one would hope, as to be meaningless.[25]

Chirac's case rested on a perverse political logic. Little justice was involved – and still less good sense. Even with the rebate, Britain remains the second largest EU contributor (after Germany), has paid twice as much as France into the EU kitty over the past twenty years, and continues to pay two and a half times as much, whereas the French, historically a substantial beneficiary nation, at present still comes out a low end of overall net contributing nations – thanks to a large CAP balance. France has always been the largest net beneficiary of the farm program – and receives about half the total payments. The others all got at least something from it, however, and only Britain benefits from the clawback. There indeed was the rub. All things being equal, the CAP recipients could be counted on to band together in defense of their payments, leaving Britain isolated.[26] Except for an alternative design for an improved EU, which never materialized, Blair found himself with nothing to offer except the threat of exit, which he, unlike the go-for-broke Chirac, never apparently considered.

An additional problem compounded Britain's situation. It was the byproduct of the nefarious 2002 stitch-up. Though receiving only a fraction of the CAP entitlements received by the old members, the easterners depended heavily on such payments because of low prevailing income levels. They were, at the same time, scheduled to receive increasing increments until reaching parity by 2013. Without such stepped-up payments, the newcomers risked becoming substantial net EU contributors. Their defection from Britain was almost a foregone conclusion. In September it happened. The Poles, and the other eastern Europeans, along with the French, went after the clawback.

Only the Polish election of November could have made a difference, but once again, an unexpected outcome tripped up the British presidency. Polish voters swept into office the right-wing Law and Government Party. Led by famous twinned child actors, the fiercely clerical party, and its reactionary coalition partners, drew heavily on Poland's large farm vote. These mainly subsistence-level private smallholders, many of them for the first time on the cash economy, vehemently objected to any reduction in the phase-in of CAP payments, which, as they reached parity in 2013, would also increase as a percentage of overall low farm incomes. Rather than end his presidency with gridlock over the budget, Blair blinked.

A concession from the purportedly non-*communautaire* Britain is what makes it possible for the EU to maintain the illusion of progress. The prime minister's humiliating climbdown will leave the CAP intact until 2013. The French have already publicly repudiated "reconsidering" the CAP in 2008, a concession Blair had wrung out at the last minute as a face-saver. The settlement was withal, an extraordinary personal triumph for a man, whom only 1 percent of the French population wanted to reelect as president. Can anything be wrong with a system that vests so much power in someone so lacking in public support?

The 2007–2013 EU budget will be 862.36 billion euros, at 1.045 percent of member state GDP actually up slightly from the target sought by the member states. An additional billion euros will help fatten up the bureaucracy. The 20 percent reduction of the British clawback of 10.5 billion euros (from a total of 50–55 billion euros) will reduce the costs of membership to the others. Britain will pay 20 percent more than France (which will become the largest net recipient) over the cycle and receive back from the EU less than any member state. The CAP will increase by two points to 46 percent of the total 2005 budget of 106.3 billion euros, and regional assistance will remain at 30 percent. Spain will continue to get over a quarter of the aid funds, twice that of any other member state. The ten poor accession nations will continue to get less than 10 percent of the program's total funding. R & D will actually be less in real terms than previously.[27]

It would be unfair to leave the impression that Tony Blair accomplished nothing as president of the European Council. Blair held Turkish accession on track – no small feat: in so doing, he kept open the same path for Romania and Bulgaria, as well as nations of the western Balkans and Ukraine. The French foreign minister's attempt in December 2005 to halt future enlargement until the case of Macedonia, the laggard among western Balkan admission candidates, can be discussed is merely a delaying tactic.

A lull has come over the EU – one more like the quiet of the graveyard than a real calm. The European Union is, as a deeply troubled Will Hutton put in the *Observer*, dangling by a thread. It resembles a cartoon character who, having charged over the cliff with legs still pumping, awaits, in ignorance, an imminent, vertiginous plummet to unforgiving reality far below. As a result of the referenda shock, the EU has in fact lost a sense of what it is for, where it is headed, how it is to be governed, and how it can secure the consent of the public. The EU has indeed become a "fragile and beleaguered" creation, which could come crashing down to earth. Like the pathetic cartoon character, institutional paralysis prevents a rescue from oblivion.[28] Stitch-up II may merely prolong the death rattles of the EU.

Decommissioned

Long past are the hard upward and forward-thrusting days of Jacques Delors; the thing now hangs limp, shriveled, and cold to the touch. Don't blame it on a bad day at the office or try to straighten it out by dreaming of past conquests: the situation is real, embarrassing, and probably not temporary. There is no getting around it. The Commission is impotent. Yet it can still be seen shuffling around. Take globalization: President Barroso warned memorably that Europe will become "nothing" if it fails to meet the challenge and succumbs instead to protectionism and xenophobia. Criticized by Chirac for failure to protect Europe's interest, however, he hedged by coming in strongly behind a proposal for a massive adjustment fund to ease the pain of unemployment brought about by foreign competition. As for his famous commitment to slashing red tape, it got nowhere because of obstruction from Berlaymont, the fortress of the Eurocracy, as well as from the Parliament, which demanded to be consulted in advance about any changes. "Canceling regulations," the president of the Commission was archly reminded, "means making political choices." No agreement could be reached within the administration about which ones should be made.[29]

To be sure, the more important commissariats continued to churn out the usual policy papers – some good, others bad – on subjects such as corporate governance, credit disclosure standards, tax harmonization, and competition policy. Under the circumstances, however, no one could act on them or, in fact, do much more than keep long-standing programs alive: lack of a budget agreement for the forthcoming seven-year cycle left all programs on hold, including, for instance, Galileo. In an attempt to buck the tide, Neelie Kroes, the competition commissioner, called for new powers to block the formation of national champions. On December 5 Charlie McCreevy, the internal market commissioner, produced a white paper with a slimmed-down program for financial reform, emphasizing simplification of cross-border money transfer and account setup; both in this and other areas, details would have to be worked out with stakeholders, and new regulations would not be issued until 2007. For his part, Barroso promoted a few liberals within the Commission, such as Catherine Day, who became director general for trade. Even a more forceful figure than he could have done little to rectify the situation. Facing the Hobson's choice of eliminating the CAP and risking the dissolution of the EU or saving it and causing the collapse of the Doha Round, he chose the latter. Could a Commission president have been expected to do otherwise, even if it meant the end of serious reform?[30]

The wheels would continue to turn in Europe's would-be capital city – work would go on like that of Margaret Wallstroem. Margaret Wallstroem is an avant-garde EU thinker. She wants to make democracy. During the "period of reflection," she learned that this was necessary. Here is her plan for reviving the constitution. Because "Plan A" (ratification) had failed and "Plan B" (intrigue) did not seem likely to succeed, she proposed a radical step. There would be no "Plan C" but a skip to "Plan D." "D" stands for Democracy! (Get it?) "There are no shortcuts," the Commission's self-styled "Mrs. PR" told the *Financial Times*. "You have to engage the citizens!" Her idea is "to put ears on the European Union." (As a matter of organic design, it would be preferable to begin with a brain able to make sense of audible signals, but the issue is technical as well as metaphorical and cannot be investigated at this point.)

Wallstroem is no slouch. Indeed she is the Commission vice president for Institutional Relations and Communication Strategy. Here is what she came up with. "Plan D," as she put it, must "inject more democracy into the Union" by stimulating dialog and debate (the other "Ds" of the triad, note well). Sounds like free-wheeling discussion? Not quite. "Plan D" will provide "a common framework for the 25 country debate," which the Commission will steer through the following schedule "Discussion and debate" will be cut off in April 2006, leaving just enough time for "feedback" at the "European Conference on the Future of Europe" (actual title) planned for May 9, 2006, which will then have a draft constitution ready for approval at the final summit of the Austrian presidency in June. Need further specifics? The Commission will select thirteen topics for discussion, work in close cooperation with other EU bodies, make visitations to each of the twenty-five member states, and appoint a celebrity "network" of European goodwill ambassadors in every one of them. The possibility that even after such indoctrination and manipulation the public might still object to vesting new powers in the EU seems to have been overlooked in "Plan D."[31]

Someone ought to put ears on Wallstroem. There is nothing very new about her harebrained proposal. The Commission has tirelessly generated numerous such self-serving schemes over the years. A campaign similar to "Plan D" failed catastrophically to win over the public to the recent constitution. The pro-EU insider blog, "Euractiv.com" – lapsing into characteristic Euro-Volapük – makes this artless comment about the cockeyed Wallstroem scheme: "The Commission has set itself high ambitions with this Plan D, but as with [the] Lisbon [Agenda], it has very little leverage over the delivery capacity and will of the member-states. Ultimately the success of Plan D lies with the national political elites in the member states.... There is a danger that if this ambition fails... the Commission will get the blame, as it mostly does when national leaders fail to deliver."[32]

Blame the Commission for the flop it devised? Unthinkable. Insufficient "delivery capacity of the member-states?" Are voters mere bags of cement, useless until carted to a building site and inert until mixed with water? Why not, then, at least offer small bribes such as a gift turkey at Christmas or, better yet, free bourbon on election day? Actually such ideas did occur to brighter lights within the Commission. Preparations have now begun, some seventeen months in advance, for fifty days of nonstop festivities to celebrate the fiftieth birthday of the EU. The costs will run high into the millions. "This," said the chair of the steering committee, "will be our way of bringing the EU closer to its citizens."[33]

A program to promote democracy like Wallstroem's Plan D, which is an insult to the intelligence of the electorate, cannot be taken seriously and does not constitute a threat to anything. It is, like the golden jubilee party, simply a stupid waste of money. Have Europe's self-anointed agenda setters still not figured out that attempts to dictate democracy will backfire? Apparently so. Upon learning that the most recent Eurobarometer poll indicated that support for the EU had continued to decline in the final six months of 2005, as she cranked up her campaign, Wallstroem complained that "citizens have seen too much selfish interest by member states [and], too little vision and solidarity."[34] The effort to put on ears sounds increasingly like one to close mouths.

Siim Kallas was another avant-garde thinker with offices at the Berlaymont, but he was in fact a man ahead of his time. Like most other eastern Europeans with memories of Soviet domination, the Estonian viscerally understood that entrenched, proliferating, self-serving bureaucracies corrupt democracy. Kallas wanted to clean up the situation in Brussels before it got completely out of hand. The commissioner for administration, audit, and antifraud, Kallas became a one-man bandwagon for EU administrative reform. In March he proposed a "European transparency initiative," which called for registering Brussels' 15,000 lobbyists, increasing investigations by Olaf (the antifraud agency), fully disclosing all recipients of agricultural and structural funds aid (80 percent of the still-unaccountable total budget expenditure), and setting "higher standards of openness for all EU institutions," including a code of conduct as well as compulsory declarations of financial interests.[35]

Kallas has met with evasion, foot-dragging, and angry opposition. Asserting the Commission was already sufficiently transparent, an official spokesperson claimed that to focus on it alone would lead to invidious public criticism; she recommended that scrutiny extend equally to all EU bodies. Barroso then sidelined Kallas by setting up an advisory committee to deal with the issue. The director general of Olaf took a more broadsided approach. Accusing Kallas of "Soviet methods" like those used in the former German Democratic Republic, he refused to cooperate. Barroso's advisory committee finally delivered a watered-down report in October 2005. It did not aim at curtailing fraud per se but simply "convincing the European Board of Auditors to approve the EU's accounts for the first time by granting a positive statement of assurance."[36] It would require the finance ministers of recipient states to sign off on all expenditures of EU monies.

Initial discussion of the plan at the EP triggered "wide-ranging hostility" and plenty of "excuses about why we can't do anything." Opposition was especially fierce from the French, German, Portuguese, Spanish, and Austrian delegations – with bottom-rankers such as Greece and Italy remaining conspicuously silent. Only the Dutch, Finns, Hungarians, and the British wanted to proceed with the matter. Although Kallas claimed to have come away from the meeting with a half-full cup, on October 25, Barroso shelved the transparency plans. The Polish *Gazeta Wyborcza* commented that "Mr. Barroso and over half the other 24 commissioners wanted to "weaken" the [transparency] document in a clash [which broke out] between a Nordic culture of openness, represented by Mr. Kallas and ... Margot Wallstroem [on the one hand] and Mediterranean traditions of government opacity on the other."[37]

On the transparency issue, Barroso might have acted to clean up the Commission but did not. On the budget matter, he was too weak to do anything. His position was purely bureaucratic – opposed to whatever might reduce the flow of revenue through his organization. He overlooked the recommendation of the Sapir Committee, maintained existing levels on the CAP, and, "rather than steer aid to the new members, ... allocated over half of structural fund spending to the fifteen old ones – even though all but two have incomes per head above the EU average."[38] The R & D agenda got quietly shelved. Funding would be less than in Framework Program 6 (FP6).

Barroso was only a bit player in the events that took place in Hong Kong from the thirteenth to the eighteenth of December – the make or break point for the Doha Round of the WTO underway since 2001. Failure at preministerial talks held in Geneva on November 9, however, cast a pall over the Hong Kong meeting. The impasse was due entirely to the refusal of the EU's trade representative to reduce tariffs on agricultural goods. As put very bluntly by one expert, "If the EU wants Doha to succeed, which as the world's biggest trading block surely it must, it will have to give up its farm protection." To the shock of economists and all others who understand that free trade is essential to growth, the EU had no such intention.[39] It was prepared to sabotage the trade negotiations in order to preserve the CAP. Such fecklessness calls into question the value of the EU. Is it signing its own death warrant?

For several reasons the CAP, rather than some other issue, was at the top of the negotiating agenda: industrial tariffs were all but eliminated at the previous negotiating round, significant trade gains could only be made in the agricultural sector, and, at the last round, the CAP was only partially reformed with the understanding that it would be the first item on the next round's agenda. Finally, consensus existed that it would be premature to attack the so-called Singapore issues: investment, competition policy, transparency (of trade rules), and trade facilitation (customs procedures). The overall stakes involved in Doha are nevertheless huge. According to one estimate, a multilateral elimination of import barriers would build up to $1.3 trillion or 2.3 percent of global GDP by 2015. But more than money is at stake. The failure of a major trade round, like Doha, could reverse progress made since the founding of the General Agreement on Tariffs and Trade (GATT), the WTO's predecessor, after World War II. It will almost certainly also lead to a system based on preferences, which normally favor the strong over the weak, and could eventually produce a world divided into trade blocs. A rise of global political tensions would result.[40]

Founded in 1948, the GATT/WTO can look back on a rich history of accomplishment, which correlates with long-term secular expansion. Originally set up with the sole aim of reducing tariff levels in successive negotiating rounds, the organization has expanded its authority to include a wide range of nontariff barriers as well. The Uruguay Round (1988–1994), the predecessor of Doha, brought world trade abreast of the globalization occurring over the previous two decades, established an agenda for "organizing liberalization" worldwide, and created a setting in which the technological breakthroughs of the 1990s could be diffused rapidly from country to country. It can also be credited with a number of important specific achievements: cutting industrial tariffs to the point of insignificance, strengthening trade rules to limit subsidization and facilitate dispute settlement, creating new ones to protect investment as well as intellectual property, and eliminating an array of nontariff barriers in textiles, leather goods, and shipbuilding.[41]

Resting more heavily than the seven prior rounds on policy inputs from producer interests, the Uruguay Round enlisted additional participation from nongovernmental organizations representing consumers, environmentalists, and labor; in other words, it created a networking infrastructure. The successful negotiating round also built in a future agenda, including the shift from price to income supports for farm products and the liberalization of services, which set the stage for the present one. Finally, the transformation from GATT to WTO entailed the creation of surveillance and enforcement machinery as well as the power to make case law. Over the past decade, international trade in goods grew twice as fast as world income, and trade in services accelerated even more rapidly, as also (at 11 percent annually) did foreign direct investment. At the same time, the composition of world trade shifted from raw materials and agricultural products to manufactured goods.[42]

When the GATT started operating after World War II, only the United States remained as a world trading power. Over time, recovery changed this, and Europe (represented by the EU) along with Japan became partners in the GATT/WTO leadership. The development was wholly in keeping with the organization's great objective of providing a mechanism for the orderly transition from a unipolar to a bipolar and eventually multipolar world. This goal remains more relevant than ever at a time when China is already an economic superpower, India is fast becoming one, Brazil is changing rapidly, and Russia – still only a candidate for WTO membership – is turning suddenly into a mighty petro-power. EU-US cooperation remains desirable in a world where influence is shifting away from the transatlantic axis. A viable WTO is essential for not only economic but political welfare. No other international organization is in a position to enforce essential rules of good business conduct, without which economic and political corruption flourish.[43]

Brazil is an example of what several emerging nations have at stake in the Doha Round. Along with India, it leads the Group of 20 (G-20), which first became a force in 2003 at Cancun, the predecessor of the Hong Kong session. For the huge perennial land of the future, it was a coming of age. Brazil has, over the past decade, finally discovered the path to modernization. Convinced until the 1980s that industrial development was an engine of modernization, Brazil's dictators financed "import substitution" by imposing a system of price and export controls, which, while channeling investment into manufacturing and providing cheap food for the urban poor, deprived the nation of comparative advantage.[44]

Since breaking with this ruinous policy in the early 1990s, Brazil has become an agricultural superpower. No nation has as rich or varied food-raising resources. Brazil's northeast can be likened to an "open-air greenhouse, with persistent sun, fertile soil, and low humidity" and plenty of water, which can count on shorter growing seasons than most anywhere else. Sao Paulo, to the south, produces the world's cheapest sugar and orange juice. The center-west is almost ideal for soybeans, Brazil's largest crop. The 60 million hectares now under cultivation could be increased by a third without touching the rain forest.

Agriculture now accounts for 8 percent of GDP, but its share is not shrinking, like that of most OECD countries, because farm exports, averaging about $5 billion annually, continue to boom. Both big food multinationals and giant grain traders have entered Brazil in force. The shift to exports is, moreover, raising product standards, improving the inadequate road system, and creating new employment. Both cause and effect of this growth, Brazilian researchers have made a number of breakthrough discoveries useful to their agriculture and farm-related technologies. The elimination of subsidies by the EU and the United States would raise Brazil's food output by 34 percent, increase farm incomes by 46 percent, and accelerate the pace of long-overdue change.[45]

As the world's leading exporter, the EU has the biggest stake of any party in the Doha negotiations. It would be supremely ironical if its policy were to destroy it. The EU and the WTO have in fact grown up together; the relationship between them has been both mutually beneficial and symbiotic. The availability of a single interlocutor with the ability to speak for Europe hugely simplifies the complicated business of international trade negotiation. It also introduces a measure of transparency into an area that otherwise would be opaque, opening it up to public accountability and responsibility and strengthening continuity and predictability – essential investment and economic security.[46]

The EU trade commissioner can, however, only act on behalf of Europe if representative. His positions must reflect the interests of stakeholders across the twenty-five member states, as arrived at in complicated bargaining. In late October the European Council, while confirming the authority of the trade negotiator, Peter Mandelson, gave him only a narrow mandate on the critical issue of agricultural tariffs: an authorization to lower them by only an average of 46 percent ("bound rate"). The offer is in fact meager. The bound rate is actually twice that of the one actually applied; moreover Mandelson's proposal excludes 70 of its most sensitive tariffs. The World Bank estimates that the average reduction would amount to no more than 1 percent. The European offer was a thoroughly inadequate counterpart to the substantially larger 60 percent cut in U.S. agricultural tariffs announced by President Bush on October 10. Chirac threatened to veto in the European Council *any* cuts that affect the CAP.[47] "French farmers," shouted the angry Australian foreign minister, "are holding the international trading system to ransom ... The French government has failed to take advantage of [a] U.S. offer, which represents a once-in-a-lifetime opportunity. ... It will be bad for the EU's standing in the world if, in the end, it cripples the Doha trade round."[48] It did, however, and nobody can do anything about it.

"The implications of France's position," commented the journalist Philip Bowring, indeed "go far beyond agriculture. They tell the world that any attempt to negotiate with the EU is futile if the antidemocratic veto powers of individual members are to be used to deprive its commissioners of negotiating authority."[49] One must also wonder how long the captains of European industry and finance will tolerate the sinking of the Doha round by a single head of state. On November 8 the chief executives of sixty leading companies published an open letter in the *Financial Times* warning of the threat of collapse and urging the governments of the Group of Eight (G-8) "to face up to their responsibilities and re-instill confidence among producers, consumers, and investors."[50] No one listened. Often accused of being a captive of European big business, the leaders of the EU pay less and less heed to its wishes. The slow-moving juggernaut is beginning to run amuck.

Although the course of trade negotiations is notoriously hard to predict, and nothing is ever really settled until the last minute, future progress in the remaining months of the Doha Round is unlikely. The round will end in April 2006, after which Congress can no longer extend the US president's "fast-track" authority.[51] A hammer blow to the WTO, the breakup in Hong Kong also undermines the credibility of the EU and could cause powerful economic agents to seek other ways to safeguard their increasingly international interests. In the face of EU intransigence in agriculture, the United States saved the Uruguay Round in November 1993, at the eleventh hour, by organizing the first Asia-Pacific Cooperation (APEC) agreement. A similar arrangement may be the sequel to, rather than the salvation of, the Doha Round. If so, a protectionist Europe will pay a high price for it. It is only a matter of time before the financial and business leaders of Europe, like those in Britain, come to realize that the EU is becoming Europe's own worst enemy.

At the Gates

Turkey not only knows what's best for itself but what's good for Europe as well. The case for Turkish accession to the EU is familiar and convincing – but should be made more forcefully. Turkish EU membership is not a burden but a blessing. Located at the confluence of cultures, Turkey is undergoing a neo-Ottoman revival, which, as with earlier ones, draws on the West for inspiration and design. This time, however, the Turks are not seeking guidance in order to field a modern armed force or build up a state bureaucracy but to establish a government under law and make democracy work; it is a slow and arduous task but one to which the government is deeply committed. The Turks harbor no superpower illusions. Reconciliation rather than domination guides foreign policy, the purpose of which is to preserve peace in the region without recourse to arms. Their goal is also that of the EU. Prominent in a geopolitically critical region comprised of often hostile and often warring nations and peoples now also undergoing a difficult transition from foreign domination and authoritarian government to self-determination and democracy, Turkey can be a welcome force multiplier of EU policy. It can also ensure that Europe plays a large role in a grand drama now unfolding: the rediscovery of historical identity by ancient peoples long oppressed by foreign and authoritarian rule.

The first point in the case for Turkish EU accession is negative in character: that the EU dare not renege on a commitment originally made decades ago, back in 1964, to admit Turkey if it could eventually meet the membership criteria – lest such a betrayal of trust produce a blowup in the Middle East. The other points are positive: (1) Turkey will provide big and growing markets, new resources, and large pools of inexpensive skilled labor. (2) Membership will stabilize the politics of a powerful neighbor and strengthen European security, not least of all by providing bridges to the Islamic world, the Caucuses, and Russia. (3) Turkey can provide a model of reform worthy of imitation.

To these three points can be added an emotionally more satisfying one: a Europe that includes Turkey will be culturally richer, more interesting, safer, and better connected to its past than it has been in recent history. Heirs to the traditions of the Ottomans, Byzantines, and Romans, modern Anatolians occupy a corner of the globe, which, for most of recorded time, has transmitted civilization westward as well as received it from thence. Why, then, should one doubt that a future Turkey might again enrich European letters, enliven art, music, and manners, and shape styles and tastes? It is true, as the president of Turkey, Recep Tayyip Erdogan, has often said, "If the Western civilization leaves the Eastern civilization aside, then the Western civilization will weaken."[52] Once in the EU, Turkey can help restore a historical relationship beneficial to both East and West.

The Turks harbor few illusions about membership in the Euro-club. They know they are not wanted as members, but they know where they are headed and are determined to get there. Brussels should no longer – as they did at the most recent marathon of nail-biting negotiations over admission to the EU – treat the Turks like intruders. The talks began in Luxembourg on October 2, 2005, and concluded late the following day, after the allotted time had lapsed, with a last-minute agreement to start the official accession process. The sessions were awful even by the boorish and Byzantine standards of the EU. Turkey secured a deal only after overcoming bitter Austrian objections and "conceding" that Croatia – accused of foot-dragging in a manhunt for a general suspected of Bosnian war crimes – could be put back on track to eventual membership. The Turkish delegates were in fact quizzical bystanders to the charade that resulted in the necessary "breakthrough." It occurred when the chief judge in the human rights tribunal at the International Court of Justice in The Hague, Carla del Ponte, retracting criticism made a week earlier, unexpectedly announced that indeed wonderful cooperation with Zagreb had for some time been taking place. With the Croats reinstated to the accession track and having pandered to the prejudices of their electorate while at the same time scoring big points with a historic ally, the Austrians grudgingly agreed to open the gates to Turkey. The journalist Yueksel Soelemez justly complained that "none of the 25 members had ever faced such a psychological ordeal and war of nerves as Turkey did in order to start membership negotiations [and] no single member had ever faced such hard terms and harsh conditions ... as Turkey had to accept under the [thirty-five separate parts] of the framework agreement."[53]

The Turks expect to be held to the strictest of admission standards, know they will receive no unofficial or special assistance, and are prepared to bear very high costs in order to comply with the *acquis*. They recognize that Turkey's CAP entitlements, even if granted on the same invidious terms received by the ten eastern European nations, would exceed their payments by $2 billion. In an interview with the *Turkish Daily News*, EU specialist Can Baydarol made no bones about the rigorousness of the accession process. It would, he said, take ten to fifteen years, involve not negotiations but declarations about "how we will adapt to the EU," and would also entail substantial expenses and adjustments – $22–72 million for environmental compliance. Every manufacturer, he added, would "have his corns trod upon" until in compliance with workplace safety requirements. Businessmen would also have to bear most of the costs of modernizing agriculture (even with anticipated CAP subsidies of $11 billion), updating food handling and processing methods; and upgrading vocational and education requirements. Well aware that such changes can generate nationalist backlash, Baydarol noted that while "all of these things have been done for the EU, they have also been done to make Turkey a contemporary country.... People should honestly be told what is done for what [purpose]. EU projects are not enough; Turkey should develop its own projects."[54] Turkey, he is sensibly saying, should put up with the EU so long is it promotes its own national interests.

Plenty of accession roadblocks remain to be knocked down in a country that denies the Armenian genocide, has threatened to prosecute its most famous novelist for exercising the right of free speech, has refused until recently to admit politically the political existence of its large Kurdish minority, and condones an unacceptable degree of both corruption and human torture. (The Turks cannot, in good conscience, be blamed for the Cyprus problem, which was not of their making.) While such long-standing issues cannot be solved in a day – and it is to be hoped that they will be aggressively attacked over a matter of years – the direction of policy is what counts. If progress in these matters is not made, Baydarol warns, Turkey will remain outside the gates.[55]

For Turkey, EU accession caps a very long and honorable reform tradition. Modernization – and Europeanization, more specifically – has been the main theme in the history of Anatolia since Mustapha Kemal (Atatürk) founded the modern Turkish Republic in 1923, and it has antecedents in the ambitious attempts at westernization, which began in the eighteenth century. Three great waves of change – under Mahmud II (1808–1839), in the so-called Tanzimat period (1839–1876), and under the guidance of Midhat Pasha and the Young Ottomans at the end of the century – transformed the Empire; over the nineteenth century. Minimal government at the level of the millet, or religious community, gave way to the centralized administration of a state with a constitution, embryonic representative government, the rudiments of a modern system of secular education, and at least the beginnings of modern transportation and communications systems. Such vast, though incomplete, change kept the long-ailing Sick Man of Europe alive; entanglement in the affairs of Europe is what eventually caused his demise.

Adaptation to modern industrial society is difficult everywhere, but over the span of nearly three decades of existence, the Kemalist state has a history that compares favorably to that of Russia, Japan, China, and Iran: Turkey has been at peace in the region, avoided the worst evils of authoritarian government, and never been the scene of famine. Modern Turkey is one of recent history's most underrated success stories and least appreciated good neighbors. Turkey became an associate member of the European Economic Community (EEC) in 1964 and in 1995 entered a customs union with the EU, as the EEC had recently been renamed. The agreement restricted labor mobility, excluded agricultural goods, and did not give Turkey the benefit of the EU's preferential trading relationships with third parties. As a result of the customs union, European manufactured goods – rather than new foreign direct investment – flooded into Turkey, which applied for full membership chiefly with a view to increasing inward financial flows. In 1999 at the Helsinki summit, Turkey finally became an official candidate. Three years later at the Copenhagen European Council, it committed itself to "applying the same standards as those of the Union." These included guaranteeing the rule of law, democracy, and respect for the rights of minorities, creating the conditions for a competitive market economy, and assuming the obligations of membership, including adherence to the aims of political, economic, and monetary union.[56]

The Turkish government has done everything short of ordering the decircumcision of the cabinet in the effort to meet these exacting criteria. The reforms serve the dual purpose of qualifying Turkey for EU admission and modernizing it politically and economically – opening markets and building democratic institutions. Whether allowed into the EU or not, Turkey comes out the winner as a result of this process of transformation: it has indeed become a more prosperous, just, tolerant, confident, happier, and civilized place. President Recep Tayyip Erdogan is uniquely responsible for this enormous accomplishment. He may well rank, alongside Atatürk, the greatest figure of the 1920s – admittedly another era of political pygmies and cretins – as the only great world statesman of his decade.[57]

Recep Tayyip Erdogan owes his national political career to the respect he earned as the "mayor of the poor" inhabiting the shantytowns on the outskirts of Istanbul, which, in addition to providing with streets, mosques, and running water, he turned into places of law, decency, and honor. He is of modest origins, popular, democratic, and honest. Erdogan became prime minister in 2001 as head of the new Justice and Development Party (AKP), an Islamist faction once banned by the strongly pro-secular military government. In office he faithfully respected the fundamental distinction, copied from French constitutionalism, between religion (as a matter of personal belief) and the state (as a neutral framework of law).[58]

Erdogan inherited an unenviable situation. The industrial and financial economy of contemporary Turkey is still largely the legacy of a protectionist inward-oriented development strategy of import substitution first adopted in 1934, which required high levels of subsidization and foreign borrowing and produced recurrent financial crises and governments bailouts of the banking sector. Shifting to indicative planning in 1960 merely aggravated the problem. Economic distortions – catastrophic inflation and unemployment rates of up to 30 percent – led in the 1970s and 1980s to chronic political instability and (twice) to military governments. In the wake of the first Gulf War and the collapse of the Soviet Union, the Turkish economy slipped to negative growth in 1994, the lira was devalued by half, and inflation shot up to 130 percent. Two devastating earthquakes precipitated a deep recession in 1999. Only an emergency intervention of the International Monetary Fund (IMF) staved off financial collapse. When Erdogan took office in 2001 Turkish GDP was shrinking by 7.5 percent, and the IMF again intervened with a loan package of $17 billion. A corner had been turned, however, and Turkey would never look back.[59]

Over the next two and a half years, Recep Tayyip Erdogan launched the most thorough wave of reform since Atatürk founded the modern Anatolian nation. Erdogan ousted a generation of corrupt, incompetent, and deeply entrenched politicians who by the mid-1990s had brought Turkey to the brink of civil war. He proceeded to adopt fundamental laws for consolidating the market economy, stabilizing democratic institutions, enforcing the rule of law as well as the respect of human rights, and protecting minorities. His government has also ended both the death penalty and press censorship, eliminated the military's authority to override parliament, abolished the notorious state security courts, and provided cultural freedom for Kurds. Erdogan has forced inflation down to the low double digits, raised tax revenues by 50 percent, and kept the economy growing at a healthy clip of 7 percent.[60]

Turkey remains very poor, with 30 percent of overall EU per capita GDP and about half the average of the eastern European accession nations. These numbers may not fully account, however, for the underground economy, estimates of whose size range wildly from 32 percent to 65 percent of GDP. Agriculture is a special problem: oversized in terms of employment (approximately 35 percent), distorted by a patchwork system of price supports, import controls, and export subsidies; able to produce at only less than export quality even in specialty lines; and suffering from undercapitalization.[61] As one expert put it, "We face feudal agriculture in the Southeast. In the west lands are divided into small plots. ... Minefields must be cleared and turned into agricultural fields, [that can be farmed] productively and properly. Because of the misuse of fertilizer, agricultural products are toxic and hormonal." Under pressure from the WTO and the EU, the support system is gradually being brought in line with the CAP. "Political will during the EU [accession] process," according to Professor Mehmet Altan, "shall ultimately decide whether society will be rescued from the peasant mentality or not." What he had in mind, the professor added, was not a "Jacobin transformation, but a transformation based on rationalism" that would depoliticize a coddled farm population treated like "state officials" and make agriculture an "economic domain."[62]

Though institutionally still quite weak, Turkey is stronger in this respect than either Bulgaria or Romania. It has also long enjoyed a limited free trade with the EU in industrial goods, has adequate laws for the protection of competition and intellectual property, and has not had to privatize whole sectors of industry. President Erdogan has already made good progress in disposing of state-owned industrial and financial assets and, in the process, strengthened a new Turkish ownership class as well as reduced the subsidy burden. A recent study by two Dutch economists concludes that while accession will raise Turkish GDP by .8 percent over the long term, substantially greater gains of 5.6 percent will result from improvements in Turkey's national institutions – from the accession process itself. Describing Turkey's current economic position as the "strongest in a generation," the IMF approved a new standby loan of $10 billion to Ankara because, in the words of the IMF's managing director, "Turkey deserves the support of the international community on the strength of its impressive track record."[63]

The EU's decision of October 3, 2005 to open membership negotiations has had a tonic affect on the Turkish economy – and even more profound implications in the political field. Company startups are occurring at the highest recorded rate, the stock market is booming, foreign interest has increased sharply, and Turkey's already improving trade with its neighbors is on an upswing. With growth rates estimated to average 6.5 percent over the next decade and the population expected to reach 85 to 90 million, Turkey will eventually be a formidable market. Even more important than the economics of the issue, the prospect of Turkish accession has changed the political configuration of Europe.[64]

Timothy Garton Ash exaggerated only slightly by asserting in an October 2005 *Guardian* op-ed piece that eventual EU membership for Turkey will banish the specter of a European superstate in favor of a future European commonwealth, yet his fundamental point was well taken. Although the threat of a superstate had become a historical artifact prior to the decision to proceed with Turkish admission, and a future commonwealth may never materialize, enlargement can be counted on to continue unless the EU collapses. The elimination of political federation as a realistic integration goal has defused much of the fear surrounding both Turkish membership and future expansion of the EU – pressure for which will not abate. Its powerful long-term drivers include Europe's need for economic growth in the face of competition from China, India, and elsewhere; the strategic desirability of moving Europe's ramparts to the east and south; and the growing influence within the EU of a strengthening bloc of new member states committed to both liberalization and defensive extension.[65]

The final driver of enlargement is the powerful urge of Turkey's neighbors to link up to the EU – to join in a common community of democratic values. This is a stirring process, fueled by exercise of freedom if also frustrated by legacies of oppression and inexperience. It has received little official encouragement from the EU. Yet like a surefooted sleepwalker, the EU is restoring territorially the Ottoman Empire in Europe. Romania and Bulgaria are on track for entrance in

2007. The decision to allow negotiations to proceed with the Turks also kick-started the accession process in the "western Balkans" – Albania, Bosnia, Croatia, Macedonia, and Serbia-Montenegro – which, once concluded, would mean that by 2020 the EU would contain 600 million people in thirty-three countries. "There is," proclaimed enlargement commissioner Olli Rehn, "a new dawn for the western Balkans and it is a European dawn." These decisions erase any ambiguity about the EU's commitment to the long-term membership of the region. To the pending new Balkan members should be added, as potential future candidates, the ancient Christian trans-Caucasian nations of Armenia and Georgia, oil-rich Azerbaijan, and, finally, Moldova and Ukraine – at least another five nations with 90 million inhabitants. The Turkish example can serve as a developmental model for these potential new members.[66]

Turkey can play a valuable role in the process of EU renewal. Painfully aware that the larger the union, the less likely they are to be bullied in it, the Turkish welcomed the verdict of the two constitutional referenda and also wholeheartedly endorsed the Copenhagen Criteria – which set out the ground rules for accession. The Turks are also prepared to help straighten out – peacefully – their own tough neighborhood. A historian of the Ottoman Empire, Ahmet Davutoglu, is President Erdogan's main advisor on foreign policy. Davutoglu's central concern is the study of how, over centuries, the Empire accommodated a wide range of conflicting minorities and subcultures and, as a result, provided long periods of peace for what was at the time the most cosmopolitan society on earth. Force does not enter into Davutoglu's explanation as often as tolerance of diversity.[67]

He advocates a "zero-problem strategy." Turning on the principle "Peace at home, peace in the world," it is keyed into the prevention of the many potential conflicts threatening Turkey in the region. The strategy includes, inter alia, forgiving Syria's Assad as a would-be reformer under pressure from his security forces; opposing Turkish involvement in the Iraq War; and courting Russia's Mr. Putin assiduously. Cooperation between such historic rivals should be welcomed so long as it respects the existence of the less powerful. Indeed it is potentially very constructive. On November 17 the Blue Stream gas pipeline, which had been in partial operation for two years, was formally opened.

Connecting Russia to Ankara, it is planned to be the first in a future network that will include another gas line for exports from Turkey as well as one to Ceyhan, on the Mediterranean. The new southern system, along with the planned Baltic trunk feeder from Vyborg to Greifswald, will strengthen Russia's hand in dealing with its central European neighbors.[68]

Now underway is a major joint Turko-Russian initiative to settle Armenia's historic conflict with Turkey (and end the Turkish embargo in exchange for recognition of the genocide) as well as with Azerbaijan (over Nagarno-Karabakh). The two major powers – the Russians historically supportive of Armenia and the Turks sentimentally allied to the Turkic-speaking Azeris – would act as guarantors of the broad settlement. Turkey also shares an interest with Russia in stabilizing central Asia where three separate Turkic-speaking tribes (Uzbeks, Kirghiz, and Tajiks) are "peoples of state" in territories carved out by the Bolsheviks on the "divide and conquer" principle; none of them are contiguous with ethnicity, and all include substantial minorities, while excluding large numbers of the dominant group. The region bristles with potential problems.[69]

Turkey's foreign policy also includes continued membership in the North Atlantic Treaty Organization (NATO) and cooperation in energy policy with Anglo-American, and other, oil multinationals – as well as amicable relations with Iran. Davutoglu, notes the columnist Christopher Caldwell, "is pitching his vision in the language of multiculturalism and globalization" and, it should be added, so casting its policy.[70] The Turks play a leading role in the Black Sea Forum (Organization of the Black Sea Economic Cooperation) and cofounded with Spain an organization called "Alliance of Civilizations," which promotes cultural pluralism through the United Nations.[71]

In a combative and contentious region, Turkey is a strong, conservative, and tolerant influence – a bridge builder between blocs and interests with a special role to play in the difficult process of nation building in a region without strong democratic traditions. The EU should solicit its help in young nations, such as Georgia, intent both on EU membership and democratization but, which, in the words of Mark Leonard and Charles Grant, have been made to feel "like a poor and unwelcome relative."[72] This is unwise. Turkish support will be needed (along with Russian) to thaw out the intractable "frozen problems" of Nagorno-Karabakh, Abkhazia, and Ossetia, help stabilize and constitutionalize the politically immature and artificial "Stans" of central Asia, and, in general, provide a voice of reason and commonsense in parts of the world the EU would like to influence but on its own cannot – and the United States probably can but should not. If the EU seriously desires a common security and foreign policy, Turkish accession will provide plenty of opportunities to play what might be called a new version, under improved rules, of the Great Game.

The Meaning of the Maidan

Europeans would like to forget about Ukraine except, perhaps, as a place to make money, a buffer to a powerful Russia, or an exotic vacation spot for the intrepid traveler. Since the Orange Revolution, they can no longer do so. Ukraine is the setting of a fantastic event at a precious moment in history: a struggle for the exercise of freedom. Kyiv's Independence Square, the "Maidan," said the political commentator Tatiana Korobova, "is about a people, who have discovered Man in themselves," by standing together for weeks of cold winter nights by the hundreds of thousands to say, with a single loud voice, "Stop you thugs. Here I stand. Look at me. I will not leave without justice."[73]

The story of this awakening nation with its simple message should not be sentimentalized. Freedom involves the exercise of choice – a luxury, which, until recently, Ukrainians have only longed for and do not yet always know how to make: it is something that must be learned. There are few helpful guideposts in Ukraine's tragic past. And since the Orange Revolution, all has not been well. Ukrainians must look beyond their borders for recognition, help, guidance, and support in becoming free for the first time in their modern history. They have earned the right to such assistance. The example of the Maidan should jar the complacency of those who take for granted what the people of Ukraine are prepared to die for and force them into reconsidering the meaning and relevance of Europe's most cherished political values. Europeans should ask themselves in particular how the EU, now drifting off into irrelevance, can be reinvented to serve the cause of freedom. Europe will be strengthened and will renew itself in the process.

Ukraine is the ground zero of human suffering in twentieth-century Europe. Although numbers can suggest the magnitude of the problem, the grim bookkeeping of mortality cannot capture the aggregated horror, misery, and wretchedness, which sets Ukraine's history apart from any other European nation's. Ukraine has not only been divided, oppressed, disrupted, and systematically stripped of identity, but it has provided consecutive settings of modern Europe's most gristly mass murders. Raw numbers, which for Ukraine are in any case only approximate, cannot account for what W. G. Sebald called the lingering death of the living: destruction of culture, obliteration of historical memory, violation of personal sanctity, and pulverization of personality.

Here is a sketch of this unhappy history from World War I to the collapse of the USSR. In 1914 Galicia was a largely Ukrainian-speaking hinterland of the Hapsburg Empire and cut off from three-quarters of the territory where Ukrainian was spoken, which was ruled like Russian provinces by the Tsar. Galicia – a place far removed from Allied headquarters in Fontainebleau – soon became the main theatre of combat on the eastern front. Russia captured Galicia shortly after the outbreak of war and then launched a campaign of deportation, mass arrests, book burnings, and religious persecution against the Ukrainian population. The retreating Austrians shot thousands of innocent Ukrainians as traitors. Galicia changed hands three times during the war in onslaughts involving hundreds of thousands on each side of the front, behind which, in the rear areas, as many civilians perished from disease as did soldiers.

All of Ukraine, including the former Austrian part, got dragged into the Russian Revolution and Civil War. Reds and Whites fought each other, but one or the other of them also fought Ukrainian nationalists, peasant anarchists, Soviet Ukrainians, and Polish nationalists. Between March 1917, when it began, and June 1920, when it officially ended, Ukraine experienced twelve changes of regime. For another eighteen months, Ukraine – the former breadbasket of Europe – suffered an induced famine, which caused another million deaths, and was wracked by warfare between bands of desperate elderly peasants fighting with scythes and pitchforks against Red Army men armed with machine guns. Three to four million lives were lost from 1914 to 1920 in the present area of Ukraine, three-quarters of them in the atrocity-filled years of the Civil War.

Things had started to improve by 1922. To replace the largely liqui-dated Russian-speaking urban middle class, the badly weakened Bol-sheviks had no choice but to resettle tens of thousands of literate Ukrainian-speaking peasants in the major cities to provide the clerical skills needed to run the proliferating state bureaucracy. For the first time, Ukrainian became an urban language. (Even today most of the nation's political leaders continue to speak Russian except when in public.) At the end of the 1920s Moscow broke with "ukrainization" and wiped out the new intelligentsia. In 1931 began the Great Famine, the Holodomor (Голодомор) – the worst of Ukraine's catastrophes. It killed another 7 to 9 million, more than a quarter of the population. The infamous Purge Trials came next. They began later in Ukraine than elsewhere in the USSR but exacted a higher price: several hundred thousand addi-tional lives.

In World War II, Ukraine was again partitioned, with the Germans incorporating Galicia (along with central Poland) into the so-called General Government, a political unit deemed unworthy even of a name of its own, while the Soviets took Volhynia and promptly sovietized it. The German occupation of Soviet Ukraine, which began in sum-mer 1941 and lasted until the Nazis were finally cleared out in October 1944, cost 5 to 7 million additional Ukrainian lives, including those of a 400,000-member Jewish community that was virtually wiped out. As in 1921 and 1922, famine again followed war. It began in 1946 and lasted for a year. Finally, 500,000 Ukrainians were sent to the Gulag, and the Ukrainian Greek Catholic church was officially dissolved in order to erase from memory a postwar resistance movement, which sought inde-pendence for Ukraine. Material losses from World War II comprised 40 percent of Ukraine's wealth and included 80 percent of industrial plant as well as three-quarters of the stock of farm machinery. Human losses due to war, famine, and the Gulag from 1939 to 1959 totaled 8.8 million. The byword for nuclear meltdown, CHERNOBYL, which still rings with apocalyptic dread in western Europe, is, for Ukrainians

Chornobyl (Чорнобиль), the scene of only one among several serious industrial accidents that took place in the dying years of the USSR.

Ukraine had no modern history as an unoccupied and peaceful independent nation until 1991 and no fully independent cultural history either. The temporary weakness of the young USSR in the 1920s would prove to be the exception to a general Soviet policy of Russification inherited from the Tsars, who forbade the use of Ukrainian as a language of political or cultural expression. The Soviets added new twists to language policy, however: they directed the infiltration of Russian words and expressions into Ukrainian and russified its grammatical structures in order to corrupt it. They also gave preferment to official speakers of Russian, many of whom rose to positions of power within the Soviet system – thereby again following a long-standing policy that attenuated the sense of a separate Ukrainian nationhood.

Viewing Ukrainians as a subspecies of the great Slav family, Russians have trouble imagining that such people could desire to be politically and culturally separate. To them it only seems natural for the little brother to copy the big one. They regard their leverage over Ukraine – by dint of size, political power, and, today, gas and oil – as belonging to the natural order of things. Ukrainians are not altogether unambiguous about nationality. Many look to the West, while others feel pride in belonging to a larger eastern Slavic culture. In politics and economics, as well as culture, the border between the two kindred peoples is highly permeable. The favorite, indeed unending, historical and philological debate between them concerns whether their putative common historical ancestor, the Kievan Rus, is, in fact, Russian or Ukrainian.

Yet there can no longer be any doubt about the underlying strength of the Ukrainian desire for independence: It has made its voice heard in national literature whose unifying theme is the struggle for freedom but whose strength has only been felt at rare moments when oppressors weaken. Such episodes have always been brief and never successful. Only once has the cry of literature become the cry of the people – and been heard. That precious opportunity gives meaning to the Maidan. "Last autumn," wrote Timothy Garton Ash and Timothy Snyder in April 2005, "Ukraine imprinted itself on the political consciousness of the world for the first time in its history."[74] Thanks to the 1.2 million

Ukrainians ready to put their lives on the line in Kyiv for democracy and the one in five Ukrainians throughout the country who demonstrated in support of them, what in 1991 had been only "a name, a capital, and a place on the map" had become a new nation, conceived in liberty and determined to survive as an independent state.

The demonstrators had come to Kyiv from all quarters of Ukraine to protest a coordinated and cynical attempt by the corrupt and criminal regime of President Leonid Kuchma to rig the run-off election held on November 21, 2004, for the presidency between Viktor Yanukovych, his designated successor, and Viktor Yushchenko. The dirty tricks hardly came as a surprise; in September, Yushchenko had been poisoned with dioxin in an attempt to remove him from the political scene. His horribly disfigured face was, as he memorably put it, "The face of Ukraine today." Yanukovych was declared winner within moments after the polls had closed. Putin congratulated him within the hour.

For a month the protesters slept in tents, ate from canteens, and tried not to freeze in subzero temperatures, the entire time facing the threat of violent repression from security forces poised to strike. There was no violence, threat of violence, or even rude or disorderly behavior on the part of the million or so men and women at the Maidan but only the display of an intense determination to hold out until Yushchenko, the man Ukrainians had voted into office, was, after a second run-off on December 26, finally allowed to take it. The security forces backed off, and the joyous protesters went home. Not a gum wrapper or cigarette butt was left behind.

Here were indeed, as Ash and Snyder put it, "ordinary people doing an extraordinary thing."[75] By being willing to die for the principles the West prided itself on upholding, the peaceful protestors of the Orange Revolution not only put Ukraine on the map but placed a moral obligation on the United States and western Europe to strengthen and defend their own deepest political values. The brave and dignified men and women of the Maidan had cast a line that could draw Ukraine – a land without a real modern history of its own and never possessing freedom but only a longing for it – from its dark and tragic past into a realm of light. That hope gives lasting meaning to the Maidan.

What at first burned with such intensity is, after a year, sadly fading into a distant glow. The tide of events beyond Ukraine's borders is also shifting in the wrong direction. The US commitment to promoting democracy as the overriding goal of foreign policy was less and less often proclaimed, as one failure in self-government followed another. The Tulip Revolution (in Kyrgyzstan) has, for instance, already withered, and the bulb must be wintered. The Bush administration's vaunted enthusiasm for democracy always took second place, in any case, to its commitment to NATO, which remains the cornerstone of US foreign policy. Membership in NATO can and should nevertheless at all costs be pursued by the Ukrainian government for reasons of domestic as well as foreign policy and, if at all possible, in tandem with the EU. The functions of the two organizations are complementary.

At this point a problem of wobbliness arises. Ukraine must help rescue the EU from its current crisis of legitimacy by demonstrating the historical utility and worthiness of the integration process. Ukraine cannot afford to let the memory of the Maidan disappear but must imprint it on historical memory by becoming an exemplary modern democracy. Thereby it can not only strengthen its own case for EU admission but reinforce the EU's commitment to political principle. Ukraine should not be merely on the receiving end of decision making but must become active as an agent of change regionally and within an expanding Europe. Kyiv must take a strong, proactive, and supportive policy toward Brussels because without the now fraying line to the West, the window of opportunity will be replaced by blackout curtains. The light will again disappear.

The Eye of the Needle

Ukraine suffers from most, though not all, of the problems faced by post-Soviet states – and some special ones as well. With a population of more than 47 million, more land than Texas, and a location at the intersection of nations and cultures, it is, first of all, too big, geopolitically critical, and militarily important to slip in under the radar like a minicountry (Greece) or a micronation (Luxembourg), for which, when necessary, exceptions can always be made, or like Ireland, which can be turned around quickly with infusions of outside money. Ukraine is also miserably poor, with a per capita income of about $5,500 per year, less than that of Turkey, half of Russia's, and a fifth of France's. About half of Ukraine's economic life takes place on the black market. Ukraine, finally, lacks both adequate legal institutions and experience in the conduct of parliamentary democracy.[76]

It is also, like every nation, divided into various regions, but its strain of regionalism is relatively benign: less virulent than the tribalism afflicting both the Caucasus and central Asia and far milder than the language division that splits Belgium and Canada into two uneasily cohabiting political communities. Nearly all Ukrainians speak Russian, which in urban areas is used interchangeably and often intermixed with Ukrainian; in the east, however, particularly in the coal-steel regions of Donbas, the majority speaks Russian but not Ukrainian. Yet from whatever region, the quarter of the overall population whose primary tongue is Russian identifies itself as, and supports, Ukrainian nationhood – a remarkable attestation, given the somewhat higher standard of living prevailing in Russia. Ukraine is distinguished, but not defined, by language. It is, rather, a nation united by suffering and hope.[77]

Ukraine is also incredibly corrupt, close to the bottom of every international survey. Like that of a fish, the rot starts at the head and moves down the body to the tail. It pervades both politics and economics – and makes one hostage to the other. The government gives away as much in tax breaks as it collects in revenue. Control of the state has given rise to a class of Ukrainian oligarchs no less relatively powerful than their counterparts in Russia; as things now are, without the support or acquiescence of big money, no government can long function. The byproduct of a degenerate socialism, such oligarchs cannot long survive in a market economy – unless they can bend the rules of the game.

In this respect, proximity to Russia presents a very acute problem for Ukraine. Permeability also extends to the oligarchs: Russian interests are often too closely interlaced to be easily distinguishable from those of their larcenous Ukrainian counterparts. Every cent of increase in the price of oil or natural gas strengthens Russian economic power in and over Ukraine. The present high level of energy prices, if lasting, will pose the clear and present danger that the transparent, equitable, and predictable framework of law and regulation needed for the smooth operation of advanced market economies could facilitate a Russian oligarchic takeover of Ukraine, increase corruption, and subvert democratic institutions.

One defense against this undesirable sort of intervention – a strong international rule-making body like the WTO – has been undermined by the Doha Round; another one, the EU, is crumbling, To escape the clutches of Russo-Ukrainian oligarchs, Ukraine will need sound and strong economic and legal institutions in order to remove obstacles to foreign investment, vast amounts of which will be needed. Local oligarchs can then either be bought out or forced to compete in the marketplace. But the best defense being a good offense, the long-term security and well-being of the nation must rest on the hope that the same infusion of foreign capital and expertise needed to weaken the economic and political hold of the oligarchs will also spur growth, provide incentives to good government, create a new class of Ukrainian managers and entrepreneurs, and, in the end, turn a reformed Ukraine into a model worth emulating – even by a big brother. Contamination from the West, via Ukraine, is surely one of Putin's greatest fears. Ukraine must do everything diplomatically possible to assuage it.[78]

When examined closely, Ukraine's window of opportunity looks more like the eye of a needle. The nation's politicians have not threaded it very deftly over the past year. For Ukrainians the letdown has been steady. Public disillusionment (*rozcharuvannia*) set in soon when, instead of getting better, economic conditions in 2005 deteriorated and promised political and administrative reform kept being deferred. Shakedowns by mobsters, racketeers, and uniformed thugs – the threats, beatings, and worse of the Kuchma years – continued to make life miserable for businessmen, both large and small. After a year, only 40 percent of Ukrainians, according to the polls, thought that the Orange Revolution had improved their lives.

Yet neither the increasingly disaffected public nor anyone else was prepared for the September Massacre, when – arguably after provocation – President Viktor Yushchenko not only unceremoniously sacked his popular prime minister, Yulia Tymoshenko, but two weeks later alarmingly signed a compact to "let bye-gones be bye-gones" with his sworn foe and former presidential rival, the brutish Viktor Yanukovych. In return for granting what amounted to a blanket amnesty to anyone, at every level of government, who committed electoral violations in the balloting for the presidency in 2004, Yushchenko received an implicit promise to support Yanukovych in defeating Tymoshenko in the March

2006 elections. It looked like a betrayal. The famous clips of a wintry Maidan draped in orange, of the smiling, courageous, pockmarked, and scarred president-elect waving joyously at the podium together with the elegant, braided lady prime minister–to–be would never again look quite the same. What once appeared spontaneous now looks staged, as indeed it was. The happy couple did not, in fact, get along. Infighting would become endemic in the government.[79]

Victor Yushchenko is a figure Ukrainians would like to admire as the George Washington of his country, but he does not yet fit the role. As one journalist put it, "The Cap of Monomakh [worn by the ruler in Kievan Rus] is too big for him."[80] Yushchenko is more technocrat than politician. He favors institutional continuity and plays a weak hand in the politics of the parliament (*Verkhovna Rada*).[81] His speeches tend to be stiff, overly lengthy, and crammed with excessive detail. He altogether lacks the common touch. Personally honest, he neither keeps the best company nor is enamored of the media, especially when it investigates friends and family. He can appear thin-skinned, vain, and spiteful. His rudeness to Yulia Tymoshenko on the anniversary of the Orange Revolution was deeply resented by the tens of thousands who had gathered at the Maidan and mocked its meaning. There is, however, no one who at present can take his place. Yushchenko is committed to a clear and sensible policy, which, given existing constraints, provides the only way forward. The September Massacre can be called a double-cross and even an act of betrayal, but without it darkness would have come over Ukraine. As it is, a distant glow remains visible.

Yushchenko's harsh chop may have been the result of a personal vendetta, may be due to the clash of oversized egos, or even may be in part the consequence of a mad rush for the spoils of office. In the ruthless world of Ukrainian politics, however such behavior is neither unprecedented nor uncharacteristic. The Orange Revolution rests on several such unsavory deals – with the security service, the old-guard politicians, and even various robber barons. The economics and politics of post-Soviet Ukraine feature continuity with the wretched Stalinist system, oligarchic abuse of power, and irresponsible behavior of demagogic politics, all of which have taken place against a background of venal and inept administration, ill-designed institutions, lawlessness, threatened as well as actual violence, and what came to be called "government by blackmail." The brutal sacking of Tymoshenko fits all too comfortably into this picture.

An uneven and fragile progress nonetheless results from this process. The very independence of Ukraine rests on a hard bargain. Without the cooperation of Ukrainian communists, the breakaway from the USSR in 1991 would probably have been impossible. The price was that the old *nomenklatura* survived in the administration and continued to occupy key management posts in the economy, especially in the heavily industrialized east. During Ukraine's formative period, the presidency of Leonid Kravchuk (December 1991–July 1994), state property shifted into private hands, but economic reform did not take place. Instead the rigid command economy inherited from the Soviets broke down, and inflation raged as the government printed excessive amounts of increasingly worthless money in a desperate attempt to keep factories operating. Kravchuk at least maintained independence and respected the outward forms of parliamentary government. Ukraine survived. It could have been worse.[82]

Kravchuk's successor, Leonid Kuchma (July 1994–December 2004), began the shift to the market economy, albeit in the face of heavy resistance from a parliament still dominated by communists and uninhibited by a sense of responsibility. The result was another dirty deal. The centerpiece of Kuchma's reforms was the creation of so-called "financial-industrial groups" (FIGs) patterned on a Russian model that, according to Robert Kravchuk, "recreated in the private sector the same kind of patronage-based economic system that Mikhail Gorbachev expended so much effort to bring down.... Cross national FIGs also re-assembled pieces of the former supply system of the Soviet economy ... the basic question remains whether FIGs are a vehicle of 'crony capitalism' or a Trojan Horse for Russian penetration of Ukrainian industry."[83] Kuchma became godfather to the Russo-Ukrainian oligarchy at the same time as he inched the nation uneasily toward the West.[84]

Although professing loyalty to the idea of the "social market economy," Kuchma never made it work and could not prevent the shrinkage of the GNP or control inflation until Viktor Yushchenko appeared on the scene. President of the national bank and backed by the IMF, Yushchenko engineered the highly successful currency reform in 1996, which replaced the worthless kupon with the strong hryvnia. The economy turned around. As prime minister in 1999, moreover, he drafted a real reform program, "Thousand Days," as well as cobbled together a majority coalition of ten separate factions needed to move it through the parliament. His cabinet included Yulia Tymoshenko as deputy prime minister for the fuel and energy sector as well as her successor as prime minister after the September 2005 Massacre, Yuriy Yekhanurov, as first deputy prime minister responsible for privatization, administrative reform, and deregulation.[85]

The Thousand Days program of 1999 would be a harbinger of Yushchenko's present policy. It called for reducing the size of government, deregulation, and the elimination of subsidies as well as special tax privileges. It further emphasized administrative reform as well as the struggle against corruption and promised to curtail noxious administrative interference with the economy. The reform plan was, in other words, an expression of pure economic liberalism. In March 2000 Yushchenko presented some eighty drafts of laws to parliament, which included long-awaited ones for the tax, housing, and criminal codes, but before they could be fully adopted, an unsavory combination of scandal and dirty politics brought down his administration.[86]

Tymoshenko was the focus of one scandal. Dubbed the Gas Princess, and an oligarch in her own right (whose former business partner languishes in a US jail), she was widely suspected of taking kickbacks on energy deals. Sacked in January 2001, Tymoshenko was subsequently jailed briefly for embezzlement. Whatever the merits of the case, which has since been dismissed by the Supreme Court, her real "sin" was to have introduced an element of competition into gas pricing, which cut into the gouging of powerful oligarchs. Tymoshenko is a brilliant woman of many gifts as well as a Sarah Bernhardt of her time. Her political slickness and unpredictability scare the pants off investors. How she would behave in office can only be conjectured. She may well be, however, the only political Ukrainian public figure capable of reconciling reform losers to the institutional and economic changes needed for democracy.[87]

The other scandal was less trivial. It was Kuchma's suspected implication in the murder and beheading of the journalist Heorhiy Gongadze. Unable or unwilling in April 2001 to defend Yushchenko ("government by blackmail") against a truly unholy alliance of oligarchs and communists, Kuchma allowed his prime minister to suffer a humiliating defeat at the hands of the *Rada*, and Yushchenko resigned. This happened, astonishingly, when after years of reverses, the economy was expanding at 7.7 percent and industrial growth had rebounded by no less than 17.4 percent.[88] Gongadze, whose popular Web page directed a drumfire of criticism against the government, made the fatal mistake of asking too many embarrassing questions at a Kuchma news conference. Audiotapes, made and leaked by a bodyguard, recorded Kuchma threatening to "do away" with the supposed troublemaker. The beheading was apparently a special touch added by the professional killers, who actually strangled Gongadze to death in the backseat of a car. How better than decapitation to warn those tempted to talk or think too much?[89]

The journalist's vicious murder set in motion the anti-Kuchma campaign that led to Yushchenko's eventual triumph. Yet Yushchenko has done little to track down or identify the men behind the plot, even though Ukrainian school children know their names. On March 4, 2005, Yuri Kravchenko, a former interior minister and one of the two men implicated in the murder, "committed suicide" by shooting himself, remarkably, twice in the back of the head. Yushchenko has not even made much effort to track down his own poisoners, though he of course remembers the company he was keeping when slipped the infamous toxic mickey. All of this smacks of other deals to let bygones be bygones – in this case, resting on détente between the government and the still very powerful and deeply sovietized security service.[90]

Some commentators regard the official Yushchenko-Tymoshenko partnership as a fraud meant from the outset to fail. This is unlikely. Not confrontational by nature, Yushchenko tried until June to maintain the appearance of outward unity with the Tymoshenko government. He supported, for example, an inflationary budget he knew to be unsound. It included substantial transfers to pensioners, salaried professionals, and soldiers but left untouched the two biggest economic problems facing Ukraine – an inefficient farm economy crippled by inadequate property laws and the archaic, subsidized, loss-making coal-steel complex in the east. It should be added that the heavy social payments in the budget derived from measures promised by Yanukovytch during the presidential election campaign, which Yushchenko had also pledged to honor.[91]

Tymoshenko's sometimes ill-considered, even reckless, economic interventions aggravated the uncomfortable situation. One was to press for the renationalization of 3,000 undesignated former state companies (Yushchenko at the time being committed to only thirty – a number after September reduced to one). It's hard not to be of two minds about this matter. A large but unspecified amount of these wealth transfers involved sweetheart deals – theft of public assets. At the same time, however, her shotgun approach sent a tremor of panic through the investment community, without whose confidence Ukraine cannot be modernized. Tymoshenko also eliminated the tax-free status of enterprise zones without any prior warning or discussion – hardly the kind of measure needed to impress long-term investors. The inward flow of capital unleashed by the Orange Revolution stopped dead in its tracks.[92]

Inexcusable on the part of the Gas Princess who made mega-millions by exploiting market imperfections, was a second of Tymoshenko's bombshells: the imposition of energy price caps at the retail level to punish alleged Russian profiteers. Setting aside the fact that the prices that Ukraine then paid were actually two-thirds below world market levels, such controls almost never work except in times of war. She acted simply to embarrass the president. Energy shortages broke out almost immediately. Yushchenko had to override the measure to preserve his crumbling authority.[93] It was indeed in serious doubt because an irresponsible parliament – including most members of his own party – refused to pass legislation required for Ukrainian admission to the WTO; it should have been a "gimme." As a result of such witless inaction, membership will have to be postponed until 2006. WTO admission was to have been the first step toward making Ukraine "EU-compatible." The next step in the process, securing "market-economy" status, would normally have been set back by at least six months.[94]

The general deterioration in the nation's economic situation is apparent even in numbers as unreliable as those for Ukraine. An astounding 12.5 percent in 2004, growth had dropped to 2.5 percent by July 2005 and was in free fall when Yushchenko finally acted in early September. Two-thirds of the sudden decline can be attributed to the drying up of foreign investment. Needing about six months to turn the economy around in time for the election, he had little choice but to move.

Precipitating his action was a slanging match over privatization and corruption, which soon spun out of control. It began with the resignation of state secretary Alexander Zinchenko, a sometime Tymoshenko ally, who, it appears, ordered the seizure of a large chemical company that had been purchased by a New York consortium in the final months of the Kuchma administration. Whether Zinchenko acted at the behest of private interests, under official authorization, or on his own is unknown. Forced to resign, he went public the same day with accusations of corruption among Yushchenko's advisors, in particular on part of the "candy king," oligarch Petro Poroshenko, chairman of the National Defense and Security Council, a shadow government that Yushchenko used to bypass the prime minister. Poroshenko and Tymoshenko thoroughly despise one another.[95]

Amidst claims from the Yushchenko faction that she was standing-in for the oligarch behind Pryvat Bank, Tymoshenko revived a campaign to renationalize the important Nikopol Steel plant, an ill-gotten property acquired and partly owned by the oligarch Viktor Pinchuk. A shadowy and shrewd player between the battle lines during the Orange Revolution – as well as son-in-law of Leonid Kuchma – Pinchuk could count in this matter on the support of a Yushchenko keen to end the still-official reprivatization policy after a single action, the sale of Kryvorizhstal, which Pinchuk (and a powerful ally) had bought at a fraction of its price during the Kuchma era.[96]

On September 8, Yushchenko fired Yulia Tymoshenko, her cabinet, and his ally Petro Poroshenko, who had been tainted with alleged impropriety. Tymoshenko did not go down without a fight. She appears to have been behind a leak disclosing that a Russian oligarch, Boris Berezovsky, had financed Yushchenko's presidential campaign, circulated a rumor that Yushchenko had considered putting out a contract on her, and all but accused Yushchenko in an interview of protecting Gongadze's killer.[97] On September 22, Yushchenko struck the deal with Yanukovych, justifying it as necessary to secure a parliamentary majority for Tymoshenko's successor, the technocrat, Yuriy Yekhanurov. As it turned out, Yekhanurov had enough votes to be confirmed in office even without the support of Yanukovych's Party of the Regions. After Yushchenko had gotten rid Tymoshenko, the Yulia Tymoshenko Bloc, still continued to vote in parliament with the president's Our Ukraine

Party. If in spite of the public mudslinging, he could gain at least a portion of her party's support, Yushchenko would have a strong incentive to get her out of politics altogether.[98]

Threading the Needle

The real purpose of Yushchenko's September Massacre was to get back to business as usual.[99] A choice between alternative reform "models" was not open to him. Nation building in post-Soviet states must begin by eliminating what remains of the corrupt and inefficient old system; it cannot change its stripes. Democracy and open societies have developed in eastern Europe only where the bureaucratic centralism of the former USSR has been reduced and replaced by the market as a mechanism of allocation. The two processes go hand in hand. Corruption cannot, however, be "rooted out"; it must be supplanted by a better – more equitable and efficient – system. There is a theoretical way to build it. The first item of business is to create legal institutions guaranteeing the rights of property and contract. The next one is to open banks that can attract money stashed "under the mattress" into savings accounts, thereby providing the raw material for credit. The third priority is to draw in foreign investment, especially, into the export economy. Economic growth in the accession states in fact correlates closely with the volumes of trade and credit.[100] Yet this gain does not come without pain: unemployment and personal hardship. In a democracy, especially a poor one, politicians associated with policies that eliminate jobs and destroy rents often find themselves out on the street. Thus elected officials "obfuscate" – conceal the truth from voters – a vice that can become a virtue only by dint of success. Ukraine needs strong political leadership as well as sound economic ideas. Can Yushchenko thread the needle?

Perhaps, if he can build on outside support, especially from the post-Soviet states of eastern Europe. The common problems and challenges they have faced provide the foundation stones of a new ideological alliance based on commitments to open markets and democracy. Ukraine would be welcomed into such a liberal association. Once the economy turns around, growth will spurt and the domestic market will expand rapidly, attracting foreign investment. As capital accumulates in eastern Europe, moreover, and incomes increase, the accession states will have strong incentives to put their money in a place "where educational standards are European and wages Chinese." Political motives are also powerful. One of them became evident during the Orange Revolution, when Poland, often an enemy, was an early, deeply committed, and eloquent supporter of Ukrainian freedom. Poland's supportive behavior comports with a general attitude within the EU that member states promote the accession of neighbors, even formerly hostile ones. Thus the Germans were the most outspoken advocates of Polish membership, the Greeks of Turkish, and so on. Such a tendency will give rise to an expanding EU and shift power within it.

This development has a profound implication: rivalries over land associated with the rise of nationalism are being superseded or supplanted by competition for expanding markets. Such a transformation provides a powerful rationale for the EU and at least partly legitimizes its existence. To close the circle and secure peace, the EU will also have to strengthen democracy both within and along the borders of Europe. One might then imagine a democratic and polycentric Europe: a fit accompaniment to a democratizing polycentric world. A new Ukraine could be an important contributing member in both spheres. It can serve as a model for a democratizing Russia and as a two-way transmission belt of culture and civilization.

But it won't be easy: to thread the needle, Viktor Yushchenko will have to stabilize government, expand the economy, put Ukraine on the accession path to the EU, secure the support of neighbors and maintain the confidence of others, strengthen the EU itself, and be both acceptable to Russia and a constructive influence on it.[101] Yushchenko faces two pressing challenges, according to a leading business consultancy, reviving investment and adopting a market-based energy policy. Both require reforms of the public sector as well as in law and administration. A number of specific measures should be adopted, like a "blue skies law," to increase transparency of government operations as well as provide for monitoring, cost-benefit analysis, accountability, and public reporting. Other laws are needed for joint-stock companies, simplification of the commercial code, and the establishment of a "guillotine process" for striking useless regulations. A privatization amnesty is necessary to protect property rights. Whenever possible, moreover, governmental functions should be transferred to local or private authorities.

The judiciary must be strengthened, finally, and business contracts made enforceable.[102]

The legislation needed to implement such basic reforms has, in many cases, been languishing for months in parliament or in ministry drawers. To pass it before the election, Yushchenko will need to herd cats – something he's never been good at. Privatization has, however, thus far been a big success. Kryvorizhstal was the first priority. Pinchuk and his partner, Rinat Akhmetov (actually the richest single Ukrainian oligarch), picked it up at the fire-sale price of $800 million in what was believed to be the most flagrant of Kuchma-era public property thefts. Since the deal had not yet been closed when Yushchenko took office, the government did not allow the transaction to be completed. Clearly, it was at the top of the reprivatization list.

In an open and contested auction, Mittal Steel, a huge Indian-owned company based in the Netherlands, picked up more than 90 percent of Kryvorizhstal at the unexpectedly high price of $4.8 billion. The sale – which Tymoshenko actually set in motion – was an unqualified success. It raised the value of all Ukrainian assets, increased government revenues by 20 percent, laid the reprivatization issue to rest, and even met with the approval of the former owners, who recuperated their original investment. Although Akhmetov continues to support Yanukovych's Party of the Regions, both Pinchuk and his father-in-law, Kuchma, have come in behind Yushchenko. Pinchuk has indeed turned into a government booster. On November 10, he popped into Brussels to visit with the Commission President Barroso, introduce Barroso to the Yalta Strategy Group (YES) – which he bankrolls – and to lobby for Ukrainian EU membership. Barroso gave Pinchuk little encouragement but apparently thanked him for helping keep the Orange Revolution bloodless.[103]

Putin was unruffled by Pinchuk's surprise visit. Is it any wonder? By the end of 2005 energy pricing had become the big international economic issue. It also loomed huge in both the Russian-Ukrainian relationship and Ukraine's future. Crisis erupted in December when the Ukrainian government refused to accept a threefold increase in the price of Russian gas, which, by bilateral treaty was being supplied at a third of market prices. The dispute took on a European dimension in early January 2006, after Putin abruptly stopped deliveries, a move that jeopardized Russia's much-vaunted reliability as an energy supplier to western Europe. It ended with a painful compromise, the implications of which are far-reaching. The EU promised to give priority to energy in future policy-making and pay particular attention to the need for multi-sourcing. Russia's hold on the Eurasian supply grid strengthened. Ukraine received assurances of a phase-in of energy pricing, gained new recognition of its vital role as a supplier, and moved up the list of EU priorities.[104]

There was another, perhaps still more significant upshot of the deal. What made it work was the role of a new sales monopoly, RosUkrenergo, owned jointly by Gazprom and a shadowy group of anonymous investors controlled by a Swiss-held trust managed by the Raiffaisenkasse, an Austrian bank which, perhaps not coincidentally, has become the second largest investor in Ukraine. Until the Yushchenko government, one pledged to ending corruption, divulges the names of the secret powers-behind-the throne, Yulia Tymoshenko will batter it with charges of selling out the Ukrainian people to the oligarchs. Putin may have given her the issue she needs to win the March election.[105]

It is hardly what he would have desired. Many western commentators will consider this outcome a just comeuppance for an overly aggressive geo-political move against a democratizing Ukraine. Putin may, however, simply have miscalculated in a more long-range policy aimed at modernizing Russia. Consider, first of all, the importance of Russia's stake in energy. This year the big energy producers (OPEC, plus Russia and Norway) will garner a net payments surplus of $400 billion, of which Russia will pocket about $125 billion. Two-thirds of this amount covers imports that include capital export, which is mostly unaccountable. The rest is used to strengthen the armed forces or pay down debt or is poured into a stabilization fund to buffer the effects of future price decreases. At the moment, Russia cannot spend more money without inflationary consequences. [106]

Putin, who must step down by law, has all but officially designated Dmitry Medvedev, the CEO of Gazprom, as his presidential successor after 2008. Russia's quasi-monopolistic producer and distributor of natural gas, Gazprom is also tying up the output of producers in the Stans. Putin is rumored to be angling to replace Medvedev as energy supremo. He would be following in the footsteps of his pal, Gerhard Schröder, who is soon to become a director of the new Vyborg-Greifswald pipeline company. With oil at $50 a barrel, Russia's GDP will double by 2013 and incomes increase from $300 per month to $1,386 per month, and GDP will pass Spain's, making Russia, in other words, nearly as wealthy as a middling western European nation.[107]

Russia now supplies about 40 percent of western Europe's gas requirements, which can be expected to increase when the new Baltic line is completed in 2010; Putin thinks his nation can and should raise its share of this market to 90 percent. The Russian president has thus far wasted little time with the EU: he can deal bilaterally. As one Moscow commentator remarked, "The notion of European values, which EU representatives used to see as an essential condition for contacts with (Russia), has faded into the background... The fundamental issue of Russia-EU relations has become the North European gas pipeline. The situation has drastically changed since 2002." The Poles and Balts can only fume about being bypassed by (and losing the transit fees from) the Baltic pipeline. Brussels has done nothing to help them.[108] It remains to be seen whether the recent crisis will change anything.

Energy is Russia's longest and strongest policy lever in the near abroad. In a practice dating from the Soviet era, Gazprom has supplied both Ukraine and Belarus with heavily-discounted gas, in the case of the latter amounting to 10 percent of the impoverished nation's GDP For its part, until 2005 Ukraine paid $50 per 100,000 cubic meters of gas as opposed to the world price of $180. The state oil and gas monopoly, Navtogaz, controls the entire flow.[109] A couple of important consequences follow from the energy subsidies. The cheap gas is over-consumed, two and half times as much by value of industrial output compared to Poland, something both inordinately wasteful and a powerful disincentive to industrial modernization. It is also the main source of Ukrainian corruption. Buy at fifty, sell at one hundred and eighty; skim and pay off! But that's only where the problem starts. More sophisticated scams are also available. Naftogaz, for instance, recently set up an immense 6-billion-euro credit line with two European banks, which up to this point seems to have been drawn down only for purported foreign acquisitions, none of them, however, yet made. The balances pile up in Cyprus banks. It appears, but has not yet been proven, that that the loan is being collateralized by revenue from future gas pipeline pass-throughs.[110]

Gas accounts for no less than 80 percent of Ukraine's energy consumption. A politician's nightmare, jacking up energy prices would pinch the consumer and force inefficient producers against the wall. By deciding in November 2005 to take Gazprom public and shift to market pricing, the Putin-Medvedev duo has saved Ukraine's politicians from having to make an impossibly difficult decision and forced the economy to become more competitive. It may even eventually undercut the oligarchy. By increasing the revenues his own country needs for modernization, he will also stimulate the rise of a new Russian middle class. Ukraine's short-term pain will yield in spades long-term gain.

The motives for Putin-Medvedev's huge move can be understood either as an attempt to force Ukraine's hand or as a belated recognition that since the Orange Revolution the subsidy-weapon has lost its power. It can also be explained in primarily economic terms. As presently run, Gazprom is vastly inefficient and far less profitable than it could be; it trades publicly at a large discount even to other Russian energy companies. "State involvement results," as the *Economist* put the matter, "in what observers politely term 'non commercial behavior.'"[111] Rather than risk antagonizing their western European customers, the Russians appear willing to accept a phase-out of the existing system. Putin has suggested, cynically, that future Ukrainian privatizations will cover the higher fuel costs. The remark may prove to be prophetic. In any case, Yushchenko is redoubling efforts to reexport oil supplies from the Caspian Sea via the heretofore unprofitable Odessa-Brody pipeline to nearby Poland and Slovakia.[112]

Ukraine cannot, and should never be, forced to make a definitive choice between East and West. But why worry? The new Gazprom pricing policy will improve the relationship with Russia. A democratic, prosperous, and proud Ukraine will never be a threat to the historic older brother but can serve as a role model for him. Russian economic success will facilitate reconciliation to a westernizing Ukraine. New wealth can be the leaven for a new class of Russian entrepreneurs and managers, who thrive not in the interstices between laws but within the framework of law. Putin's controversial former economic advisor, Andrei Ilarionov, estimates that Russia's "state capitalist interventionism would shave no less than 9 points off the Russian GDP in 2005." Ending this unnecessary waste could trigger a future boom.[113]

When he speaks of "security," Putin seems less concerned by external than internal threats.[114] The Orange Revolution has plenty of Russian admirers, such as Natalya Gevorkian of *Kommersant*, who praise Ukraine for its "fully democratic and many-voiced parliament, [not] an [obliging] 'as you please, the way it is' [rubberstamp] in Moscow" but which politicians follow with trepidation because "the press in that country works normally." She concludes that "those people in Russia, who have not yet been finally and completely brainwashed, follow the ups and downs of the turbulent political life of out neighbors with cheerful envy ... those people, the ones who have not been castrated yet, are secretly harboring an orange fruit, which is what the Kremlin fears most of all."[115]

The prospect of Ukrainian NATO membership does not give Putin nightmares. Ukraine should pursue it at all costs. Membership can be gained relatively easily. It raises few of the distribution issues problems (who gets what?) arising in the economy. NATO's rules are established and must be accepted by those who join it. Only rarely does the alliance directly affect the lives of people, and it thus dwells most of the time in comfortable obscurity, except when a lightening rod for generalized discontent. NATO is not a war-making but a regional collective security organization, which never entered into combat during the Cold War; at the same time, it spared the nations of western Europe the costs of defending their borders from potentially hostile neighboring countries. Ukrainian NATO membership is less a threat to Russia than a restraint on unilateral action; it will increase the security of Russia's borders and lower its defense expenditures. These matters have a particular relevance in light of China's military buildup.[116]

Membership in the alliance requires accepting rules similar to those of the "Copenhagen Criteria" and especially civilian control of the security services. The current director of the Ukrainian Security Service (SBU) claims that the SBU is currently being "professionalized" in preparation for NATO membership and promises that corruption and coercion will be eliminated. Membership in the alliance is also important, because common training methods and compatible technologies will advance the careers of new men linked to the welfare and standards of western Europe and the United States. Ukrainian membership in NATO does, however, have a hitch: The public opposes it. Ukraine should not try to join the alliance unless this attitude changes.[117]

At the EU-Ukraine summit in early December, the Yushchenko government finally received the friendly nod for which it had long been waiting, but in fact had not yet earned, because of the Rada's refusal to pass the measures required for WTO admission. This was an EU granting of market economy status, which permitted the duty-free importation of Ukrainian steel into the EU. The gesture also indicated that Brussels was well disposed to the country's eventual admission into the Euro-club. President Barroso frankly stated as much. Whether he can speak for the EU as a whole in this matter is, however, questionable. In a radio address the following day, President Yushchenko, in any case, depicted the status upgrade as a major triumph and pledged that Ukraine would "live and play" by European rules and begin the overhaul of the judiciary. This was a step in the right direction.[118]

"The bigger the EU, the bigger the political role and prestige of the bureaucracy," notes Czech President Vaclav Klaus, adding that "Brussels is [thus] more in favor of enlargement than individual member countries."[119] "Enlargement fatigue" from which some of them suffer at this point need not be an obstacle to Ukrainian accession progress – though it may later become one. At this early stage in the process, the Commission runs the show. If the long string of EU policy failures continues, its one noteworthy success, enlargement, will receive increasing attention. The real danger is the Commission outracing public sentiment and making commitments it cannot keep. In a weakening EU, however, the value of membership will shrink and, as a result, opposition to taking in new members diminish accordingly. Like Turkey, Ukraine's overriding interest is at this point simply to remain on the accession path in order to keep hope alive. Prospective admission to the EU is invaluable as a lever for necessary reform – more important than membership itself.

The Orange Revolution is vulnerable at many points. The Yushchenko government now in office, and its successor, must get the economy rolling by attracting foreign investment in order to dilute the power of the oligarchs and create new centers of power. It must also better working conditions and improve management standards, strengthen the enforcement of laws and administrative regulations, broaden international contacts, increase social opportunity, and drive brutality and coercion out of public life. The present and future Ukrainian government must also navigate between a strengthening Russia and a weakening EU as well as overcome resistance from entrenched oligarchs, the venal politicians who do their bidding, and the foreign influences that encourage the unholy alliance between them. Ukraine's democratic institutions are still weak and will remain so even after the completion in 2006 of a reform already under way, which concentrates additional power in the office of the prime minister. Neither President Yushchenko nor the new prime minister can count on much help from the parties or the individuals after whom many of them are named. He or she who would lead Ukraine at this special moment in history must speak and answer to the Maidan, which is the spirit of Ukraine. Only thus can democracy eventually take hold and freedom be secured.

Not a Bang and Nary a Whimper

The British presidency of the EU began with hope and ended with a shrug. The dual constitutional referenda rejections discredited the claim of President Chirac to EU leadership, and the events that unfolded over the latter six months of the year made its resurrection impossible. The French public turned decisively and irreversibly against "Europe." The immigrant rioting of late October and early November, moreover, exposed, as never before, the shortcomings of the French economic and social model and the intellectual poverty of the political class. President Chirac also suffered a stroke, and his two contesting heirs, Sarkozy and de Villepin, waged an obsessive campaign for an election still well over a year and a half away.

In Germany, "gridlock" is the operational word: The inconclusive results of the September election, which resulted in two months of exhausting negotiation for a grand coalition, ruled out anything more ambitious than a caretaker role for the Federal Republic in the affairs of the EU. The lack of forward movement in the politics of the "duo" had its counterpart in the economic field. Growth did not pick up appreciably over the half-year, and only optimists imagined that, with a European Central Bank bent on increasing interest rates and Germany adopting a deflationary policy, 2006 would be the long-awaited year of recovery.

Britain, it would seem, alone held the field – and could even count on the support of the Commission, for what little it was worth.[120] Yet a funny thing happened on the way to Brussels: with the important exception of Turkey – which received a flashing yellow light for eventual EU admission, brought the Balkans along with it, and kept the door open for Ukraine – Britain went limp (or was it rigid?). In any case, Blair did not seriously tackle the issue of structural reform. The ugly budget settlement will keep it on ice for years to come. A post-Lisbon agenda never developed. The weakened French won the day. The WTO – an organization whose role in international economic governance should grow in a multipolar world – took a hit. As a result, Europe will loom smaller and the emergent superpowers of Asia, along with rest of the world, larger in the future. The EU tripped itself up in attempting to preserve the status quo. One leg of the EU's triad – the representation of Europe in trade policy is buckling. The other two, competition and internal market policy, cannot support the heavy structures of official Brussels much longer.

Gordon Brown, the chancellor of the Exchequer, provides the clue to Britain's lackadaisical conduct of its presidency. "Europe," he said, is obsolete: a regional trade block like the EU counts for less and less in a globalizing world. It is dispensable, at least economically, and worth paying for only when Brussels can deliver better than any alternative. Judgments as to what an ideal EU can or should do naturally vary from country to country. What Brown stated openly is being acted on in different ways by other key players. To secure the German energy supply, Schröder did not meet with Barroso in Brussels but with Putin in Moscow: the pipeline deal was an instance of pure bilateralism. Similarly, France, which can no longer make the rules, is taking its marbles, leaving Brussels, and going home. In a revival of the *planisme* thought to have become extinct after the 1970s, Villepin openly promotes the creation of national champions, and Sarkozy fears doing otherwise.

The new attitude is equally evident in trade negotiations. The French stance on the CAP is not only contrary to the economic interests of Europe and the world but to those of France itself. But so what? The

French could care less, at least for now. They are turning inward and are prepared to go it alone rather than be enslaved to that (purported) equivalent of Stalinism, Anglo-American capitalism. A consensus on this matter links traditional Left to traditional Right; it will exist until the intellectual bubble pops and reality intrudes. The French cannot of course stop the onward rush of either technological change or liberalization but only, by undermining what remains of the EU's regulatory authority and international influence, reduce Europe's voice world affairs.

A cogently argued book by the political philosopher Glyn Morgan has recently revived interest in the EU as a security organization, the term being used in the broad sense of including whatever contributes to a sense of well-being by reducing uncertainty and increasing operational independence.[121] Europe will not end its anxiety by raising and maintaining a military establishment along US lines but by creating conditions of political stability along its borders – by the encouragement of democracy. The moment is opportune.

The Turkish government's campaign to reform itself along the lines of modern European politics has been breathtaking in scope, exemplary in its sincerity, and extraordinary in its results. Yet Turkish admission is something that Europeans may accept but cannot like. This should change. The Turks have more to offer Europe than Europe does the Turks. Forget, for a moment, the historic ties linking the eastern to the western Mediterranean and the orient to the occident. Bear in mind the importance of Turkey as the indispensable stabilizing force in a region that touches on the Middle East, the Caucuses, and the Balkans, in which it has shared power historically with Russia and Iran, and whose people have ethnic and religious ties with central Asia. To imagine that Europe, or the United States, can for long be a major "presence" in this region, where warfare is endemic and real blood is often shed, is foolhardy. The wisest course for the West is to link up with a strong, modernizing, and democratic Turkey – and give it a leading voice in overall policy in its region.

A democratic Ukraine can also enhance European security. Ukraine is, of course, unencumbered by a colonial past and has been for centuries subject to outside domination. Ukraine has never waged war against its powerful neighbors but only provided battlefields for them. It faces complicated problems of international settlement (Transdnistria, Crimean extra-territoriality, etc.) but has no war-threatening conflicts with any of surrounding nation, least of all Russia. Yet it is too big for even the Russians to occupy and rule by force in the face of mass opposition. The Maidan can serve as a warning: it is Europe's security as well as Ukraine's. In the words of Zbigniew Brzezinski, "As soon as Ukraine turns into a truly democratic and European nation, Russia will have to follow suit. Ukraine's mission transcends Ukraine ... [it] is a prerequisite for the formation of a transcontinental Europe."[122] The path to EU accession must be kept open and Ukraine's new democracy be given a chance to strengthen. Even with plummeting growth, malfunctioning legal institutions, endemic political squabbling, and the persistence of corruption at every level, Ukraine has just experienced the best year in its history. A nation founded on hope and suffering is acquiring a new democratic identity. That is the ultimate meaning of the Maidan.[123]

The fall of communism, the expansion of the EU, and the springtime of peoples in the Eurasian landmass are moving the borders of Europe southeastward and in the process expanding the definition of Europe itself. It is no longer limited to Western Rite Christianity but almost serendipitously has come to include most traditional places (outside Russia) of Orthodoxy. It is thus reweaving a human tapestry frayed thin by western colonialism and brutally ripped apart by Soviet communism. What an odd way to end the Schism! The culturally richer, larger, and reunited Europe of the future can also be more confident and secure and its many voices fuller, more harmonic, and stronger than before, even in a world it will never again dominate.

Postscript: Neither Superstate
nor New-Market Economy

What is said of old soldiers also applies to bureaucracies that have had
their day: they never die, just fade away. Will the same also be true of
the European Union (EU)? The EU is entering a period of hibernation.
It will last until, at some future date, the temperature rises, birds sing,
bees buzz, fish hatch, the sun shines again, and tourists return to national
parks. During this extended period of rest and regeneration, the heart
rate drops low enough to sustain only vital functions and does not rise
again until the massive fat accumulated from the feeding season has
burned off and hunger returns.

The EU cannot advance until it has a popular mandate and will
remain gridlocked in the foreseeable future. It's time for triage, to decide
between what is worth keeping and what can no longer survive. The EU
had become nearly dysfunctional even before the two referenda exposed
its widespread unpopularity. The Brussels machinery sputtered and mis-
fired, gasped and wheezed, and got nowhere. Individual member states
have since turned inward and gone their separate ways in foreign policy. The notion of Europe as a single economic and political bloc is also,
because of globalization, rapidly becoming obsolete. In a world gallop-
ing ahead, Europe is falling by the wayside because institutions designed
for economic and political union retard growth and weaken democracy.
Every recent attempt to improve the situation has worsened it. The
repeated failures of elitist methods have gone far to discredit the European Idea. The budget deal of December 2005 is a new nadir, which
threatens to paralyze the EU. Yet "Europe's great experiment in political and economic union" can still be revived, redefined, and rescued – if

the public so wishes. The EU must first, however, rediscover a sense of purpose and earn a new legitimacy.

No longer can the Commission, the member states represented in the European Council, or any single bloc of them, lead the EU, which, if it were a real nation state, could be described as ungovernable. This being the case, the serious action takes place behind the scenes, without mandate, supervision, or accountability, and outside the framework of law. Policy making by stealth results, now more than ever. In December 2005 President Merkel's personal foreign affairs advisor proposed implementing administratively all the parts of the discredited constitution that "do not rely on ratification," such as the European Defense Agency and the European Space Agency. "Do we still need a text when we have the political will?" asked rhetorically the French Defense Minister Michèle Alliot-Marie. Portraying confidence that Europe could be built from behind the scenes, 100,000 pamphlets printed for Belgian school children in December treated the rejected document as a done deal: "With this new constitution," it reassured the kids, "everything will go like clockwork, just like in your own club." Such stupidities usually backfire. Intrigue often only amounts in the end to mischief making.[1]

As Council president in 2005, Prime Minister Blair seemed content to have demonstrated that by keeping Turkish accession on track, the EU is, indeed, still alive and well. In that one respect, he succeeded. Had the German election of September not resulted in a demoralizing deadlock, he might have done more: as it was, however, Merkel could not form a grand coalition until late November, and even then her hands were tied. Blair made little attempt to link the economic liberals of western Europe with a like-minded bloc forming in the accession nations of the east and no effort whatsoever to restructure European institutions. The budgetary impasse, reached in June, lasted for the remainder of the year. To resolve it the British prime minister capitulated pitifully to Chirac: the CAP will remain unscathed until 2013, EU institutions will rust solid, and European public life spiral downward. The locus of world power will shift elsewhere.

The only accomplishment of the British presidency other than keeping Turkish accession on track was an end-of-the-year goodwill gesture towards Ukraine. The EU granted it "market economy status," even without the preliminary of World Trade Organization (WTO) admission. Commission President Barroso declared that "the future of Ukraine is in Europe."[2] Whether he could deliver on the proffered suggestion is, of course, another matter altogether. Nor could any one else in the near term: optimists expect the EU is likely to remain immobilized through 2006.[3] The rotating presidencies will be held by Austria and Finland, neither of whom is likely to exercise a strong hand. Germany, which takes the helm in 2007, remains the great hope of Euro-constitutionalists. It will be their also last one unless public opinion can be turned around this year.[4]

Operating from behind the scenes, with a compliant Schröder in tow and an obliging Juncker often in the wings, Chirac hatched a plot, which unfolded in 2003 and 2004, to hijack the EU. Its success would have prevented the democratic development of a future European government. Thanks to the referendum, the unprecedented power grab ended in ignominy. Chirac envisaged nothing less than the creation of a French-led European hyperpower able to compete with the United States for world supremacy. Underlying the scheme was a vain hope that new state-of-the-art high-tech space-age weaponry would enable Europe (united around the French atomic bomb and a Franco-German dominated military-industrial complex) to skip a generation of costly rearmament and emerge dramatically on the superpower scene, too late for a complacent United States to prevent an epochal shift in the balance of power.

The plot unfolded at the interface of the semisecret French national security state and the unaccountable European Commission. It generated an imaginary European defense agency, a miniscule rapid reaction force dependent on US logistical support, and an unbudgeted global positioning satellite (GPS) system. Even if the GPS scheme were eventually to see the light of day, it would be militarily and economically useless. Finally, Chirac sought a "strategic partnership" with China, which roiled the already stormy diplomatic seas of east Asia, damaged Taiwan without doing China any good, and has now been shelved by the Chinese.

The French public's rejection of the constitution, of political Europe, and of Jacques Chirac personally revealed the emptiness of France's Napoleonic pretensions. The three weeks of general mayhem, which in late October broke out in the high-rise ghettoes of immigrant France, exposed the failure of the French "social and economic model." A week after the fires went out, a Sino-American détente set in, as the Chinese apparently concluded that Europe would not, contrary to what Chirac had so often intimated, soon become a superpower. His seventy-third birthday was not a happy one. Three quarters of the French public, according to a poll taken on that day, thought him a nullity.[5] The implications of Chirac's overweening ambitions for the future of Europe are more memorable than his shoddy posturing. His was a blueprint for a modern Sparta, a Euro-garrison state with war-waging as the bond of community. The abortive constitution would have provided a mandate to proceed. Thank God it crashed, along with Chirac's reputation.

The Commission spills ink, generates paperwork, and stands in the way of real leadership. Progress in completing the internal market has come to a halt. Reform of the CAP seems more remote than ever, regional funding is more inequitable and corrupt than ever, and the European Commission continues to make commitments it cannot keep. Yet plans, projects, and programs continue to spin out of the Berlaymont. Some of them, such as Registration, Evaluation, and Authorization of Chemicals (REACH), are potential bureaucratic nightmares. Others, such as biotech policy, have been destructive and work at cross-purposes to other policies. Protectionist schemes have a powerful deterrent effect. It is the threat, even more than the reality, of such restrictive measures that drives research and development out of Europe, lowers investment, and acts as a drag on the economy. The policies themselves, being unworkable, eventually break down. This is not surprising. The Commission often trips over its own feet.

Maladministration characterizes official accession policy. The *acquis communautaire*, the corpus of EU administrative regulations, is too costly, time-consuming, and intrusive for most new member states to implement. (Nor, in the absence of new revenues, will the EU be able to meet its growing financial commitments to the accession states.) Yet a conspiracy of silence keeps such secrets under lock and key. The vulnerable eastern Europeans fear jeopardizing membership in the EU-Club, the Commission fears publicizing that it struck an impossible deal with them, and the governments of protectionist member states fear disclosing that the easterners cannot be saddled with the full costs of the *acquis*.

The accession states must also reckon with the economic and political absurdity of the membership sine qua non, adoption of the euro. Quite simply, the fiscal and monetary tightening needed to comply with the European Monetary Union's (EMU) growth and stability criteria would shrink economies and topple governments in eastern Europe. Since half of Euroland – including Germany, France, and Italy – cannot meet the European Central Bank's (ECB) strict monetary and fiscal targets, the easterners face the impossibility of being "whiter than white." This gives rise to the politics of appearance.

Accession policy is sparring – a mock combat. The Commission browbeats noncompliers with the threat of cutting off regional funding and CAP transfers but does little in the end. The accession governments prostrate themselves before the EMU and try to spend EU money before it dries up. So convoluted are the bureaucratic procedures of Brussels and so inefficient the local authorities in eastern Europe that only half of the allocated funds can actually be spent before the statutory expiry date of twenty-four months. The magnitude of the muddling is greater than any party to it cares to admit.[6]

The relevant sections of the Commission, or a successor organization, should be maintained as linkage to new and future member states on whom the EU's own future depends. Further enlargement to the east is economically and geopolitically desirable. It will not only extend the borders and increase the wealth of Europe but enrich its culture as well as spread and strengthen its political values. Such a new Europe would be diverse, polycentric, genuinely ecumenical, and not the property of any single nation or group of nations, peoples, religions, or languages, but of all of them. It would create, and rest on, acceptance of a shared set of fundamental rules. The new Europe would be a community of principle.

A reformed EU would have to be radically downsized to focus on important, new responsibilities. The CAP must go: it has warped the institutional development of the EU and misallocated and squandered funds for decades, is undermining the WTO, will paralyze the EU unless drastically cutback, and may eventually bankrupt Brussels. No member state is willing to pay more into the foolhardy scheme. To demand doing so would cause pointless aggravation. Dripping with sleaze, regional funding likewise undermines member state integrity and, along with the

CAP, will undo EU finances as claims grow and revenues remain constant or shrink. The elimination of these two transfer programs would free up balances that national governments need to bolster their own authority. Other wasteful programs, such as fisheries policy and foreign aid, could also be repatriated to the states. Involving only financial transfers, these matters could be settled without great fanfare by the European Council.

The Council could also set up a new "European Agency for the Liquidation of the European Union" to arrange for the orderly disposal of EU assets. They consist largely of oversized office buildings in Brussels and other European cities. The proceeds could be placed in a sinking fund to cover the generous pensions of retiring Eurocrats. Because the Commission refuses to reform itself, it must be dismantled and later, as necessary, be rebuilt. Barroso's "bonfire of the inanities" was, as it turns out, a meaningless gesture: not a conflagration but a flare-up in a waste-basket caused by a carelessly tossed burning cigarette butt.[7] There is no alternative to the vertical chop: Brussels' regulations and directives entangle government, overload business, and are both duplicative and economically disruptive. The EU's attempt to harmonize laws should end, and the principles of subsidiarity and mutual recognition should be respected.

The Commission's biggest problem is a blinkered mindset. Euro-speak and Euro-thought are too deeply engrained to airbrush out of a mental portrait. Official Brussels' frame of mind reflects the "blocistic" vision of the world decried by Czech President Vaclav Klaus. It overlooks that Europe is an aggregate of countries, pretends it consists of a unified people, and incorrectly assumes that the EU is a single economic entity, which produces, trades, innovates, invests, redeploys resources, and reduces cost. This viewpoint is blind not only to the complexities of Europe but to the significance of globalization.[8]

To reform the EU by assigning the Commission a vast new "competence" in research and development would be like handing a chimpanzee a clock to tinker with: the results are amusing, except to the owner of the clock. In pursuit of a campaign against "Frankenfoods," the Brussels authorities wrecked much of the European biotech industry, caused major collateral damage elsewhere, saddled Europe's food producers with a whole new set of unnecessary controls, and failed, in the end, to prevent the rest of the world from developing a new and immensely valuable technology. Thanks to this inane EU policy, the revolution in biotechnology, like its predecessor in information technology, will largely bypass Europe.

Pouring more money into "European" science and technology reflects "blocistic" thinking of the worst kind. It will burn cash and entrench bureaucrats but not save either the EU or the European economy. To speak of a special "European science" is nonsense. Scientific knowledge is universal. Imagining otherwise exposes the Euro-elites as out of touch not only with the public but with reality. Anyone who has doubts on this score should be sentenced to writing a doctoral dissertation about Margaret Wallstroem's idea of democracy, Philippe Busquin's strategic space initiative, or the economics and administration of the Registration, Evaluation, and Authorization of Chemicals (REACH) program.

A reformed Commission should be set up to operate at the same scale as organizations with similar powers. Skeleton crews must be kept on hand to enforce competition law, coordinate the legal and institutional changes needed to develop the single market on the basis of mutual recognition, and conduct international trade negotiations. The Surveillance Authority of the European Free Trade Association handles these tasks with fifty officials. The much larger EU would need at least three times as many. A reformed EU would also face additional responsibilities in connection with enlargement and nation building. These tasks would require an equal number of officials. The 18,000 grey-suited functionaries at the Berlaymont could nonetheless be reduced to about 300, at the very most 500. The 17,500 recent retirees would then be free to write memoirs blaming others for the decline of the EU.

Unless member states are prepared to make a new commitment to the EU and increase their dues, they should press hard for an orderly winding down of operations. The first option is unrealistic. While supporting the European Idea, the member states themselves distrust the Brussels institutions. All of them refuse to grant the Commission the investigative powers needed to desleaze the CAP and regional funding; they fear the EU will treat such an authorization as a blank check. Increasingly, member states go their own ways. Schröder did not ask Barroso for permission to cut a pipeline deal with Putin. The French openly flout EU rules; the Greeks, Italians, and others do so less overtly. And in eastern

Europe, the wink-wink culture has quickly taken hold. The virtuous Nordics, the Dutch, and the British are fed up with subsidizing crooked behavior.

In a recent editorial, Timothy Garton Ash recommended shutting down the European Parliament (EP) in Strasbourg, because he thought it "ludicrous and simply incomprehensible...that the entire European parliament still commutes between two vast buildings in Brussels and Strasbourg at a cost to the European taxpayer of well over 200 million euros per year."[9] He's got a point. But rather than just shut down one of its two oversized facilities, the institution itself should be reconfigured to fit the needs of the new Europe. Let's take a stab at it. The EP is of course not a real legislature, because it lacks the power to tax, has little authority to make law, and talks far too much. It should be slimmed down from 732 members to an even 100, one for each of the 25 EU countries, with the remainder allocated between them on the basis of population.

Like the House of Lords, the new body should have no powers but be purely consultative and composed of distinguished senior statesmen and stateswomen. To minimize sleaze and as an act of solidarity in commemoration of the "European social and economic model," the new Members of Parliament should be compensated at lower net rates than they could command in the marketplace. Savings from such "salary compression" would accrue in a special fund set up to support the "active labor market policy" championed by the EU's Economic and Social Council (ECOSOC). It would be spent specifically to "upgrade the skill sets" of unemployable former Community bureaucrats. A certified public accountant, the Senior Cloakroom Attendant (*Oberklosetttürwart*), would check attendance and verify the legitimacy of travel and other reimbursement requests at the foyer to the new EP facility.

The EP should no longer be located on the fringes of an expanding Europe but at its center, in an ancient seat of power, and at a rampart of culture. It should be moved to a member state unlikely to split, with a hard-working, well-educated, multilingual labor force, affordable housing, an untainted local language, good discount airlines connections, and close proximity to recreational facilities. The location best meeting these criteria is Székesfehérvár, located near scenic Lake Balaton in Hungary.

The EU's new consultative body will replace the old EP and have several official languages. This accurate demographic microcosm will reflect the numbers speaking them, minimize historic conflicts, and protect the diversity of Europe's tongues and the identity of its peoples from the corrosive Anglosphere. Turkish, of course, must be an official language. To prevent unnecessary disagreements between the historically dispersed and divided Slavs, a similar status should be given the one language easily understood by all of them, Church Slavonic. The same principle can also be applied to the Nordics. Faced with the prospect of endless historical-philological wrangling, they will, preferring silence, agree on Icelandic, which has few words but is grammatically pure and close to ancient Norse. The romance languages present a more difficult problem: Spanish and Portuguese are, of course, the only two surviving genuinely international Latinate tongues, but French has strong historical claims, as does Italian. If unable to follow the Slavic and Nordic precedents and adopt Mediaeval Latin, the romance language group will have to sort out the contending claims by itself.

English of course cannot have official status and will be allowed only in the corridors. It is the sole official language of no more than a single country, the United Kingdom, and even there it is giving ground to Welsh, Cornish, and Pictish; otherwise it is only spoken in Ireland (along with Gaelic) and Malta (along with Maltese). The British should quickly relinquish any claim to official status on one condition: to prevent future language abuse, all publications in English bearing the imprimatur of the EU will need the approval of a committee appointed by the press Syndics and Delegates of Cambridge and Oxford, which are the only two European institutions of higher education that consistently make the prestigious list of the world's hundred best universities, published annually by the Chinese government. Finally, the old EP needs a new name, which should be in the language of the host nation and accurately describes its function: Az új nagy vendéglő kiürítése.[10]

Although voting majorities in most EU countries would support an orderly phase-out of the Eurocracy, parties of both the Right and Left still almost universally oppose it. Even British Tories worry that an "opt-out agenda" could destroy the EU, leaving a trail of wreckage behind. This need not happen if timely action is taken. Electorates must be made aware that withdrawal from the EU is not an act of aggression or a betrayal of the European Idea but a simple political and economic necessity. Growth requires reforms that only the individual states can make. They must, above all, reduce "social protection" – slim down the welfare state and introduce flexible labor markets. The conclusion is inescapable. Governments need more, not less, control over fiscal and monetary policy in order to manage this difficult feat. Buck-passing to Brussels no longer works: elected officials must regain responsiveness to constituent needs for democracy to remain vibrant.

Today's sharp division between political elites and citizens must end. The European public consists of the best educated, most prosperous and humane generation in history. Such civilized men and women are not going to backslide into war, fascism, or violent revolution. The spillage of blood has become a European taboo. Europeans do not require tutorials from Brussels or any other self-anointed, entrenched political elite, nor do they look forward to the removal of decision making from the public forum by means of an international "constitutionalization process" presided over by judges, lawyers, academics, and technocrats. The same is true of any form of judicial activism that strips the public of self-determination. The prospect of such governance by experts also went up in smoke with the European Constitution.[11] The peoples of Europe need a chance to make their own decisions. The lack of self-government has become demoralizing as well as economically and politically crippling.

The EMU is a special case of misbegotten EU policy making. It cannot, like the CAP or regional funding, simply be re-jiggered or, like many Commission programs, halted without further ado. The European Monetary Union is real and must be taken seriously. Careless tampering might trigger a financial panic. The EMU was built on an imagined future European federal union as well as on unsound operating principles. The need for action is imminent. The EMU has for years slowed down growth because the Eurozone is not an optimal currency area. Its faulty structures compound governance problems and leave it vulnerable to attack. The European Central Bank's sole task is currency stabilization. Neither the ECB nor any other European authority has the macroeconomic tools needed to promote growth. The ECB also has an inbuilt deflationary bias and cannot adjust to changes in the economic cycle because it is bound by the growth and stability pact.

The inadequate Maastricht Criteria provide its only means of disciplining spendthrift politicians. Fearing slowdowns and unemployment, most Eurozone governments now flout these rules. Yet the ECB treats all Euro-denominated sovereign debt as equivalent. The ECB does not, in other words, factor in risk. This is a red flag. The bank's room for maneuver in this situation is very limited: To allow bonds to trade at market value would – by exposing the intrinsic flaws in the EMU's design – undermine its authority, encourage speculation, and trigger the dreaded event – a run on the currency.

No administrative or political authority can alter the ECB's policies or modify its rules, nor has any provision been made to permit a member state to leave the Eurozone. Conceived as a rung on the ladder leading to economic and political union, such omissions were deliberate. The institutional design of the bank did not allow for either "voice" or "exit," in keeping with Jacques Delors's policy of *engrenage*. Often translated into English as "gearing," the term really means "entanglement." *Engrenage* entails making procedures so complicated, political tradeoffs so complex, and operations so opaque that the costs of evading, breaking, or dissolving them would be prohibitive; such procedures were thereby over time institutionalized and became permanent, enabling the integration process to continue advancing along a one-way track. In this scheme, provisions for voice and exit are unnecessary and unwelcome temptations. Such practices may have prevented minor breakdowns, but they increase the likelihood of catastrophic failure.

The danger of financial panic and the long-term threat to growth call for the immediate preparation, under the auspices of the European Council, of a "Plan B" for the euro. This may already have begun behind closed doors. In connection with the first rate increase in five years, the ECB president Jean-Claude Trichet announced in December 2005 that the bank would no longer hold as collateral sovereign Eurobonds issued by countries with deteriorating credit ratings. Trichet's statement indicates an awareness of a potential problem. The first priority of a Plan B should be to set up procedures for national opt-outs from the Eurozone. The second concern should be even more basic – one of institutional redesign. Such a Plan B should also recognize that Eurozone membership does not serve either the interests of the accession states, which cannot fulfill the strict Maastricht Criteria at acceptable economic costs, or meet the needs of the present members, whose chronic rule breaking has already gravely weakened the monetary union.

The ladder toward economic and political union having broken apart, the EMU can no longer be thought of as a rung on it. The political rationale for it has disappeared. Yet a vestigial euro can be saved, the EMU be salvaged, ailing economies be let off the hook, and the monetary and fiscal policies of accession and future member states be kept in line by floating reissued national currencies against both one another and a virtuous euro. An economically functional Eurozone can then help revive the European Idea.

As the EU hibernates, the individual member states will go their separate ways. Some countries will play by its rules, others will pay lip service to them, and still others will break them. There will be twenty-five national variations on a common theme. Not every state can be expected to adopt a liberal reform policy, and surely some, such as France, will try to adopt a form of mercantilism. A hibernating Europe will not, however, become a centrifugal Europe but will be disciplined by a growing world market. The weakening of the WTO or other international regulatory agencies can only strengthen globalization. It will give rise to summit deal making by interdependent giants operating on too vast a scale to tolerate national or regional protectionism. Their power will be be irresistible.

The new importance of the world market is only a matter of degree. Exogenous influence has always been the main driver of European economic integration, which is an epiphenomenon of deep-seated longer-term trends at work both nationally and internationally. By most calculations, at least two-thirds of the "integration dividend" derives from either incoming investment or the effect of foreign competition on European markets. This was the case both before and after the Single European Act (SEA) of 1986, which has gone about halfway toward creating a single European market. The erection of new barriers can delay but not prevent the globalization of the European economy: Technological development, reductions in information costs, and increases in labor productivity impel it forward. Their points of diffusion are now extra-European.

The new competition need not lead to "a race to the bottom" but can strengthen welfare states by building confidence in the political system, adding to intellectual capital, and increasing longevity and productivity. Yet this will happen only where governments are trusted. The Nordic model was not designed as an export product. The superior performance of market economies will determine most outcomes. As Friedrich Hayek explained in "The Economic Conditions of Interstate Federalism," the competition principle will eventually lead to market erosion of state economic sovereignty and political reorganization at a higher level.[12]

The horse that slips harness must be coaxed back into it. The posthibernation Europe will have to be built not on opt-outs but on opt-ins, building up by accretion a sturdy network of treaties entered into in order to accomplish specific tasks efficiently and cheaply. Such a system would be flexible and convenient but not transparent. A measure of public supervision, even if costly, should be provided to enforce accountability. Private activities could then remain within the purview of responsible democratic governments and be made subject to public control as necessary.

Strengthening democracy, both at present and in an enlarged future EU, should become the overriding purpose of the integration process. No theory, scenario, or roadmap will bring about its revival and extension. So long as the EU remained an elite project, which an admiring public was expected to applaud at a distance, the integration phenomenon could be explained theoretically (although not predictably). Both process and outcome, it involved an ongoing contestation between two principles of social organization, market competition and bureaucratic centralism. Each of them had the upper hand at one time or another. Integration was tantamount to a struggle for supremacy between superstate and new-market economy.[13] The effort to organize the European superstate ran the integration process into the ground in the 1990s, delayed the rise of the new market economy, and, by dint of its failure, changed the rules of the game. The future of the integration process now rests with the peoples of Europe. They will determine how it unfolds.

Progress, to use Hayekian phraseology, occurs not by human design but by human action.[14] The truism, which applies normally to the market process, has a broader relevance in our time. It can advance human freedom. Recent history witnesses extraordinary ways that people can serve the cause. The unyielding Polish resistance to Soviet domina-tion eventually drove out a foreign oppressor. An unorganized Swedish electorate, opposed by the entire establishment, voted to stay out of Euroland. The referenda on the proposed constitution were a largely spontaneous popular response to institutional failure. Fighting for politi-cal freedom they had never enjoyed, the frozen multitudes on Kyiv's Independence Square demonstrated that a peaceful people, united in purpose, confident of the justice of their cause, and courageous enough to die for values Europeans too readily take for granted can bring a vicious dictator to heel. The meaning of the Maidan is universal. Love of freedom can also move ordinary men and women elsewhere to do extraordinary things. The lesson should be taken to heart in western Europe when politicians go deaf. It can also become the inspiration of a new Europe of principle.

The EU often claims more credit than it deserves. The North Atlantic Treaty Organization (NATO) – and not the EU – guaranteed peace in western Europe for over a generation. Foreign enterprise and money, along with plenty of hard work – and not the EU – brought Europe to unprecedented levels of prosperity. A desire to be free – and not the accession process – is behind the new democratic revolution taking place in eastern Europe. Unless it can be said, however, that all of these developments would have occurred in the absence of the EU (and its predecessors), one must conclude that the integration process has been postwar Europe's crowning political achievement. To be worth saving, the Brussels institutions must be drastically reformed or, failing that, be replaced with better ones. Unless the politicians are up to the job, Europe's peoples should do it. The EU stands between Europe and a more promising and richer future than imagined. The tribulations of the EU may mark the end of an old era, but they can also herald the beginning of a new one.

Acknowledgments

The author has received help of more kinds and from more persons and organizations than can be appropriately acknowledged in a few lines. He benefited from the support of not one but two major Harvard institutions, the Minda de Gunzburg Center for European Studies (CES), where he was a fellow in 2004–5, and the Harvard Ukrainian Research Institute (HURI) where he has been a senior research fellow since fall 2005. He would like to thank their tireless and helpful staffs as well as their directors, Professors Peter Hall and Michael Flier. The pages of *Design for a New Europe* attest to the heavy intellectual debt I owe both CES and HURI.

Without the release time provided by my parent institution, the University of Missouri/St. Louis, it would have been impossible to write the book. I would at this point like to thank Professors Louis Gerteis (Chair, History Department), Mark Burkholder (Dean, College of Arts and Sciences), Nasser Arshadi (Director, Office of Research Administration), and Joel Glassman, (Director, Center for International Studies [CIS]). Professor Glassman also arranged a study trip to China in summer 2004, which was co-sponsored by the Chinese Academy of Social Science (CASS). He and his staff at CIS have been a source of encouragement and research assistance for many years.

Peter Acsay, Dominic Cummings, Anne Gillingham, Lubomyr Hjada, Robert Kravchuk, Harm Schröder, Roman Szporluk, Marian Tupy, and Tom Zwart all read and commented on portions of the manuscript, as did four anonymous readers for Cambridge University Press. Their help was very welcome. Peter Acsay, Lubko Hajda, and my wife, Barbara, deserve special commendation: each of them patiently listened to the author's book prattle on a daily basis.

He would also like to thank a number of institutions that provided opportunities to discuss the research project at various stages of its development in 2004–2005. At Harvard, they include CES, HURI, the John F. Kennedy School, and the Boston Harvard Club. In Europe, the author had the opportunity to lecture at the universities of Utrecht, Leiden, and Bergen, as well as at a number of think-tanks: the Telders Foundation, the Netherlands Institute for International Affairs, the New Frontiers Foundation, and the Institute for Economic Affairs – the latter two in London. He was also the guest of the Aspen Institute of France, for a special weeklong conference on trans-Atlantic relations.

In China, he held seminars at the State Council, the Ministry of Foreign Affairs, and the Chinese Academy of Social Science. Finally, he had a chance to speak on panels at the annual conventions of both the American Political Science Association and the German Studies Association.

None of the persons or organizations mentioned above can be blamed for the book's remaining shortcomings. They are the fault of the author.

Notes

I. GOVERNANCE

1. "The Tower of Babble: The Curious Cabbalistic Language of Those Who Run the European Union (Charlemagne)," *The Economist*, July 31, 2003.
2. Laurent Cohen-Tanugi, "The End of Europe?" *Foreign Affairs*, November–December 2005.
3. John Gillingham, *European Integration, 1950–2003: Superstate or New Market Economy?* (Cambridge, 2003), 157–164, 228–237, 259–289.
4. Ibid., 303–357; Ian Ward, "A Decade of Europe," Some Reflections on an Aspiration." *Journal of Law and Society* 30, no. 2 (June 2003): 236–257.
5. "The Return Journey: After Five Years of Tussles in Brussels, Romano Prodi Plans His New Mission in Italian Politics," *Financial Times*, October 26, 2004.
6. Commission of the European Communities, "European Governance: A White Paper," July 25, 2001.
7. Commission of the European Communities, "Green Paper: Entrepreneurship in Europe," January 21, 2003.
8. "EU Looking for a New Industrial Policy Slant," *European Report*, February 25, 2004; "Prodi Shortlists Projects for Growth," *Financial Times*, October 17, 2003.
9. "'Mickey Mouse' Forum Lambasted," *Financial Times*, September 2, 2004; "Preparation of the Competitiveness Council of Ministers, Brussels (3 March 2003)," RAPID, February 28, 2003.
10. "An Agenda for a Growing Europe: Making the EU Economic System Deliver," Sapir Report (July 2003); Jean Pisani-Ferry et al., "Europe Must Spend Its Money More Wisely," *Financial Times*, July 29, 2003; "Protests Greet Call for Radical Reforms at EU," *Financial Times*, July 18, 2003; "Call to Scrap CAP and Rethink Structural Policy," *European Report*, July 19, 2003.
11. Jasper Gerard, "Don't Panic – the EU Superstate is Dead," *Sunday Times*, October 17, 2004; "Le retour politique de Romano Prodi en Italie provoque une polemique à Bruxelles," *Le Monde*, November 13, 2003.

12. "Europe's Failing Economy Threatens Political Turmoil," *Sunday Times*, October 17, 2004; Graham Bowley, "A Grim Report on Future Grabs Europe's Attention," *International Herald Tribune*, November 12, 2004.

13. "Frugal Dutch Take the Helm as EU Sails Towards Choppy Waters," *Manchester Guardian Weekly*, July 16–22, 2004; "EU Outlines New Business-Friendly Vision," *EU Business*, February 2, 2005; "Meet the President," *The Economist*, February 17, 2005.

14. "Jubilant Luxembourg Seals Savings Tax Deal with a Kiss: The Grand Duchy is Elated by European Union Concessions to Banking Secrecy," *Financial Times*, January 23, 2003; Joachim Fritz-Vannahe, "M.Euro. Mit Jean-Claude Juncker bekommt die EU einen Ratspräsident, der Europa fast so sehr liebt wie die Bankgeheimnisse," *Die Zeit*, March 2005; "A Turning Point in EU History," *The Guardian*, August 14, 2004; "How Barroso Secured the Reformist Team He Wanted. Old Europe Loses Out," *The Guardian*, August 13, 2004.

15. "In Europe's Name," *The Times*, July 24, 2004.

16. "Barroso Under Pressure to Jettison EU Nominee," *International Herald Tribune*, October 21, 2004; "Barroso's Bombshell," *Spiegel Online*, October 28, 2004.

17. Alisdair Murray, "An Unstable House? Reconstructing the European Commission" (working paper, Centre for European Reform, March 2004).

18. Ibid.; "Fill Eur Boots with Cash," *The Sun*, March 31, 2005; "Interview: Why There's Still Plenty of Work Needed to Turn Europe into a Class Act," *Accountancy Age*, May 27, 2004; "Brussels Accused of Failing to Tackle Fraud: Chief Auditor," *Financial Times*, July 9, 2003; "EU Is Forced to Reveal 'Obscenely High' Salaries," *Daily Telegraph*, June 12, 2005.

19. "EU Wouldn't Listen to Me, Reveals Whistleblower," *Sunday Times*, September 28, 2004; "EU Fraud Office Investigates Aid Diversion to Bombers," *The Independent*, November 27, 2003.

20. Stephen Grey. "Tackling Fraud and Mismanagement in the European Union" (working paper, Centre for European Reform, n.d.); "EU Auditors Blast Budget Failings," *Daily Telegraph*, November 18, 2003; "EU Slow to Recover Misspent Money," EUObserver.com (June 8, 2005).

21. "Auditor Blames Politicians of EC for Waste and Corruption," *Sunday Herald*, August 8, 2003; "A Fragile Financial Future," *The Economist*, August 9, 2003; "Commission Accounting System Still Open to Abuse," *Financial Times*, January 22, 2004.

22. "EU Slow to Recover Misspent Money," EUObserver.com (June 8, 2005); "Olaf Ineffective, Reports Say," EUObserver.com (July 13, 2005).

23. "Kinnock's Shameful Treatment of Whistleblower," *Yorkshire Post*, October 22, 2004; "Do We Really Need Lord Windbag," *Daily Mail*, October 16, 2004; "You Can't Hear the Whistles if You're a Eurocrat," *The Times*, July 11, 2003.

24. "EU Court Whistleblower Sacked," EUObserver.com (July 18, 2003).

25. "Cursed, Spat at, Ignored. The Ordeal of an EU Whistleblower," *Daily Telegraph*, September 29, 2003.

26. "Eurostat Whistleblower Goes to Court to Clear Her Name," *Financial Times*, December 15, 2004; "Brussels Reporter Loses Battle to Protect Sources," *Media Guardian*, April 22, 2005.

27. Tobias Buck, "Was Action Taken Quickly Enough?" *Financial Times*, June 16, 2003.

28. Ibid.

29. Jens-Peter Bonde, "Responsibility and Guilt in the Eurostat Scandal," Bonde.com; *"Officials at European Statistic Agency Caused Diversion of Money for Lavish Dinner, Other Perks"* (Associated Press, September 25, 2003).

30. "Brussels Finally Moves to Quell Critics over Financial Services Scandals at Eurostat," *Financial Times*, July 10, 2003; "EU's Kinnock Widens 'Eurostat' Fraud Probe," AFX.COM (July 17, 2003); "Prodi Dismisses Resignation Calls over EU Fraud Scandal" (Agence France Presse, September 25, 2003); "Letter to Deepen Eurostat Scandal," August 28, 2003; "EU Corruption Body Confirms Alleged Misconduct" (Deutsche Presse-Agentur, September 24, 2003); "Affaire Eurostat: les deputés européens acceptant de temporiser," *Le Monde*, September 27, 2003; "Statisticians Exposed Fiddling with Their Figures," *The Times*, September 26, 2003.

31. "Fraud Politically Correct in the EU?" EUObserver.com (July 18, 2003); Marta Andreasen, "Brussels and a culture of corruption," *The Times*, December 6, 2004; "Kinnock May be First Whistle Blower in Last Act" (Press Association, September 29, 2004); "Suspended Chief Accountant Fears Dismissal for Going Public on Potential Waste and Fraud," *Financial Times*, October 1, 2004.

32. Carl Mortished, "Who Will Have the Last Laugh After Bad EU Joke," *The Times*, June 30, 2004; "Barroso Sets Out Pragmatic Agenda for EU," *Financial Times*, January 27, 2005; "Le plan Barroso pour créer 6 million d'emplois en Europe," *Le Figaro Economique*, February 2, 2005; "Barosso to Focus on Jobs and Growth," *Financial Times*, February 2, 2005; "EU to Outline Business-Friendly Economic Plan" (Agence France Presse, February 2, 2002); "European Social Model Must Be Modernized, Says Barosso," EUObserver.com (December 14, 2004); "Brussels Lays Out Road Map for More Competitive Union," *Lloyd's List*, August 4, 2004; Danuta Hubner, "Europe's Institutions Must Make Lisbon Work," *Financial Times*, January 31, 2005.

33. Allister Heath, "EU Admits Growth and Jobs Reforms Have Failed," *The Business*, January 23, 2005; "Barroso's 'Liberal' Economic Plan Faces Protests," *Financial Times*, January 25, 2005; "The European Commission President Tells George Parker and Andrew Gowers That He Detects a 'New Sense of Urgency' About the Need to Deliver Economic Reforms," *Financial Times*, February 2, 2005.

34. Gillingham, *European Integration, 1950–2003: Superstate or New Market Economy*, (Cambridge University Press, 2003). 250–258, 473–480.

35. Daniel Dombey and Toby Shelley, "Europe's Competition Authorities Used to Strike Fear into Business, but a Series of Defeats is Curtailing Their Powers";

"Monti's Cave-in: A Squalid Deal Has Jeopardized EU Competition Policy," *Financial Times*, February 14, 2003; "Trustbusters on Trial," *Business Week*, October 1, 2003; "Setback for Monti on Mergers Scrutiny," *Financial Times*, October 10, 2003; "Last Stand for Mario Monti? After Earlier Rulings Were Overturned, the EU's Competition Czar is Going After Microsoft with Zeal," *Business Week*, November 17, 2003; "Monti and Microsoft Get Personal," *Financial Times*, September 30, 2004.

36. "Rescuing Alstom: State Aid in Europe," *The Economist*, September 27, 2003; "EU Allows France to Rescue Alstom," *Wall Street Journal*, September 23, 2003; "Neelie Ventures Forth: A New Crusade Against State Aid," *The Economist*, February 3, 2005; "EU States Renege on Promises to Reduce State Aid," *The Times*, April 21, 2005; "Decline in EU State Aid Grinds to a Halt," *Financial Times*, April 19, 2005; "Alstom Turns Gradually Away from Ship of State," *The Business*, April 3, 2005.

37. "Europe's Tough Girl," *Financial Times*, October 2, 2004; "Holland's Iron Lady Defies 'Lies' to Fight for Her EU Job," *Daily Telegraph*, September 29, 2004; "EU's Kroes Puts State Aid Reform at Top of Competition Agenda," AFX.COM (June 6, 2005); "Brussels Can't Seem to Squeeze Government any Further," *Financial Times*, April 19, 2005.

38. Frits Bolkestein, "*Grensverkenningen, Dagboek van een Eurocommissaris*" (Amsterdam, 2005); Gillingham, op. cit., 328, 330, 332, 449, 468–469.

39. "Speech by Frits Bolkestein: Actions Speak Louder than Words," RAPID, November 3, 2003; "Frits Bolkestein Slams Competitiveness Council's Inaction," *European Information Service*, November 11, 2003; Frits Bolkestein, "Company Tax Law Must not Be Made in Court," *Financial Times*, October 21, 2003; "Bolkestein Attacks Disastrous Spat on Euro Rules," EUObserver.com (November 7, 2003); "Bolkestein Slams Ministers for not Honoring Commitments," *European Information Service*, September 24, 2003; "EU Bolkestein Accuses States of Hypocrisy on Lisbon Reforms," *Market News International*, March 2, 2004.

40. Christa Randzio-Plath, "Europe Prepares for a Single Financial Market," *Intereconomics* 39, no. 3 (May–June, 2004); Frits Bolkestein, "Learning the Lessons of the Financial Services Action Plan," RAPID, January 30, 2004; "A Crucial Year for the Single Market," *Financial Times*, January 12, 2004; Testimony of Marc E. Lackritz, President Securities Industry Association, "The European Union's Financial Services Action Plan" (before the House Financial Services Committee, May 22, 2002).

41. New Frontiers Foundation, "Historic Shift in Business Opinion: Large Majorities Reject Euro and Constitution," April 27, 2005; David Lascelles, "The City and the EU: There Must be a Better Way," December 2004; Philip Booth, "Who Should Regulate Financial Institutions?" *Economic Affairs* September 3, 2003; Allister Heath, "Business Turns Against Europe's Single Market," *Knight Ridder Business News*, October 31, 2004; David W. Green, "Harmonization and Integration: Regulation of EU Cross-border Financial Integration" (speech,

November 8, 2002); Financial Services Authority (UK), "After the EU Financial Services Action Plan," September 2004; "A Breath of Fresh Air from Brussels," *eFinancial News*, January 30, 2005.

42. "Services Directive to Break Down Single Market Barriers Tabled," *European Report*, January 14, 2004; "Commission Pushes for Single Market in Services," EUObserver.com (January 14, 2004); "EU Sets Out to Harmonize Legal Rules Across Europe," *Legal Week*, November 13, 2003.

43. "Barroso Insists Pro-Business Reforms Must Go Ahead," *Financial Times*, March 13, 2005; "The Week in Brussels," *Financial Times*, March 13, 2005; "Not at Your Service: The Franco-German Rejection of the Services Directive," *The Economist*, March 10, 2005.

44. "A French Call for the EU to Raise Military Outlays," *International Herald Tribune*, June 10, 2005.

45. "Le Triumphant SNLE" FAS.WMD, (Around the World Web site); "France's Nuclear Weapons: The Current French Arsenal" nuclearweaponrchive.org; Mary Bird Davis, "Nuclear France: Materials and Sites" francenuc.org; Richard North, "The Wrong Side of the Hill: The Secret Realignment of UK Defense Policy with the EU" (Center for Policy Studies, October 2005).

46. "Network-centric Warfare: Revolution or Passing Fad?" *Armada International*, May 2004; David A. Fulgham, "Catch a Wave: Small Communications Sigint Payloads Refined for Combat," *Aviation and Space Technology*, November 8, 2004; David A. Fulgham, "Network Wars," *Aviation and Space Technology*, October 25, 2004; Robert Wall, "Standard-Bearers," *Aviation Week and Space Technology*, October 4, 2004.

47. "European Say Yes! to a Strong Europe in Space," RAPID, June 24, 2003; "Strategic Value of Space Access Emphasized," *Flight International*, March 18, 2003; "Brussels Calls for Genuine Commitment to Space Policy," *Lloyd's List*, March 21, 2003; *"EU Seeks Separate Space Path"* (United Press International, August 22, 2003); "A Giant Leap for the EU," eureferendum.blogspot.com (September 12, 2004); *"Enlarging EU Looks to Ultimate Frontier"* (Agence France Presse, November 11, 2003); "Space: White Paper Recommends Firm European Commitment," *European Information Service*, November 13, 2003; "What's This...Scotch Bloody Mist," eureferendum.blogspot.com (June 8, 2005); "EU Economy: Toward a European Space Program," *EIU ViewsWire*, June 10, 2005.

48. "Chinese Buildup Assessed as Threat to US," *Washington Times*, February 18, 2005.

49. "Retired NATO Generals Blast European Military," *Financial Times*, October 11, 2005.

50. "Hi-tech Weapons Help Europe to Close Military Gap with US," *The Times*, March 2, 2005; "EU Armies Not Up to Bloc's Ambition: Defense Agency," DefenseNews.com (February 15, 2005); "So the Integration Continues...," eureferendum.blogspot.com (April 23, 2005); "New Military Staff HQ in Lille to be Capable of Commanding Multinational 50,000 Man Force," *Financial Times*, September 27, 2003; "A Symbolic Step Toward Real EU Defense," *International*

Herald Tribune, December 23, 2003; "ESDP: The State of Play" (working paper 11, European Policy Center, September 2004); "Divide and Fall," *The Economist*, October 23, 2003; "US, EU Divided on High-Tech Issues," *China Daily*, March 9, 2005.

51. Thomas Pedersen, "Keynote Address: Recent Trends in the Franco-German Relationship," *Annual Review of Common Market Studies* 41 (2003): 13–25; Charles Grant, "Germany's Foreign Policy: What Lessons Can Be Learned from the Schröder Years?" (Centre for European Reform, September 2005).

52. Jean-Pierre Maulny and Burkard Schmitt, "Joining Forces," *Financial Times*, July 16, 2002; "Revamping Fortress Europe," *The Economist*, July 19, 2003; "Getting it Together: Europe's Defense Companies Cannot Go It Alone," *The Economist*, July 20, 2002; "EADS beendet Führungsstreit," *Spiegel Online*, December 17, 2004; "L'Europe unit les forces de ses industriels pour lancer Galileo er défier l'Amerique," *Le Figaro*, June 28, 2005; Leslie Wayne, "US Weapons, Foreign Flavor," *New York Times*, September 27, 2005.

53. Richard North, "Galileo: The Military and Political Dimensions," brugesgroup.com.

54. Allister Heath, "US Threatens to Take Space War to a Third Dimension," *The Business*, November 1, 2004; "Air Force Seeks Bush's Approval for Space Weapons Programs," *New York Times*, May 18, 2005; "New US Weapon Can Jam Enemy Satellites," *The Business*, November 20, 2004; "US Ready to Put Weapons in Space," *The Observer*, November 7, 2004; "Space War – Now We're Jammin'!," *Bulletin of the Atomic Scientists*, March–April 2005; "Bush Seeks Ways to Shut Off Galileo," *The Business*, December 19, 2004; "Where It's at: Galileo and GPS," *The Economist*, January 31, 2004; "US Deploys Satellite Jamming System," *People's Daily Online*, November 1, 2004; "Pentagon Would Attack EU Satellites in Wartime," *The Business*, October 24, 2004; "Pentagon Wants Mini-Killers in Space" Defensetech.org/archives/001144html; "Blair's Contribution to History," eureferendum.blogspot.com (September 25, 2005).

55. "Earth to Galileo: Spread the Word," *The Engineer*; "Who Do They Think They're Kidding?" eureferendum.blogspot.com (November 8, 2004); "Would You Buy a Used Satellite from This Man?" eureferendum.blogspot.com (December 14, 2004); PriceWaterhouseCoopers, "Inception Study to Support the Development of a Business Plan for the Galileo Program," November 20, 2001; North, "Wrong Side," op. cit., 12.

56. "New Row at EC over Funding Conviction of MEP," *Daily Telegraph*, November 20, 2004; "EU Economy: Toward a European Space Program," op. cit.

57. "A Question of Money," eureferendum.blogspot.com (September 25, 2005); "EU Budget: No New Compromise on 2007–13 Funding Before November," *European Report*, September 10, 2005.

58. "Space: White Paper Recommends Firm European Commitment," *European Report*, November 13, 2003.

59. "Chinese Navy Buildup Gives Pentagon New Worries," *New York Times*, April 8, 2005; "China Builds a Stronger, Smaller Military," *Washington Post*, April 12, 2005; "Chinese Nuclear Forces, 2003," *Bulletin of the Atomic Scientists*, November– December 2003; "Transparent It Ain't" (from International Institute of Strategic Studies), eureferendum.blogspot.com (October 27, 2005).

60. "China Prepares to Re-arm with Help from EU," *The Business*, January 16, 2005; "A Bold Move by Paris and China?" *Business Week*, March 29, 2004; "Vice-PM Zeng Peiyan Stresses Sino-European Comprehensive Strategic Partnership," BBC Monitoring, International Reports, November 29, 2004.

61. Martin Walker, "With Friends like Chirac ..." (United Press International, October 13, 2004).

62. "Arms and the EU," *Daily Telegraph*, March 23, 2005; "The EU Feels the Heat on China Embargo," *International Herald Tribune*, March 23, 2005; "In Europe, Public Turns Toward US on China," *International Herald Tribune*, March 25, 2005.

63. "Jiang: Hu's Takeover Natural and Convincing," *China Daily*, September 21, 2004; "Jiang Yields Last Official Title to Hu," *International Herald Tribune*, March 14, 2005; "Japan-China Sub Escapade Raises Hackles," *Spiegel Online*, November 22, 2004; "Unidentified Submarine Trespasses into Japan Waters," *Financial Times*, November 10, 2004; "China Allows More Protests in Shanghai Against Japan," *New York Times*, April 17, 2005; "Thousands Hold Anti-Japan Protests in Eastern China," *Financial Times*, April 16, 2005; "Japan Moving Towards Describing China as Military Threat," AFX News Limited, September 15, 2004.

64. David Howell, "Again a Land of the Rising Sun," *International Herald Tribune*, January 22, 2005; "So Hard to be Friends," *The Economist*, March 23, 2005; "Japan's Rivalry with China is Stirring a Crowded Sea," *New York Times*, September 11, 2005.

65. "Le président Hu Jintao exhorte l'armée chinoise a se 'preparer à un conflit arm," *Le Monde*, March 14, 2005; "China Will Crush Taiwan Independence Moves," *Financial Times*, December 28, 2004; "Own Goal: Has China Blundered," *The Economist*, May 31, 2005.

66. "China's Leader Meets with Taiwan's Opposition," *New York Times*, April 29, 2005; "Sixty Years Later, China's Enemies End their War," *New York Times*, April 30, 2005; "A Step too Far?" (from Xinuanet news agency), eureferendum.blogspot.com (September 20, 2005).

67. "EU Ministers Discuss New European Gender Institute," *European Report*, May 12, 2004; "Commission Floats Plan for New European School of Administration," *European Report*, May 12, 2004; "Pulled Report on Diplomatic Corps Showed Council Divisions," *European Report*, June 22, 2005; "Judicial Training Network Headquarters Inaugurated," *European Report*, October 1, 2005.

68. "European Satellite Navigation Gets off the Ground," *The Times*, December 28, 2008.

69. Alberto Alesina and Roberto Perotti, "The European Union: A Politically Incorrect View" (working report 10342, National Bureau of Economic Research,

March 2004); Giandomenico Majone, "Europe's 'Democratic Deficit': The Question of Standards," *European Law Journal* 4, no. 1 (March 1998): 5–28.

70. Gillingham, op. cit., 120–124; Richard Howarth, "The Common Agricultural Policy," in *The Cost of Europe*, ed. Patrick Minford (Manchester, 1992), 51–83; Elmar Rieger, "The Common Agricultural Policy," in *Policy-Marking in the European Union*, 4th ed., ed. Helen Wallace and William Wallace (Oxford, 2000), 179–210.

71. Gillingham, op. cit., 262f; Dmitri A Sotiropoulos, "Southern European Public Bureaucracies in Comparative Perspective," *West European Politics* 27, no. 3 (May 2004): 405–422; Marta Andreasen, "Brussels and a Culture of Corruption," *The Times*, December 6, 2004; "Report on the Activities Financed from the General Budget," *Official Journal of the European Union*: 155–193.

72. "Free the Strasbourg 626," *The Economist*, February 7, 2004; Alexander Hagelüken, "Europas Dunkelmänner," *Süddeutsche Zeitung*, September 27, 2003; "The European Parliament at Fifty: A View from the Inside," *Journal of Common Market Studies* 41, no. 2 (2003): 253–273.

73. Alesina and Perotti, op. cit.

74. David J. Bailey, "Obfuscation through Integration: Legitimating the 'New' Social Democracy in the European Union," *Journal of Common Market Studies* 43, no. 1 (2005): 13–35.

75. Ibid.; Fritz W. Scharpf, "The European Social Model: Coping with the Challenges of Diversity," *Journal of Common Market Studies* 40, no. 4 (2002): 645–670; Herbert Obinger et al., "Bypasses to a Social Europe? Lessons from Federal Experience," *Journal of European Public Policy* 12, no. 3 (2005).

76. Daniel Hannan, "The Gravy Train Starts Here," *Daily Mai*, August 6, 2004; Daniel Hannan, "What Are We MEPs Good For? Only Sticking Together, It Seems," *Daily Telegraph*, November 28, 2004; "Don't Mention the Allowances," *Daily Telegraph*, April 17, 2004; "It's the Eurocrats Who Really Ride the Gravy Train," *Daily Telegraph*, August 15, 2004; "Bad News from Brussels," *Daily Mail*, August 6, 2004; "The Bottom Line," *The European Foundation*, (from *Le Monde*, June 23, 2005).

77. "Apathy and Protest Mark Historic Vote for European Union's Parliament" (Associated Press, June 14, 2004); "Wins en verlies in uitgebreid Europees Parlement," *NRC Handelsblad*, June 14, 2004; "Euroskeptik Mavericks and Fundamentalists Thrive as Czechs and Poles Stay at Home," *The Independent*, June 15, 2004; "Electorates Use EU to Punish Their Rulers," *The Times*, June 15, 2004; "EU Voters Send a Message: In Historic Elections, Governing Parties are Drubbed," *International Herald Tribune*, June 14, 2004; "Old Order Shaken as 'the Misfits' Gain Ground'," *Daily Telegraph*, June 14, 2004.

78. "Europe Speaks," *The Times*, June 15, 2004; Vernon Bogdanor, "Europe Needs to Connect to the Electorate," *Financial Times*, June 15, 2004; "Leaders Vow to Do More to 'Sell' Benefits of Membership," *Financial Times*, June 15, 2004.

79. Andreas Broscheid and David Coen, "Lobbying Systems in the European Union" (working paper in progress); David Coen, "The European Business Interest and

the Nation State: Large-Firm Lobbying in the European Union and Member States," *International Public Policy* 18, no. 1 (1998): 75–100.

80. David Coen, "Environmental and Business Lobbying Alliances in Europe: Learning from America?" 23pp.; Barbara Gunnell, "In Brussels the Lobbyocracy Rules," *New Statesman*, February 7, 2005.

81. Youri Devuyst, "The European Union's Constitutional Order? Between Community Method and *Ad Hoc* Compromise," *Berkeley Journal of International Law* 18, no. 1 (2000): 1–48.

82. "The EU's Judicial Land Grab," *The Business*, March 6, 2005; Francisco Astenngo, "The Europeanization of the Italian Constitutional Court," *European Integration* 26, no. 2 (June 2004); Martin Howe, "The European Court: the Forgotten Powerhouse Building the European Superstate," *Economic Affairs* 24, no.1 (March 2004); "The EU Stops Here: Germany's Constitutional Court Puts European Integration to the Test," *The Economist*, April 14, 2005; Karen Alter, "*Establishing the Supremacy of European Law: International Rule of Law in Europe*" (Oxford, 2001).

83. Ibid., in passim.

84. "Government by Judges?" *The Economist*, January 17, 2004.

85. Ibid.

86. Alter, op. cit., 208.

87. Gian Luigi Tosato and Ettore Greco, "The EU Constitutional Treaty: How to Deal with the Ratification Bottleneck" (Istituto Affari Internazionali, November 15, 2004).

88. Allister Heath, "Big Brother and the EU Art of Double-speak," *The Business*, June 27, 2004; Ambrose Evans-Pritchard, "The EU Has Had No Real Mandate for This Extraordinary Leap Forward," *Daily Telegraph*, June 19, 2004; David Heathcoat-Amory, "The European Constitution and What it Meant for Britain" (Center for Policy Studies, June 2003); Simon Wolfson, "Vote No to the Constitution. And Save Europe from Itself (Again)," *Daily Telegraph*, October 29, 2004; "A Flawed Document," *The Times*, June 19, 2004; Edward Rothstein, "Europe's Constitution: All Hail the Bureaucracy," *New York Times*, July 5, 2003.

89. The New Frontiers Foundation, "Guide to the Key Questions on the Constitution," 44pp.; "Highlights of New EU Constitution," *EU-business*, January 31, 2005; Stephen G. Breyer, "Europe's Constitution is Welcome, but Very Different from Its US Counterpart," *European Affairs*, Spring 2004; Paul Craig, "Constitutions, Constitutionalism, and the European Union," *European Law Journal* 7, no. 2 (June 2001).

90. The New Frontiers Foundation, "Guide to the Key Questions on the Constitution," 44pp.; Richard Baldwin and Mika Widgren, "Europe's Voting Reform Will Shift Power Balance," *Financial Times*, June 22, 2003; "Treaty Establishing a Constitution for Europe: Main Provisions," *Irish Times*, June 19, 2004.

91. "Draft is Still 90% Intact, Says Giscard," *The Times*, June 22, 2004; "Autocratic Giscard Seeks Compromise," *Financial Times*, June 12, 2003; Hans-Jürgen

Leersch and Andreas Middel, "Empörung über Giscard d'Estaing. Präsidium will übrige Konventsteilnehmer ausschliessen," *Die Welt*, June 5, 2005.

92. 'Where to File It: Europe's Constitutional Convention Has Produced a Lamentable Piece of Work," *The Economist*, June 19, 2003; John Major, "Why We Must Veto This Constitution," *Spectator*, May 24, 2003.

93. John Gillingham, "Economics Eurotrouble: Sweden's Rejection of the European Monetary Union Signals Deep Problems. US Policies May Have to Change if Europe's Economic Stability Wavers," *St. Louis Post-Dispatch*, September 16, 2003.

94. Ibid.

95. "Why Is This Happening?" *The Economist*, October 11, 2003.

96. "Who Killed the Constitution?" *The Economist*, December 20, 2003; "EU Talks on Charter 'Urgent'," *International Herald Tribune*, January 7, 2004.

97. "Back from the Dead: European Union Constitution," *The Economist*, February 7, 2004; "Try, Try Again," *The Economist*, June 10, 2004; "The Battle in Brussels Is over, Now the Fight at Home Begins," *Daily Telegraph*, June 19, 2004; "Squabbles Replace any Celebrations," *Financial Times*, June 19, 2004; "Europe Debate: The Key Issues," *The Independent*, June 18, 2004.

98. "Hardest Part Is yet to Come in Risky Referendums," *The Times*, June 19, 2004,

99. "France Is Self-Destructing Prior to EU Constitution Vote," *New York Times*, May 25, 2005; Charles Bremner, "On the Spot: France's Referendum Campaign," *The Times*, May 19, 2005; Tim King, "Franco-Euro Flap," *Prospect*, May 2005; "Französischer Poker," *Frankfurter Allgemeine Zeitung*, May 25, 2005; "Brussels Looks into the Abyss as 'No' Vote Surges: Turkey Has Most Reason to Fear Referendum Results," May 25, 2005.

100. "Waiting for the Guillotine to Fall," *The Guardian*, May 26, 2005; "Barroso Appeals to Europeans over Constitution," EUObserver.com (September 23, 2004); "The Ultra-Liberal Socialist Constitution: French Socialists Join British Conservatives in Disliking the EU Constitution," *The Economist*, December 16, 2004; "Chirac Toils to Stem Tide of 'No' Voters in EU Constitution Poll," *The Times*, April 13, 2005.

101. "Burger geen inspraak met referendum Grondwet," *Het Financieele Dagblad*, April 11, 2005; *"Europese grondwet Frans 'nee' brengt Nederlands referendum in gevaar"* (Algemeen Nederlands Persbureau, April 5, 2005); John Gillingham, *Europe at the Tipping Point*, (Den Haag), 2005; "Wary Dutch Prepare to Strike Fatal Blow," *The Times*, April 16, 2005; "Staying Dutch: Why the People of the Netherlands May Well Say 'Nee'," *The Times*, April 28, 2005.

2. ECONOMICS

1. "The World Economy: Still Gushing Forth," *The Economist*, February 3, 2005; Mickey D. Levy, "Ending Europe's Underperformance," *Cato Journal* 24, no. 1–2 (2004): 71; "Facing the Challenge: The Lisbon Strategy for Growth and

Employment," Wim Kok Report, (November 2004), 15; Jeffrey Sachs, *The End of Poverty: Economic Possibilities for Our Time* (New York, 2005); (U.S.) National Intelligence Council, *Mapping the Global Future* (December 2004), 32; "A New World Economy," *Business Week* August 22, 2005; EU Commission, "The Economy for the Euro Area, the European Union, and the Candidate Countries in 2004–2006," no. 2 (2005); "Upbeat Signs Hold Caution for the Future," *New York Times*, November 30, 2005.

2. Gordon Brown, "Global Europe: Full-Employment Europe" (HM Treasury, October 2005); "Why It Is Make or Break for European Social Reform," *Financial Times*, October 13, 2005.

3. Wolfgang Munchau, "Why Economic Renewal Will Have to Wait," *Financial Times*, October 17, 2005; "Power Vacuum in West (Leading Comment)," *The Business*, October 16, 2005; John Gillingham, "Neither Superstate nor New Market Economy: The Impact of the European Constitutional Referenda – A Preliminary Appraisal," *Merkurious: Utrecht Journal of International and European Law 22*, no. 61 (December 2005).

4. Anatole Kaletsky, "A Hard Truth: The Future of the Single Currency Is Now Far Beyond Our Ken," *The Times*, August 25, 2005.

5. Vaclav Klaus, "Why Europe Must Reject Centralization," *Financial Times*, August 30, 2005; John Gillingham, "Europe's Crisis Is Britain's Chance" (NFF/CASS lecture, October 27, 2004).

6. "Immigration Can Help Europe Support Its Ageing Population: EU Commissioner Calls for Changes to Labor Market," *Financial Times*, October 25, 2005.

7. Ibid.

8. "Facing the Challenge," op. cit., *Mapping the Global Future*, op. cit.; Allister Heath, "Europe Must Reform or Die, the CIA Warns," *The Business*, January 16, 2005; "Social Affairs Commissioner Eschews 'Typology' Debate," *European Report*, October 8, 2005; Gunther Zichy, "Die Risikogesellschaft – Ein vernachlässigtes Konzept in der europäischen Stagnationsdiskussion, Institut für Technikfolgen-Abschätzung" (ITA-03–02, November 2003).

9. Martin Wolf, *Why Globalization Works* (New Haven, 2004), 105.

10. Martin Wolf, "A Bigger Playing Field Needs New Goalposts," *Financial Times*, October 20, 2005.

11. Andrew Scobell and Larry Wortzell, ed., *Civil-Military Change in China: Elites, Institutes, and Ideas after the 16th Party Congress* (Strategic Studies Institute, U.S. Army War College, September 2004), 1–377; "China and the Key to Asian Peace," *The Economist*, March 23, 2005; Joseph Kahn, "China's Leader, Ex-Rival at Side, Solidify Power," *New York Times*, September 25, 2005; "Wrong Definition of Democracy in China," October 21, 2005; Yonglin Zhang, "China Goes Global" (The Foreign Policy Centre, April 2005).

12. Evan S. Medeiros and Taylor M. Fravel, "China's New Diplomacy," *Foreign Affairs* 82, no. 6 (November–December 2003); "China and the Key to Asian Peace,"

The Economist, March 23, 2005; "China Leaps to Third Place in Global Trade," *The Business*, November 21, 2004; "Top 10 Trade Partners of China's Mainland," *Business Daily Update*, July 22, 2004; John Burton, Victor Mallet and Richard McGregor, " A New Sphere of Influence," *Financial Times*, 9 December 2005.

13. Allister Heath, "Jobs Threat as Europe falls down League Table," *The Business*, December 4, 2005.

14. *Mapping the Global Future*, op. cit.; "The BRICs and Global Markets: Crude, Cars, and Capital" (working paper Goldman Sachs Global Economics, October 14, 2004).

15. "Hu's in Charge," *The Economist*, August 18, 2005.

16. "China and India," *Business Week* 22, no. 29 (August 2005, special section): 50–144; "New Enhanced Powers Leave Hu Free to Focus on Macro-Economic Reform," *Financial Times*, September 23, 2004.

17. Martin Jacques, "The End of the West. Europe Is No Longer the Center of the World – The Future Belongs to Asia," *The Guardian*, December 4, 2003; John Gillingham "Column: De Europese Unie: de Aziatische uitdaging," *Knack*, February 25–March 2, 2004.

18. John Gillingham, *European Integration, 1950–2003: Superstate or New Market Economy* (Cambridge, 2003), 269–278; Bernard Connoly and John Whittaker, "What Will Happen to the Euro," *Economic Affairs* 23, no. 1 (March 2003); International Monetary Fund, *World Economic Outlook*, (September 2004), 33–66; Allister Heath, "Disunited States of Europe," *The Business*, February 20, 2005; "Single Currency but Many Prices," *The Times*, October 13, 2004; Peter Hoeller, Claude Giorno, and Christine de la Maisonneuve, "One Money, One Cycle? Making Monetary Union a Smoother Ride" (working paper, Organization for Economic Cooperation and Development, September 1, 2004); Manuele Croci, "Integration of the Euro Equity Markets: An Empirical Analysis" (unpublished manuscript, October 2004), 3, 19.

19. Ruth Lea, "Under the Eurozone Calm, Tensions Are Building Up," *Daily Telegraph*, October 24, 2005.

20. Gillingham, *European Integration*, op. cit., in passim.

21. Heather Stewart, "Fudge Making Europe Sickly," *The Observer*, December 19, 2004; Allister Heath, "Disunited States of Europe," *The Business*, February 20, 2005; "The Euro May Have a Single Currency, but It Still Has Many Different Real Exchange Rates," *The Economist*, February 17, 2005; "Rate Rise Is Opposed in Europe," *New York Times*, November 25, 2005.

22. Gillingham, *European Integration*, op. cit., 180–221.

23. Carl Gjersem, "Financial Market Integration in the Euro Area" (working paper, Organization for Economic Cooperation and Development, October 8, 2003); Jean-Pierre Casey and Karel Lannoo, "Time to Enforce Europe's Financial Market," *Financial Times*, February 16, 2005; Marco Pagano and Ernst-Ludwig von Thadden, "The European Bond Markets Under EMU" (unpublished paper, November 2004), 29; Hossein Askari and Joydeep Chatterjee, "The Euro and

Financial Market Integration," *Journal of Common Market Studies* 43, no. 1 (2005): 1–11.

24. Christopher Fildes, "Don't Bet on the Grand Project – Europe Would be Better Off Without It," *Spectator*, January 31, 2004; Ambrose Evans-Pritchard, "EU Economists Look in Vain for Benefits of Euro," *Daily Telegraph*, October 9, 2004; "Europe Crippled by Single Currency," September 23, 2004; Henrik Enderlein, "Break It, Don't Fix It!," *Journal of Common Market Studies* 42, no. 4 (2004): 1039–1047; "Hungary Deficit May Delay Adoption of Euro," *Financial Times*, September 30, 2005.

25. Joachim Fels, "Euroland's Fiscal Morass" (Morgan Stanley Equity Research, February 27, 2004); "Europe: Fiscal Surveillance in EMU – Allow Markets to Do the Job" (Morgan Stanley Global Forum, March 25, 2005); "One Money but Many Nations," www.stanford.edu/-wacziarg/articles (December 22, 1997); Ambrose Evans-Pritchard, "Eurozone May Have a Reverse Gear," *Daily Telegraph*, February 7, 2004; Bertrand Benoit and George Parker, "Budget Deficits Heighten Sense of Crisis in EU," *Financial Times*, September 29, 2005.

26. Martin Feldstein, "The Euro and the Stability Pact" (working paper 11249, National Bureau of Economic Research, March 2005); Wayne Walker, Europe's Cheerful Voice (United Press International, February 16, 2004).

27. Vincenzo Guzzo, "Maybe More Growth, Certainly Less Stability" (Morgan Stanley Global Forum, March 23, 2005); Vincenzo Guzzo and Eric Cheney, "Revamped Stability Pact: Easier Said than Done" (Morgan Stanley Global Forum, September 3, 2004).

28. Anatole Kaletsky, "Stability Pact Reform Stirs New Misgivings," *The Times*, September 7, 2004; "Stability Pact's Ghost Will Return to Haunt EU," *The Times*, July 20, 2004; Wolfgang Munchau, "Six Lessons in Five Years of Monetary Union," *Financial Times*, January 5, 2004; "A Treaty to Undermine the Eurozone," *Financial Times*, December 1, 2003.

29. Sheila Dawson, "Could the EU Constitution "No" Vote Herald a Breakup?" *Reuters*, April 13, 2005; "France and Germany Smash Stability Pact," *Daily Telegraph*, November 26, 2003; "Stability or Instability," *The Economist*, November 6, 2003; "Most Countries Flouting the Rules," BBC News, September 11, 2003; "Don't Mention the Euro. The Euro's Deficit Rules Are Apparently Unenforceable yet Unchangeable," *The Economist*, October 2, 2003; "Dollar-Style Management Urged for Euro," *Financial Times*, September 17, 2004; Eric Chaney, "Fiscal Alert" (Morgan Stanley Global Forum, March 14, 2005).

30. Wolfgang Munchau. "Is the Euro forever?" *Financial Times*, June 8, 2005.

31. "Exit 'Fess,' The Credit-Rating Consequences of Quitting the Single Currency," *The Economist*, November 24, 2005.

32. Pierre A. Messerlin, "A European Economic Agenda After the NO Votes" (35th Wincott Lecture, October 3, 2003).

33. House of Lords, European Union Committee, "Future Financing of the European Union, Report with Evidence," March 9, 2005.

34. Dominique Strauss-Kahn, *Building a Political Europe: 50 Proposals for Tomorrow's Europe* (April 2004), 1–65; Dominique Strauss-Kahn, "A Sense of Common Interest for the Eurozone," *Financial Times*, September 14, 2004; "Strauss-Kahn Jumps on a Soapbox," *Financial Times*, May 19, 2004; "Strauss-Kahn Urges 'Political Theatre' to Assure Future of EU," *European Report*, May 20, 2004.

35. "Building a Political Europe," op. cit.

36. "How to Blow a Trillion Euros (Charlemagne)," *The Economist*, January 24, 2004.

37. Christopher Haskins, "CAP Can Reshape the EU Budget," *CER Bulletin*, no. 44 (October–November 2005).

38. Oxford Economic Forecasting, *Trade Liberalization and CAP Reform in the EU* (October 2005), 3; "Future Financing of the European Union," op. cit., 21–26.

39. David Kernonen, Jorge Nunez Ferrer, and Andraes Schneider, "The EU Budget Process and International Trade Liberalization" (working paper, Centre for European Policy Studies [CEPS], October 2005).

40. Gillingham, *European Integration*, in passim.

41. "Future Financing," ibid., 26–32; Richard North, "Why Nobody ever Does Anything About Brussels' Great Financial Scandal," *The Business*, November 20, 2005.

42. Ibid., 32–34.

43. "Decision of the EP and of the Council Concerning the Seventh Framework Program ... (2007–2013): Building the Europe of Knowledge," April 6, 2005, 1–47; "7th Framework Program Geared Towards Efficiency," *European Environment*, April 14, 2005; "Expert Group Identifies 23 Priority Infrastructures," *European Report*, April 13, 2005; Jeffrey Matsu, "Unlocking the Growth Behind R&D" (Morgan Stanley Global Forum, September 26, 2005).

44. "EU Falls Behind in Research," *Financial Times*, October 23, 2005; "R&D Spending Falls Further Behind Target," *Financial Times*, October 24, 2005; "EU Accounts Still Riddled with Fraud and Error, Say Auditors," *The Times*, November 16, 2005.

45. Tamim Bayoumi, Douglas Laxton, and Paolo Pesenti, "Benefits and Spillovers of Greater Competition in Europe," Federal Reserve Bank of New York, Staff Report No. 182 (April 2004); European Commission (Enterprise Publications), "European Competitiveness Report 2004" (November 8, 2004), 1–358.

46. "Brussels Originates 80 Percent of New Laws Passed in Europe," *The Business*, May 8, 2005; "Snoring While a Superstate Emerges? (Charlemagne)," *The Economist*, May 10, 2003; "Bonfire of the Diktats Sputters into Life as Brussels Lights the First Match," *The Times*, November 25, 2004; "This Time It's Serious, Say Ministers in Renewed Onslaught on Red Tape in EU," *The Times*, December 7, 2004; "Financial Executives Say Growing Burden of Regulation Is Biggest Risk Facing Banks," *Financial Times*, February 21, 2005; Mark A Pollack, "The End of Creeping Competence? EU Policy-Making Since Maastricht," *Journal of Common Market Studies* 38, no. 3 (September 2000): 519–538; "Euro-Politician Wants

Hands-off Commission," *The Lawyer*, October 20, 2003; George Parker, "Brussels Moves to Slay Image of 'Bureaucratic Monster'," *Financial Times*, October 26, 2005.

47. "Politicians as Technologists," *Printed Circuit Design and Manufacture* 21, no. 1 (November 2004); Angela Lagomasini and Henry Miller, "REACH and Risk," Tech Central Station Web site (August 2, 2005); Noelle Eckley and Henrik Selin, "All Talk, Little Action: Precaution and the European Chemicals Regulation," *Journal of European Public Policy* 11, no. 1 (February 2004): 78–105; "No Thanks, We're European. A Piece of European Legislation That Will Affect Industry Across the World," *The Economist*, November 24, 2005.

48. Eckley and Selin, op. cit., 99; "Chemical Industry Skeptical of Value of EU's R&D Policy," *Chemical Market Reporter*, October 4, 2004; Angela Lagomasini, "Europe's Global REACH: Costly for the World, Suicidal for Europe" (Institut Heyek, November 2005); "Deal on Chemical Register Proposal," November 10, 2005.

49. World Economic Forum, "Global Competitiveness Report 2005–2006," September 2005; John Rossant, "How Europe Could Grow Again," *Business Week*, November 17, 2003; "Putting up Walls," *Business Week*, December 30, 2002; Nigel Grimwald and Isabelle Joumard, "Tax Systems in European Union Countries," *OECD Economic Studies*, 2002; "Developments in the Economies of the European Union," *Annual Review of Common Market Studies* 42 (2004): 169–185; Oliver Blanchard, "The Economic Future of Europe" (working paper, National Bureau of Economic Research, February 2004); Jean-Philippe Cotis, "Population Aging: Aging Will Make It Hard for Governments to Deal with Mounting Financial Pressures," *OECD Observer*, September 2003; Jens Lundgaard, "Competition and Efficiency in Publicly Funded Services," *OECD Economic Studies*, 2004; Francisco Daveri, "The New Economy in Europe" (working paper, Università Bocconi, April 3, 2002); Raghuram G. Rajan and Luigi Zingales, "Banks and Markets: The Changing Character of European Finance" (paper prepared for 2nd ECB Banking Conference, January 2003); European Commission, "The Economic Costs of Non-Lisbon," March 2003; EFN Report, "The Euro Area and the Lisbon Strategy," 2004.

50. Andre Sapir, "Globalization and the Reform of European Social Models" (Bruegel Policy Brief, October 2002).

51. Douglas Alexander, "Europe in a Global Age" (The Foreign Policy Centre, October 2005).

52. Anatole Kaletsky, "The People of Europe Have Voted for Paralysis – and Perhaps Slow Obliteration," *The Times*, October 13, 2005.

53. Herbert Kitschelt and Wolfgang Streeck, "From Stability to Stagnation: Germany at the Beginning of the Twenty-first Century," *West European Politics* 26, no. 14 (2003); Charley Jeffery and William E Paterson, "Germany and European Integration: a Shifting of Tectonic Plates," *West European Politics* 26, no. 4

(October 2003); Patrick Jenkins, James Mackintosh, and Richard Milne, "Shield for Corporate Germany or a Family Affair? V W and Porsche Close Ranks," *Financial Times*, September 27, 2005.

54. "Germany Faces Five Years of Stagnation," *Daily Telegraph*, October 6, 2004; "If Not Now, When?" *The Economist*, April 28, 2005; "Odd European Out," *The Economist*, February 21, 2004; "Germany: the Case for Reform," *OECD Observer*, May 2003; "How to Pep Up Germany's Economy," *The Economist*, May 8, 2004; "Bad Schools Red Tape and the Dole – Germany Today," *The Business*, September 19, 2004; "Mit Bildung können arme Laender Reich warden," *Die Zeit*, 2004, 39; "House Prices Still Falling," FAZ.NET (March 4, 2005); "5216 Millionen arbeitslos," ZDFheute.de (March 1, 2005); Floyd Norris, "A Bright Spot in Germany's Economy Seems to be Fading," *New York Times*, September 17, 2005; Floyd Norris, "U.S. Still Firmly on the Down Side of the Charts," *New York Times*, November 12, 2005.

55. Stephen J. Sylvia, "Reinventing the German Economy," AICGS Policy Report No. 8 (August 2003); "Sturm und Drang," *Forbes*, July 26, 2002.

56. Adam S. Posen, "Germany," *International Economy* 17, no. 4 (Fall 2003).

57. Wolfgang Streek and Christine Trampusch, "Economic Reform and the Political Economy of the German Welfare State," Working Paper, MPIfG (February 2005), 2; Eswar S. Prasad, "The Unbearable Stability of the German Wage Structure: Evidence and Interpretation," Staff Papers No. 51 (IMF, 2004), 2.

58. Stephen Liebfried and Herbert Obinger, "The State of the Welfare State: German Social Policy between Macroeconomic Retrenchment and Microeconomic Recalibration," *West European Politics* 26, no. 4 (October 2003).

59. Wolfgang Streeck and Anke Hassel, "The Crumbling Pillars of Social Partnership," *Western European Politics* 26, no. 4 (October 2003).

60. "For Years Germany Did Not Trust Private Equity. Now There Is a Flood of Deals," *Financial Times*, January 14, 2005; "Germany's Surprising Economy," *The Economist*, August 18, 2005; "Abhaengig vom Rest der Welt," *Die Zeit*, January 2005.

61. John Gillingham, *European Integration*, op. cit., (Cambridge, 2003), 395.

62. Ibid., 395–399.

63. "Schröder Quitting Party Post, Citing Need to Pursue Reform," *New York Times*, February 7, 2004; *"Main Points of German Reform Package"* (Agence France Presse, December 19, 2003); "Unpopular Reforms Were a Necessity" (Interview with Gerhard Schröder), *Financial Times*, February 26, 2004; "A Resigning Matter," *The Economist*, February 14, 2004; "Schröder und Gewerkschaften auf Konfliktkurs," *Financial Times (Deutschland)*, March 2, 2004.

64. "German Unemployment Hits Postwar High," *Guardian Unlimited*, March 31, 2005; "Confidence Dives in Europe's Economy," *Financial Times*, March 31, 2005; "German Joblessness Rises as Benefits are Reduced," *New York Times*, February 3, 2005.

65. "Top Parties Are Losing Supporters," *Frankfurter Allgemeine Zeitung* (English Edition), October 1, 2004; "Slow Implosion. The Sad State of the Ruling Party," *The Economist*, November 20, 2003; "The Great Disintegration Act," *Spiegel Online*, October 22, 2004; "Pride in the Fatherland," *Spiegel Online*, December 8, 2004; "Christlish-demokratische Verunsicherung," *Die Zeit*, 2004, 52.

66. "Germany's Election: Let the Battle Commence," *The Economist*, August 18, 2005; "German Voters Rebuff Main Parties," *Financial Times*, September 20, 2004; "Landtagswahlen. Die Erosion der politischen Mitte," FAZ.Net (September 20, 2004); "Schröder's Surprise," *The Economist*, May 28, 2005; "German Leader Gambles in Call for Early Election," *New York Times*, May 25, 2005.

67. "German Unions Under Attack as Jobs Disappear," *The Business*, October 24, 2004; "Union Leader Retires Early in Feud Fallout," *New York Times*, July 22, 2004; "A German Union Takes Stock," *New York Times*, July 9, 2003; "Heavy Metal: Jürgen Peters sah sich schön als Chef der IG Metall," *Die Welt*, July 5, 2003; "Germany's Arthur Scargill," *The Economist*, December 29, 2004.

68. "Deutsche Bank Denies Reports That Its Chief Will Quit if Faced with New Fraud Trial," *New York Times*, May 20, 2005. "Bogus Backlash: Attacks by a Leading German Politician on Investors Have Been Hysterical and Misguided," *The Economist*, May 5, 2005; "Locust, Pocus," *The Economist*, May 5, 2005; "New Accusations Against Deutsche Bank Boss," *Frankfurter Allgemeine Zeitung* (English Edition), April 9, 2004; "The Trials of Josef Ackermann," *Fortune*, January 26, 2004; Wolfgang Munchau, "Market Economies in the Dock in Germany," *Financial Times*, January 26, 2004; "Germany's Fat Cats on Trial," *The Economist*, September 25, 2003; "Ackermann to Face Retrial, *Financial Times*, 22 December 2005.

69. "The Federal Knot," *The Economist*, March 23, 2005; "Jeder für sich. Keiner für alle. Die Reform des Föderalismus scheiterte an dem, was sie beseitigen sollte: Am Egoismus von Bund und Ländern," *Die Zeit*, 2004, 53; "What's Paralyzing Reform: the Opposition's Grip on the Upper House is Blocking Any Action on the Economy," *Business Week*, November 17, 2003.

70. "Das Projekt ist tot," *Spiegel Online*, January 15, 2005; Fritz W. Scharpf, "Der deutsche Föderalismus – reformbedürftig oder reformierbar?" Working Paper, MPIfG (May 2004), 2; "Untangling the System," *The Economist*, November 6, 2003; "Müntefering und Stoiber erklären Reform für gescheitert," *Spiegel Online*, December 17, 2004.

71. "Russia and Germany to Seal Dollars 5 billion Gas Pipeline Agreement," *Financial Times*, September 7, 2005.

72. "Schröder Adamant on Chinese Embargo," *International Herald Tribune*, April 1, 2005; "The Big Business Chancellor," *Spiegel Online*, December 13, 2004; "Schröder Ready to Fight Parliament over China," FAZ.NET (April 1, 2005); "Gerhard's Comrade," *Spiegel Online*, December 8, 2004.

73. "Juggernaut Wal-Mart Goes Slow in Germany," *The Business*, September 26, 2004; "Die letzte Runde beginnt," *Die Welt*, July 26, 2003.

74. Analole Kaletsky, "Germany Risks Japanese-Style Lost Decade," *The Times*, November 14, 2005; "German Coalition Opts for Dose of Fiscal Probity," *Financial Times*, November 14, 2005.

75. Jorgen Beyer and Martin Hopner, "The Disintegration of Organized Capitalism: German Corporate Governance in the 1990s," *West European Politics* 26, no. 4 (October 2003); "La crise du modèle social allemande: un défi europeen," *Le Monde*, January 4, 2005; "Wir brauchen Überzeugungstäter" (Interview with Hans-Werner Sinn), *Die Welt*, June 4, 2005.

76. John Henley, "Milestone for the President Who Mirrors His People," *The Guardian*, March 14, 2005.

77. Nicolas Baverez, "Chirac Vendetta Is Hurting France," *EIU Viewswire*, July 27, 2004; "Chirac Gives Countrymen Plenty to Talk About," *International Herald Tribune*, January 7, 2005; Floyd Norris, "Europe's Excessive Economic Gloom," *International Herald Tribune*, July 23, 2004.

78. "Jacques Chirac and the Politics of the Past," *The Economist*, January 13, 2005; (Editorial), *The Business*, November 12, 2005.

79. Perry Anderson, "Dégringolade," *London Review of Books*, September 2, 2004.

80. Perry Anderson, "Union Sucrée," *London Review of Books*, September 23, 2004, in passim.

81. "To Have and to Hold," *The Economist*, November 14, 2002; "It Has to Happen but Will It?" *The Economist*, April 24, 2003; "Testing Raffarin's Resolve," *The Economist*, June 3, 2003; Martin Rhodes and David Natali, "France's Dialog of the Deaf over Pensions," *Financial Times*, June 12 2003; "Jacques Chirac – First," *The Economist*, January 17, 2004.

82. Robert Graham, "The French Presidential System Established Under De Gaulle Lacks Checks and Balances and Is Ill-Suited to the Needs of Modern Democracy," *Financial Times*, September 1, 2004.

83. Stein Ringen, "Why *Le Monde* Should Toughen Up Its Act" *The Times*, August 29, 2003.

84. "Allegations of Vote-Rigging Haunt Chirac," *The Guardian*, November 20, 2004; "Tarnished Glory," *The Economist*, November 14, 2002; "Schwarze kassen und Firmenspenden," *Handelsblatt*, January 17, 2005; "Sleaze Trial Swirls Around Chirac," *The Guardian*, March 21, 2005; "Reflections on Things Past: Jacques Chirac's Future Plans Are Upset by the Conviction of His One-Time Protege, Alain Juppé," *The Economist*, February 5, 2004.

85. "France in the Dock as Bad Boy of Europe," *The Guardian*, May 31, 2004.

86. John Rossant, "The Pernicious Rise of Core Europe," *Business Week*, May 10, 2004.

87. "Europe Likely to Approve French Aid for Company," *New York Times*, August 28, 2004; "Side Effects of Dehecq's Beautiful Deal," *The Guardian*, April 27, 2004.

88. "France's Public Sector: They Love It," *The Economist*, May 24, 2001; "Coming Home to Roost," *The Economist*, June 27, 2002; "The Last State Mammoth in France Faces Its Extinction," *The Business*, September 12, 2004; "Paris Cedes

Control of Telephone Company," *International Herald Tribune*, September 2, 2004; Stefan Thies and Tracy McNicoll, "Close the Door." *Newsweek*, November 7, 2005.

89. "Mythos des Erlöseres: Nicolas lässt sich zum König der französischen Konservativen krönen," *Die Zeit*, 2004, 49; "Chirac Feels the Heat as His Former Protege Goes on the Offensive," *Sunday Telegraph*, June 20, 2004; "Nicolas Sarkozy and the Reform of France," *EIU ViewsWire*, July 19, 2004.

90. "French Must Work Harder, Says Study," *The Business*, October 17, 2004; "Paris Urged to Reform Labor Market," *Financial Times*, October 19, 2004; "Sarkozy Leaves Mixed Legacy Behind as He Sets Out to Win the Presidency," *The Business*, November 21, 2002; "Does France's Master Pragmatist Have a Head for Figures?" *The Economist*, April 15, 2005; "Sarkozy Talks Up the Notion of Cooperation: French Finance Minister's Plan for EADS-Style Franco-German Alliance May Have Ulterior Motive," *Lloyd's List*, October 26, 2004; "Sarkozy Defends French Backing for Alstom," *The Guardian*, November 10, 2004.

91. John Carlin, "Hail Berlusconi!," *The Observer*, January 18, 2004; Ulrich Ladurner, "Ein Thron für König Silvio I.," *Die Zeit*, 2003, 27; Jane Kramer, "All He Surveys: Silvio Berlusconi Liked Italy so much He Bought the Country," *New Yorker*, November 10, 2003; "From Parma to Milan: Berlusconi's Long Trail of Gaffes," *The Times*, July 3, 2003; "The Strange Cases of Silvio Berlusconi," *The Economist*, November 24, 2005.

92. "The Eurozone's Sickest Patient," *Business Week*, June 6, 2005.

93. "Political Jitters Raise Notion of Euro's End," *Wall Street Journal*, June 2005; "The Real Sick Man of Europe," *The Economist*, May 19, 2003; "A Test of Credibility," *Financial Times*, June 9, 2005; David Natali and Martin Rhodes, "Berlusconi Has Failed to Heed the Lesson of History," *Financial Times*, October 24, 2003.

94. "Italian Reforms in Jeopardy as Berlusconi Cuts Cause Strike," *The Business*, December 5, 2004.; "Eine Million Italiener auf der Strasse," *Spiegel Online*, November 30, 2004; "Five Public Grievances That Could Spell End for Italy's Great Survivor," *The Times*, April 21, 2005.

95. Perry Anderson, "Land Without Prejudice," *London Review of Books*, March 2, 2002.

96. Ibid.

97. "Berlusconi and the Failure of Forza Italia," *The Business*, May 1, 2005; "La dolce vita sours for Italy's new poor," *The Guardian*, December 28, 2004; "An Italian Lesson for Europe," *The Observer*, September 26, 2004; "Twinges of Foreboding," *The Economist*, April 7, 2005; "Berlusconi Planning Radical Tax Cuts in Bid to Boost Flagging Popularity," *The Business*, May 16, 2004; "Gloom Could Ruin Rome's Budget Plans," *Business Week*, July 12, 2004; "You Can't Win, Why Italian Politics Is Impossible," *The Economist*, February 24, 2005.

98. Gillingham *European Integration*, op. cit., 336–374; "Structurally Unsound. So Easy to Pinpoint What Is Wrong, so Hard to Put It Right," *The Economist*, November 24, 2005.

99. "Business in Italy: In Need of Repair," *The Economist*, May 19, 2005.

100. "Protectionism Is on EU's Agenda," *Wall Street Journal*, August 22, 2003; "Italy: Review" (Janet Matthews Information Service, October 20, 2003); "The Gatekeeper: The European Commission Tells Italy to Open Up Its Banking Market," *The Economist*, February 17, 2005; "HVB Close to Approving UNICredito Takeover," *Financial Times*, October 25, 2005.

101. "Spilt Milk: The Fallout from Parmelat May Be Costly," *The Economist*, February 5, 2004; "Italy: The Land of Bilk and Money," *Fortune*, January 26, 2004; "To Err Is Human," *The Economist*, July 24, 2004.

102. Desmond Lachman, "Italy in Argentina's Shadow," Tech Central Station Web site (August 1, 2005); Anatole Kaletsky, "A Hard Truth: The Future of the Single Currency Is Beyond Our Ken," *The Times*, August 25, 2005; "Berlusconi Blames Inflation on the Euro" (Deutsche Presse-Agentur, January 23, 2004).

103. "The Next Target?" *The Economist*, July 14, 2005; "Mafia Infiltration of the Banking System," *The Economist*, July 14, 2005; "Pleas to Pope from God's Banker Revealed as Murder Trial Begins," *The Times*, October 6, 2005;

104. "The Fiat Heir, the Transsexual and a Sordid Backstreet Drugs Overdose," *The Times*, October 12, 2005; "Italians Dismayed at Berlusconi's Low-Key Response to Slaying," *Financial Times*, October 22, 2005.

105. "Berlusconi Wins Re-Jig of Italy's Voting Laws," *Financial Times*, October 13, 2005; "Parties Pull Together as Poll Campaign Kicks Off," *Financial Times*, October 20, 2006; "Silvio Berlusconi's Parliamentary Games," *Spiegel Online*, October 21, 2005; "More Ballots, More Bullets. While Deepening Italy's Democracy, the Primaries Showed a Dark Side too," *The Economist*, October 20, 2005.

106. "Italians Find That Breaking Up with Fazio Is Hard to Do," *Financial Times*, September 26, 2005; "Fazio's Folly," *The Economist*, November 24, 2005.

107. Alberto Alesina and Luigi Zingales, "Italy's Fazio Problem Is a Symptom of Its Perverse Bank System," *Financial Times*, September 28, 2005; "Another Year, Another Scandal," *The Economist*, August 4, 2005; "Italian Bank Governor Snubbed," *Financial Times*, October 19, 2005.

108. "Dutch Win May Not Clear Way for More Deals," *Financial Times*, November 8, 2005; "Exit Sinasalco, Scandalized," *The Economist*, September 22, 2005; "Market Fiddles While Rome Burns," *Daily Telegraph*, September 23, 2005; "Siniscalpo," *Financial Times*, September 23, 2005; "Fazio Shamed out of Office," *The Economist*, December 20, 2005.

109. Anatole Kaletsky, "Italy Wonders if It's Time to Cut and Run," *The Times*, August 8, 2005; "ECB Targets Its Problem Nations," *Financial Times*.

110. "Hedge Funds Bet on Italy Leaving Euro," *The Guardian*, November 10, 2005.

111. Kaletsky, op. cit.

112. Ibid.; "Some Countries Better Off Leaving Eurozone, Leading Bank Says," EUObserver.com (July 12, 2005).

113. Ivan Miklos, "Europe Must Look Within for Ways to Compete," *Financial Times*, March 23, 2005; "Reaping the European Harvest: Central Europe," *The Economist*, January 8, 2005.

114. "The Flat Tax Revolution," *The Economist*, April 14, 2005; Marian L. Tupy, "EU Enlargement: Costs, Benefits, and Strategies for Central and Eastern European Countries," Policy Analysis No. 489 (CATO, September 18, 2003), 1–19; "East Meets West" Tech Central Station Web site (September 15, 2005).

115. Alina Mungiu-Pippidi, "Enlargement and Democracy Progress," in *Democratization in the European Neighborhood*, Michael Evans (Brussels, 2005), 28; Gillingham, *European Integration*, op. cit., 410–445; David R. Cameron, "The Challenges of Accession," *East European Politics and Society* 17, no. 1 (2003): 24–41; ibid., Stephen Holmes, "A European *Doppelstaat*," 107–118; ibid., Anna Grzymala-Busse and Abby Innes, "Great Expectations: The EU and Domestic Political Competition in East Central Europe," 64–73; ibid., Lazlo Brust and David Atark, "Who Counts? Supranational Norms and Societal Needs", 74–82; Sean Hanley, "From Neo-Liberalism to National Interests: Ideology, Strategy, and Party Development in the Euroskepticism of the Czech Right," *East European Politics and Societies* 18, no. 3: 513–548; ibid., Kristi Raik, *EU Accession of Central and Eastern European Countries: Democracy and Integration as Conflicting Logics*, 567–594; Roger Schoenmann, "Captains or Pirates? State-Business Relations in Post-Socialist Poland," *East European Politics and Societies* 19, no. 1: 40–75.

116. Mingiu-Pippidi, op. cit., 18

117. Ibid., 27.

118. Ibid., 23; Marian Tupy, "Slovakia and the Euro: No Need to Rush In" (Conservative Institute of M.R. Stefanik, June 2005).

119. *"Tax Revolution Takes Hold in Central Europe"* (Deutsche Presse Agentur, March 4, 2004); "Turbulent Times for Social Democrats in Central Europe," *Financial Times*, May 10, 2005; Michael Kapoor, "Eastern Europe Countries Destined to be Poor Partners in Union." *The Business*, October 31, 2004; "Why Europe, Inc. Is Jumping Ship, Its Booming Multinationals See More Profits in Newer, Less Sclerotic Economies," *Business Week*, January 10, 2005.

3. INNOVATION

1. "Research and Innovation: New Reports Reveal Deterioration in European Performance" (European Information Service, October 28, 2003).

2. Philip S. Anton, et al., *The Global Technology Revolution. Bio/Nano/Materials Trends and their Synergies with Information Technology by 2015* (RAND, National Defense Research Institute, 2001).

3. Ibid., 25–31.

4. Ibid., 1; "Climbing the Helical Staircase," *The Economist*, March 27, 2003.

5. Lynne G. Zucker and Michael R. Darby, "Socio-Economic Impact of Nanoscale Science: Initial Results and Nanobank" (working paper 11181, NBER, March 2005).

6. Ibid., 3.

7. Ibid., 16.

8. "Inside Washington," *Feedstuffs*, March 31, 2003.

9. Dick Taverns, "Safety Quacks," Steve Davies, *Prospect*, March 25, 2004; review of *The Gifts of Athena: Historical Origins of the Knowledge Economy*, by Joel Mokyr, *International Affairs*, September 3, 2003, 59.

10. Francis Fukuyama and Caroline S. Wagner, "Information and Biological Revolutions: Global Governance Challenges – Summary of a Study Group," RAND, 1999; John Krebs, "Seeds of Hope," *New Scientist*, August 5, 2000.

11. "Genetically Modified Food Items Are Common but Little Noticed," *Wall Street Journal*, March 24, 2005.

12. Robert Paarlberg, "Reinvigorating Genetically Modified Crops," *Issues in Science and Technology* (Spring 2003): 87–93.

13. Lawrence A. Kogan, "Exporting Europe's Protectionism," *National Interest* (Fall 2004): 91; Derek Burke, "The Dead Hand of Regulation," *Biologist*, no. 2 (2004): 51, 63; Klaus Amann, "Report Looks at Biotech's Impact on Biodiversity," *Feedstuffs*, July 7, 2003; "Genetically Modified Weaklings. GM Crops Are Less Weed-like Than Weedy," *The Economist*, February 8, 2001; "Study Finds No GM Corn in Mexico," *Crop Biotech Update* (August 12, 2005); "In a Stew: The Latest Research Suggests That, Even for Europeans, GM Food Is Safe," *The Economist*, July 24, 2003; Jonathan Reich, "Will Frankenfood Save the Planet?" *Atlantic Monthly*, October 2003.

14. "Sour Taste: Britons Don't Want Scientists Meddling with Their Crop. It's Official," *The Economist*, September 2003; "Knowledge of Foods Remains Low, Opinions on Food Safety Still Split," *Feedstuffs*, September 22, 2003; "Agricultural Biotech Faces Backlash in Europe," *Science* (July 8, 1998): 768; "Genetically Modified Food," *The Economist*, April 3, 2003; "Blech," *The Economist*, January 13, 2000.

15. "Genetic Food Fight," *Wall Street Journal*, May 15, 2003; Rodney W., Nichols, "Biotech on the Farm," *Science* (July–August 2000).

16. "Danger at the Manger," *The Economist*, August 14, 2003.

17. Peters, Pringle, *Food, Inc Mendel to Monsanto – The Promises and Perils of the Biotech Harvest* (NY, 2003), 144–151; Robert Anderson, "Thought for Food," *Natural History*, October 2003.

18. "Genetically Modified Company," *The Economist*, August 15, 2002.

19. Pringle, op. cit., in passim.; Graham T. T. and Molitor, "Food and Agriculture in the 21st Century," *Futurist*, September–October 2003, 40f.; "Man and Superman," *The Economist*, March 27, 2003.

20. Pringle, op. cit. in passim.; "Planting a Seed," *The Economist*, March 27, 2003.

21. "A Happy Ending: Crops Genetically Engineered to Produce Sterile Seeds Have Been Roundly Condemned. Michael Le Page Thinks Critics Are Missing the Point," *New Scientist*, February 16, 2005; "Corn Cuts Contamination," *Des Moines Register*, July 17, 2005; "How to Distinguish GM Crops from Space," *Food Production Daily*, May 7, 2005.

22. "Taking the Fear Out of 'Genetically Modified'," *Business Week*, July 5, 2004.

23. "EU's New Biotech-Crop Laws May Raise, Not Lower Barriers," *Wall Street Journal*, January 20, 2004; "Butterfly Balls. Genetically Modified Maize Is Not That Bad for Monarchs," *The Economist*, September 20, 2001; "Trade Trouble Ahead," *The Economist*, January 13, 2005; "The GM Gamble," *The Economist*, May 15, 2003; Kym Anderson et al., "Implications of Genetically Modified Food Technology Policies for Sub-Saharan Africa," Working Paper 3411 (World Bank Policy Research, September 2004), 3.

24. Paarlberg, op. cit.; Roger Bate, "The European Union's Confused Position on GM Food," *Economic Affairs* 23, no. 1 (March 2003): 58; "EU's New Biotech Crop Laws May Raise, Not Lower, Barriers," *Wall Street Journal*, January 20, 2004.

25. "More Trouble Ahead; GM Food and Trade," *The Economist*, July 5, 2003; Henry Miller, "A Rational Approach to Labeling Biotech-Derived Foods," *Science* (May 28, 1999); "Europe to Allow GM Foods with "Farm to Fork Labels," *Christian Science Monitor*, July 3, 2003.

26. "US Fury at EU Rules," *New Scientist*, December 7, 2002; "One Cotton-Pickin' Mess," *Forbes*, October 14, 2002.

27. "European Food Safety Agency Takes One more Step Closer to Reality," *Lancet*, December 15, 2001.

28. "Food Safety: European Authority Can Start Work Following Appointment of Scientists," *European Report*, May 10, 2003; "The Self-Inflicted Wound of EU Biotech Rules," *International Herald Tribune*, July 2, 2004; "EU Passes Labeling and Tracking Laws for GM Foods," *Chemical Week*, July 30–August 8, 2003.

29. "Genetic Engineering: European Network of GMO Laboratories Launched" (European Information Service, December 6, 2002). "EU Aide Suggests Labeling Products," *Washington Times*, October 19, 2003.

30. "Food Safety: Accession State Food Establishments Almost Ready," *Europe Agri*, April 16, 2004.

31. Martin Callanan. "We're Watching What You Eat!" Tech Central Station Web site (April 19, 2005); Christopher Booker, "Disease Control: SARS Gives the EU a Chance to Extend its Powers," *Daily Telegraph*, July 27, 2003; September 29, 2001; "Life Sciences and Biotechnology – As Strategy for Europe: Progress Report and Future Orientations," March 5, 2003.

32. "More Trouble Ahead; GM Food and Trade," *The Economist*, July 5, 2003; "Trans-Atlantic GMO Trade War Delayed," EUObserver.com (August 27, 2004).

33. Norman E. Borlaug, "Science vs. Hysteria: Responsible Biotechnology Is Not the Enemy – Starvation Is," *Engineering and Technology for a Sustainable World* (July 2003): 29; "Put Down the Genetically Modified Tomatoes: It's No Time to Pick a Trade Fight over Biotech Foes," *Legal Times*, September 1, 2003; Norman E. Borlaug, "Science vs. Hysteria," *Wall Street Journal*, January 22, 2003.

34. Paarlberg, op. cit.

35. Ibid.
36. Nigel Purvis, "Building a Transatlantic Biotech Partnership," *Issues in Science and Technology* 21, no. 1 (Fall 2004): 67; "Grain Traders 'Deathly Afraid' of Cartegena Biosafety Protocol," *Pesticide and Toxic Chemical News*, March 3, 2003; "EU Parliament Moves Toward Implementing Cartegna Protocol," *Pesticide and Toxic Chemical News*, June 9, 2003; "Cartegena Ratification Will Strengthen EU Position," *Agra Europe*, June 6, 2003; Grant E. Isaac and William A. Kerr, "Genetically Modified Organisms at the World Trade Organization: A Harvest of Trouble," *Journal of World Trade* 37, no. 16 (December 2003): 1083–1096.
37. "New European Group Lobbies for Support," *Science* (July 7, 2000); "European Commission Finds Severe Drop in Biotech Research," *Pesticide and Toxic Chemical News*, Marcy 31, 2003.
38. "EU Should Not Fall Behind in Biotech, Says Fischler," *European Report*; "Fall in Biotech Investment Worries EU," *Manufacturing Chemist*, May 2003; "Commission Calls on EU Member States to Intensify Efforts in Life Sciences and Biology," RAPID, March 5, 2003; "EU Warns Biotech Sector in Europe under Danger from Lack of Funding, Public Opposition"(Associated Press, March 5, 2003).
39. "EU Schedules Meeting on Biotech Co-existence," *Pesticide and Toxic Chemical News*, April 14, 2003; "Biotechnology Commission Wants States to Take Responsibility for Coexistence," *European Report*, April 26, 2003.
40. "Farm Council: Member States Split over Co-existence Approach to GMOs," *European Report*, May 29, 2003; "EC Says No Biotech Approvals Until the Fall," *Pesticide and Toxic Chemical News*, March 17, 2003; "Biotechnology: National Rules to Resolve Problem of Co-existence," *European Report*, March 8, 2003; "Co-existence Issue Bedevils EU Biotech Debate," *Pesticide and Toxic Chemical News*, June 2, 2003; "Farm Council Members Deeply Divided on Co-existence," *European Report*, October 1, 2003; "Unable to Reach an Agreement, Ministers Close Debate on Stem Cells," *European Report*, December 6, 2003; eureferendum.blogspot.com (October 18, 2005).
41. "No Decision on GM Maize," *European Chemical News*, March 14–20, 2005; "Biotech-Based Food Products at a Crossroads," *Chemical Market Reporter*, July 5–12, 2004; "Stalking Genetically Modified Corn," *Spiegel Online*, April 18, 2005.
42. "EU Approves Biotech Feed Products" (Western Farm Press, May 7, 2005); "Stalking Genetically Modified Corn," *Spiegel Online*, April 18, 2005.
43. "Modifying GM Food Perception" (Interview with Simon Barber), *Technology Review*, December 2004, 78f.; Julian Gardner, "Light Fading on European GM Crops," *Crops*, April 23, 2005.
44. "Tough Times for European Biotech," *New Scientist*, July 28, 2003.
45. "German Biotechs Blast Government GMO Stance," *Chemical Market Reporter*, September 1, 2003; "German Biotechs Return to Health," *Financial Times*, September 2, 2004; "Grey Clouds Gather in the Clear Blue Skies Above Bavaria's High Technology Heartland," *Financial Times*, September 17, 2003.

46. EuropaBio, "Biotechnology in Europe: 2005 Comparative Study," passim.; EuropaBio, "Biotechnology in Europe Poorly Financed Says Study," April 13, 2005; "L'Amerique se construit un quasi monopole dans les biotechnologies," *Le Monde*, April 22, 2005.

47. "Biotechnology in Europe," op. cit., 22f.; "Serono: Big Ambitions in Biotech," *Chemical Week*, April 27, 2005.

48. "These Biotechs Need Time to Ripen. A Rush to the IPO Market in Europe Won't Do the Industry Any Good," *Business Week*, July 12, 2004.

49. "Britain Is in the Vanguard of Genetics Research and the Government Wants to Put This to Practical Use," *The Economist*, June 26, 2003; "Biotech Sector Loses to US Rivals," *Financial Times*, July 16, 2004; "Trailblazing in Europe," *New Scientist*, March 19, 2005; "Suppliers to Bioscience Group Get Protection," *The Times*, November 18, 2003; Syngenta Shuts GM Labs in UK," *Financial Times*, July 1, 2004; "The Grim Reaper," *The Economist*, August 22, 2002; "Extremists Are Driving Drug Forms Out of UK," *The Times*, April 6, 2005; "Britain May Pay Price for Botched GM Debate," *Daily Telegraph*, April 16, 2005; *"UK Government: New Study Demonstrates Why Companies Cannot Ignore Research and Development"* (M2 Presswire, October 20, 2003); "Will the Harsh Financial Climate Shape European Biotech into a Fitter, More Competitive Sector?" *New Scientist*, November 6, 2004; "Crops Giant Retreats from Europe Ahead of GM Report," *The Independent*, October 16, 2003.

50. Biotechnology: Recommendations on Co-existence of GM and Non-GM Crops," *European Report*, July 26, 2003; "Biotechnology: Council Calls for Strategy to be Applied Soon," *European Report*, September 24, 2004.

51. "Spain: Trade Policy Monitoring. Biotechnology Coexistence Update 2005 (SP5023)" (USDA Foreign Agricultural Service); "EU Officials Nix Efforts to Lift Biotech Bans," Pew Initiative on Food and Biotechnology (news summary), June 27, 2005; Lene Johansen, "Crop Circles," Tech Central Station Web site (August 3, 2005).

52. "EU Acts to Block Flood of GM Food from East," *Manchester Guardian Weekly*, February 19–25, 2004.

53. European Academies Science Council, "Genomics and Crop Plant Science in Europe (Vesentini Study)," May 2004, in passim.

54. Ibid., 11.

55. Ibid., 1, 11–15.

56. Ibid., 7.

57. Ibid., 25.

58. John Gillingham, *European Integration, 1950–2003: Superstate or New Market Economy?* (Cambridge, 2003), 246f.; "UK May Play Smaller Part in Europe's Next Framework," *Times Higher Education Supplement*, March 28, 2003; Philippe Busquin, "Respect Research and Watch Economy Boom," *Times Educational Supplement*, February 24, 2004; "EU Research Commissioners Urges More

Research Efforts to Close Gap," BBC Monitoring International Reports, November 26, 2003; "Education: Higher: Show Me the Money" *The Guardian*, December 9, 2003.

59. "Brain Drain Robbing Europe of Its Brightest Young Scientists," *Lancet*, June 28, 2003; "Europe Strives to Keep Its Scientists at Home," *Chronicle of Higher Education*, September 3, 2004.

60. "Research: Calls for Proposals for the Sixth Framework Program," *European Report*, December 18, 2002; "Higher Education: Get Rich Slowly," *The Guardian*, April 15, 2003.

61. "EU Research Analyses: The New 'Development Model' for Europe," RAPID, March 14, 2003.

62. "Food Safety: EU Backing for 24 Projects and Research Networks," *Europe Agri*, September 12, 2003.

63. "Commission Supports Visionary Research," RAPID, European Commission, February 27, 2003.

64. "EU Urged to Create European Research Council," *Lancet*, October 18, 2003.

65. "Verheugen Backs Biotech as an EU Economic Backbone," *European Report*, April 16, 2005; "European Union's Proposed $87 Billion Research Budget Gets Mixed Reviews from Academe," *Chronicle of Higher Education*, April 8, 2005; "Seventh Framework Program Geared Toward Efficiency," *Europe Environment*, April 14, 2005.

66. "EC to Pay for Defense Research," *Flight International*, October 14, 2003; "Brussels Earmarks Euro 65 Million for a 'Security Culture'," *Irish Times*, October 8, 2003; "European Industry Leaders and EU Policymakers Meet to Plan for Security Research," RAPID, October 7, 2003; "Euro Plan Needs Cash to Take Off," *Times Educational Supplement*, October 10, 2003; "Commission Launches Debate on Future European Policy," January 25, 2003; Philippe Busquin, "Past, Present, Future: A New Nuclear Generation," *Nuclear Engineering International*, March 31, 2003; "Philippe Busquin Calls for Military Research Income under EU Wing," *European Report*, September 17, 2003.

67. "Research: Commission Keen to Double Budget for 2007–2013 Period," *European Report*, February 14, 2004.

68. "Le système francais d'enseignement superieur handicape la croissance, selon des deux chercheurs," *Le Monde*, January 21, 2004; "Europe's Failing Universities" (United Press International, September 27, 2004); Collapsing Ivory Towers," *Spiegel Online*, November 17, 2004; "Europe's Troubled Universities," *The Economist*, September 25, 2004; Ivar Blieklie, "The University, State, and Civil Society," *Higher Education in Europe* 24, no. 4 (1999): 509–526; Hans N. Weiler, "States, Markets, University Funding," *Compare: A Journal of Comparative Education* 30, no. 3 (October 2000): 7f.; "Survey: Universities," *The Economist*, September 8, 2005.

69. "Bund will Hochschulreform anschieben," *Die Welt*, November 3, 2004; "EU Commissioner's 9.5 Billion Pounds," *Times Education Supplement*, January 21, 2003; "Der Bologna-Prozess. Noch nichts davon gehört?" *Die Welt*, April 15, 2004; "Does Europe Need Its Own Technology Institute?" *International Herald Tribune*, March 10, 2005; "European Universities Unite to Welcome Super Scholars," *International Herald Tribune*, February 17, 2004; "Standard CVs for EU Graduates," *Times Higher Educational Supplement*, June 11, 2004; "Commission Hosts Seminars and Awards Label to Promote the Bologna Process," *European Report*, November 20, 2004.

70. "The Issue Is Explained," *The Times*, September 30, 2003; "In sechs Semestern durchs Studium jagen," *Spiegel Online*, April 6, 2005; "Students in Europe Line Up to Fight Tuition," *International Herald Tribune*, February 5, 2004; "Quatre etudiants jugent avec sevérité la mise en place de Bologne," *Le Temps*, August 27, 2004.; "Titres academiques: la révolution 'bachelor-master,'" *Le Temps*, October 21, 2004.

71. "Commission Launches Debate on How to Turn European Universities into a World Class Reference," RAPID, February 5, 2005; "Bachelor ist nicht gleich Bachelor," *Frankfurter Allgemeine Zeitung*, January 24, 2004.

72. "Deutscher Bechelor in Amerika nicht anerkannt," *Frankfurter Allgemeine Zeitung*, October 13, 2004.

73. "*Students from EU Countries Choose British Universities*" (Deutsche Presse Agentur, July 15, 2004); "Rules and Regulations Will just Cramp Our Style," *Times Higher Education Supplement*, August 1, 2003; "Reforms Spark French Student Strikes," *The Independent*, November 21, 2003; "Le CNRS, dans la douleur, à se reformer," *Le Monde*, April 22, 2005; "Europe: Lower Education; German Universities," *The Economist*, January 10, 2004.

74. "Introduction: Looking Back: Higher Education Reform in Germany," *German Policy Studies* 2, no. 3 (July 2002).

75. "Pay or Decay; Universities," *The Economist*, January 24, 2004.

76. "Can Foreigners Prop Them Up?" *The Economist*, January 13, 2005.

77. Ibid.

78. Ibid.

79. "US Style Universities for Germany," *Science* (June 19): 1098; "Hessen scheitert mit Eilantrag in Karlsruhe," *Spiegel Online*, April 12, 2005.

80. ISAA Briefs No. 32–2004: Executive Summary, "Global Status of Commercialized Biotech/GMJ Crops: 2004; "Sometimes a Bumper Crop Is Too Much of a Good Thing," *New York Times*, December 8, 2005.

81. "Enjoying Prosperity and Some Powerful Friends," *Financial Times*, December 9, 2003.

82. "In Search of Global Recognition," *Financial Times*, December 9, 2003.

83. "Galvanized into Action," *Financial Times*, December 9, 2003; C. Ford Runge, "The Global Diffusion of Plant Biotechnology: International Adoption and

Research in 2004" (report prepared for the Council on Biotechnology Information, Washington, DC, December, 2004).

84. "Learning to Love Lula," *Fortune*, January 11, 2004; "Watch Out for Brazil," *Weekly Times* (Australia), April 13, 2005; "South American Seeks to Fill the World's Table," *New York Times*, December 12, 2004.

85. Antonio Salazar Pessoa Brandhao et al., "Agricultural Growth in the Period 1999–2004, Outbursts in Soybeans Area and Environmental Impacts in Brazil" (Texto Para Discussao 1062, January 2005).

86. "GM Crops in Brazil: An Amber Light for Agri-Business," *The Economist*, October 2, 2003; "Genetically Modified Food and the Poor," *New York Times*, October 12, 2003; "One Cotton-picken' Mess," *Forbes*, October 14, 2002; "Argentine Soy Exports Are Up, But Monsanto Is Not Amused," *New York Times*, January 21, 2004.

87. "Scientists Push GM Rice Commercialization," *Business Daily Update*, June 8, 2004.

88. "Government Determined to Develop Biotech," *China Daily*, August 26, 2004.

89. Need note

90. "China's Problem with 'Anti-Pest' Rice," *New York Times*, April 16, 2005; "Illicit Rice Trade Endangers Biotech Barriers," *The Guardian*, June 14, 2005; "Ripe for Research: GM Is One of Many Ways to Fix Poor Countries' Agricultural Problems," *The Economist*, July 24, 2003; "A Sweet Rice Pudding: Genetically Modified Rice Seems to Deliver the Goods," April 2, 2005.

91. Kym Anderson et al., "Genetically Modified Rice Adoption: Implications for Welfare and Poverty Alleviation" (working paper 3380, World Bank Policy Research, August 2004); "Reaping the Rewards: China's Genetically Modified Crops Are Proving a Success," *New Scientist*, February 2, 2002.

92. "China Develops Fast in Life Science Research," *Business Daily* Update, February 3, 2004; "Biotech's Yin and Yang," *The Economist*, December 12, 2002; 'Country Report: China," *Scientific American*, June 27, 2005.

93. Ibid.

94. "Asian Biotech Sector Making Rapid Strides," *Business Line*, June 9, 2004.

95. "Crouching Tigers, Hidden Dragons," *Business Week*, August 22–29, 2005.

96. "Monsanto Tries to Win Indian Farmers over to Biotechnology Seeds," *St. Louis Post-Dispatch*, June 20, 2004; "Biotechnology: A Blueprint for a Policy," *India Business Insight*, July 2, 2004; "India Companies Bank on Biotechnology to Transform Nation's Agricultural Sector," June 20, 2004.

97. "India Right on Track," *Indian Express Online*, June 9, 2004; "The Growing Bio Marketplace," *Businessline*, July 29, 2004; "Biotech Industry Grows in India," *Research Technology Management*, July–August 2003.

98. "India Forsakes World Trade Organization for Bilateral Free Trade Deals with Its Neighbors," *Financial Times*, October 16, 2002; "Monsanto Withdraws from Europe, May Target India," *Times of India*, October 17, 2003.

99. Kym Anderson "Implications of Genetically Modified Food: Technology Policies for Sub-Saharan Africa," (Paper, Conference on African Development, Somerset, South Africa, 13–15 October, 2004).

100. "Genetic Engineering Industry Extols Virtues of Biotechnology for Developing Nations," *European Report*, February 1, 2003; "What Green Revolution? Genetically Modified Food Could Save Lives in Africa," *Newsweek International*, September 15, 2003.

101. "Scientists Here Hope Bioengineered Crop Will Help African Food Supply," *St. Louis Post-Dispatch*, December 20, 2003; "Gates Foundation Gives $25 Million to Bring Nutrients to World's Poor," St. Louis Post-Dispatch October 20, 2003.

102. "Sea of Dreams. Genetically Modified Microbes Will Lead to a Revolution in Industrial Biotechnology," *The Economist*, April 29, 2994; "Big Science: Wallflower No More," *Genomics and Proteomics*, January 1, 2004; "Ego Men," *The Economist*, January 24, 2004; "Human Genome Project Completed," *Washington Post*, October 22, 2003; "Life Story," *The Economist*, June 29, 2000.

103. "Political Science: Stem Cell Researchers Hope for a $3 bn Boost from US Voters," *Financial Times*, October 28, 2004; "Threat to Global Lead in Stem Cell Research," *Financial Times*, November 4, 2004; "Baywatch," *New Scientist*, March 12, 2005; "R&D's Scientist of the Year Uses His Strong Interdisciplinary Research Background to Build New Paradigms for Future Academic Growth," *R&D*, November 1, 2004; "St. Louis Waits for Bio-Belt to Bloom," *Chicago Tribune*, May 1, 2005; "Coming Up on the Inside," *New Scientist*, March 5, 2005; "Other Communities Try to Attract Biotech Firms from Research Triangle Area," *Knight Ridder Tribune Business News*, March 31, 2005.

104. "Genetically Modified Food: A Taste of the Future," *MedSurg Nursing*, October 2002; "Rice Genome Fully Mapped," *Washington Post*, August 11, 2005; "Dry Season," *The Economist*, November 2, 2000; "Biotech Farming for Development," *OECD Observer*, May 2003; "Monsanto Sows Seeds of Food Revolution in Europe," *Financial Times*, March 19, 2002; "Why the New Genetically Modified Crop Is Really Quite Conventional," *New Scientist*, March 19, 2005; "Biotech Foods: No Going Back Now?" (Interview with Anthony Shelton), *Business Week*, August, 14, 2003; "Biting the Hand That Feeds You (Interview with Mark van Montague)," *Eurinvest*, Summer 2003.

105. "Reinventing Yesterday: Biotech's Biggest Use May Be to Rebuild Basic Industry," May 27, 2003; "Personalized Biotech Cures," *Pharmaceutical Technology Europe*, November 2004; "The Quest for Custom Cures," *Fortune*, February 5, 2005; "Biotech's Billion Dollar Breakthrough: A Technology called RNAi," *Fortune*, May 26, 2003; "Repairing the Engines of Life," *Business Week*, May 24, 2004; "The Race to Computerize Biology," *The Economist*, December 12, 2002.; "Man and Superman: Biology Could Transform Humanity – Provided Humanity Wished to Be Transformed," *The Economist*, May 27, 2003; "A Voyage of Discovery," *The Economist*, May 27, 2003.

106. "Boomtown Wannabes," *American Demographics*, February 1, 2024; "Industrial Biotech, Biology Lessons," *Engineer*, January 28, 2005; "Future Role for Non-Food Crops?" *Farmers Guardian*, April 15, 2005.

107. "In Brazil, Sugarcane Growers Become Fuel Farmers," May 24, 2005; "Saving the World in Comfort," *The Economist*, March 2, 2003; "Non-Food GM: The Men in White Coats Are Winning, Slowly," *The Economist*, October 7, 2004; Ted C. Fishman, "Cars That Guzzle Gas," *New York Times*, September 25, 2005; "A Tank Full of Sugar," *The Economist*, September 22, 2005.

108. "Environmentalists Want Ethanol to End America's Oil Addiction," *Top Producer*, April 11, 2005; "Stirrings in the Corn Fields," *The Economist*, May 12, 2005; "Is Turning Crops into Fuels and Chemicals the Next Big Thing," *The Economist*, April 7, 2004; "Ethanol Growth Factor: Plan Capacity Is Set to Swell Again in 2005," *Farm Journal*, March 10, 2005.

109. "Beyond the Nanohype," *The Economist*, March 13, 2003; "Nanotechnology Promises Great Benefits, but Safeguards Will Be Essential," *The Economist*, December 29, 2004; "Barred and Larthed," *The Economist*, February 3, 2005; "Nanotech: Is Small Scary?" *Bulletin of Atomic Scientists* (September–October, 2004); "Nanomaterials Move Up a Notch," *The Economist*, September 4, 2003; "Viral Workhorses," *Scientific American*, September 2, 2002. "Nanoparticles Pass Muster as Vectors for Gene Therapy," *Scientific American*, July 26, 2005.

110. "Raising the Stakes," *European Chemical News*, February 9–15, 2004; "Looking at Big Picture in the Nanotech Revolution," *Insurance Day*, June 22, 2005; "Towards a European Strategy for Nanotechnology" (Mondaq Business Briefing, December 7, 2004); "Think-Tank Calls for Debate on Nanotechnology to Avert Backlash," *Financial Times*, September 1, 2004; "Can We Overcome Nano-Fear," *Financial Times*, January 15, 2004; "Nanotech Won't Suffer GM Fate," *Times Higher Education Supplement*, June 27, 2003; "Nanofunding: The Next Big Thing Isn't Small at All," www.laserfocusworld.com (August 2005).

4. DEMOCRACY

1. André Sapir, "Globalization and the Reform of the European Social Model," Breughel Policy Brief 02 (October 2005).

2. "Blair's European Speech," *The Gurdian* June 23, 2005; "Tony Blair's Big Speech to Euro MPs Was (a) Visionary, Modernizing Performance," news.bbc.co.uk; "EU Must Reform or It Will Risk Massive Failure, Blair Warns," *The Times*, June 24, 2005.

3. "UKIP Hails Blair's Europe Speech," news.bbc.co.uk; "Blair Speech Stirs EU Debate," newsvote.bbc.co.uk; "European Press Reviews," newsvote.bbc.co.uk; "A Wind of Change Starts to Blow Across Europe," *The Times*, June 25, 2005.

4. "Blair May Walk into a Trap of His Own Making," *The Times*, June 24, 2005; "Astride His Horse, Our Hero Fights for Pro-European Euroskepticism," *The Times*, June 21, 2005.

5. Ibid.; Quentin Peel, "Blair Must Not Neglect the Big Debates on Europe," *Financial Times*, September 29, 2005; Gordon Brown, "Global Europe: Full-Employment Europe" (HM Treasury, October 2005).

6. "Tony Blair's Speech in Full," *Daily Telegraph*, September 27, 2005; "Four More Bold Years, Vows Blair," *The Times*, September 28, 2005.

7. Timothy Garton Ash, "Can Hampton Court Be Europe's Great House of Easement?" *The Guardian*, October 27, 2005; Martin Wolf, "A Bigger Playing Field Needs New Goal Posts," *Financial Times*, October 20, 2005.

8. Wolfgang Munchau, "Why Economic Renewal Will Have to Wait," *Financial Times*, October 17, 2005; "The Error of Germany's Budget Plan," *Financial Times*, November 7, 2005.

9. "French Taxes. When Cuts Aren't Kind Enough," *The Economist*, September 22, 2005; "French Flunk Labour Reforms," *The Guardian*, September 8, 2005; "French Facing Tidal Wave of Protest," *The Guardian*, August 25, 2005; "Chirac's Illness Sets Off Power Battle," *The Guardian*, September 10, 2005; "Can Thierry Breton Get France Working Again?" *International Herald Tribune*, September 28, 2005; "French Protests Raise Pressure on PM," *Financial Times*, October 5, 2005; "Envoys Admit Taking Oil for Payoffs," *The Times*, October 14, 2005; *"Thales Denies Corruption, Selling Arms to Saddam"* (Associated Press, September 26, 2005); "President's Men Tumble in Chirac Sleaze Trial," *Daily Telegraph*, October 27, 2005; "Quatre ans de proson requis contre l'ex depute europeene Marchiani," *Le Figaro*, October 11, 2005.

10. "A Very One-Sided Transatlantic Love Affair," *The Times*, October 1, 2005.

11. Andreas Noll, "Europe's Lost Future," www.dw-world.de; Charles Bremner, "Social Divide and Unrest: An Epitaph for Chirac's Presidency." *The Times*, November 9, 2005.

12. Catherine Field, "The Sickness in France's Heart," *International Herald Tribune*, November 8, 2005.

13. "Unions Urge End to Strike That Halted French Trains," *New York Times*, November 23, 2005; "Rail Workers Strike over 'Sell-Off' Plan," *The Times*, November 21, 2005; "To the Barricades," *The Economist*, November 24, 2005.

14. David Brooks, "Gangsta, in French," *New York Times*, November 10, 2005; "After the Riot," *The Economist*, December 14, 2005.

15. "Immigrant Polygamy Is a Factor in French Unrest, a Gaullist Says," *New York Times*, November 12, 2005; Charles Bremner, "Curfews in France, Too Little, Too Late," *The Times*, November 8, 2005; John Thornhill, "The Impetuous Gambler. The Interior Minister's Reckless Streak Could Cost Him the Prize He Covets Most," *Financial Times*, November 12, 2005.

16. "De Villepin Under attack for Imposing Riot Law," *Financial Times*, November 8, 2005.

17. "Target of Critics, Chirac Says He'll Discuss French Rest After Order Prevails," *New York Times*, November 11, 2005.

18. "France Fights Back with More Police and Curfews," *The Times*, November 8, 2005; "While Paris Burns," *New York Times*, November 8, 2005; "Chirac Says France Must Strive for Diversity," *International Herald Tribune*, November 16, 2005; "Chirac's Influence Sinks to New Low," *Daily Telegraph*, November 28, 2005.

19. "France Tops Euroskepticism League," *European Foundation Intelligence Digest*, October 13, 2005 (from *Le Monde*, October 4, 2005).

20. John Gillingham, *European Integration, 1950–2003: Superstate or New Market Economy*, (Cambridge University Press, 2003), 442–445.

21. Oxford Economic Forecasting, "Trade Liberalization and CAP Reform in the EU" (October 2005), 82 pp.; "Farmer Prince Reaps EU Subsidies," *The Times*, November 4, 2005.

22. Open Europe Briefing Note, "EU Budget/Rebate Briefing," October 2005; Richard E. Baldwin, "Who Finances the Queen's CAP Payments" (CEPS Policy Brief 88, December 2005).

23. Peet, op. cit., "Blair to Refocus EU Presidency on Budget Strategy," *Financial Times*, September 27, 2005.

24. "British Rebate Prompts Bitter Cross Channel Exchanges," *The Times*, June 11, 2005; "Old Europe Must Reform or Crumble, Blair Warns Leaders," *The Times*, June 15, 2005; "Europe Turns on France as Britain Wins New Allies," *The Times*, June 17, 2000; 'Blair's New Best Friend in Europe Comes to Britain's Aid over Rebate," *The Times*, June 17, 2005..

25. George Trefgarne, "Budget Row Is Britain's Weapon of Reform," *Daily Telegraph*, June 11, 2005; "Å Wholly Different Game," eureferendum.blogspot.com; Blair and Brown Turn up Heat in EU Rebate Row with French" *The Times*, June 10, 2005; George Parker, "Blair Pushed to Give up Part of Rebate in EU Deal. France Is Being Urged to Accept Subsidy Cuts in a Budget Compromise," *Financial Times*, June 8, 2005; "Fieberhafte Suche nach Lösung in EU-Finanzstreit," *Die Welt*, June 8, 2005; "Le budget pour la periode 2007–2013, l'autre bataille," *Le Monde*, June 7, 2005.

26. "French Farmers, the British Rebate and a European Moment of Truth," *The Times*, June 14, 2005; "Blair Stands Alone on Rebate but with Friends n Reform," *The Times*, June 13, 2005.

27. "How the Money Is Spent: Regional Aid," BBC News, December 17, 2005; "Open Europe Bulletin," November 30–December 20, 2005.

28. Will Hutton, "Europe Is Hanging by a Thread," *The Observer*, October 23, 2005.

29. "Whipping the Commission into Shape," *The Economist*, November 17, 2005; "Irish Official Takes Top Post in Brussels," *Financial Times*, November 10, 2005; "We Cannot Hide, EU Must Accept Globalization or We Are Nothing," *The Times*, October 24, 2005; "Bad Start to the Most Difficult Job," *The Times*, October 25, 2005; "EU Plant Anti-Globalisierungsfonds," *Spiegel Online*, December 19, 2005; "EU Commission Failing to Protect Europe – Chirac," *Reuters*, October 4, 2005; "Barroso to Scrap a Third of Pending EU Laws," *Financial Times*,

September 28, 2005; "Don't just Bash the Bureaucrats," *The Economist*, October 13, 2005; "Finance Ministers Pledge Clampdown on EU Waste," *Financial Times*, November 8, 2005; "Single Tax Base Planned for Companies," *Financial Times*, October 28, 2005; "Brussels Starts Third Attempt to Harmonize Credit Rules," *Financial Times*, October 11, 2005; "Galileo Faces Suspension as Workshare Talks Stall," *Flight International*, October 4, 2005.

30. "Brussels Seeks Power on Mergers," *Financial Times*, November 16, 2005; "Banking on McCreevy," *The Economist*, November 24, 2005; "Europe's Satellite System is Wobbling Perilously Off Course," *Daily Telegraph*, October 29, 2005.

31. "EU Leaders Urged to 'Engage' Their Citizens," *Financial Times*, October 12, 2005; "Plan D in Place but Will Member States Deliver?" EURactif.com (October 15, 2005).

32. Ibid.; " European Commission Launches PLAN D for Democracy, Dialog, and Debate" (Commission Press Release, October 13, 2005); " The Commission's Contribution to the Period of Reflection and Beyond: Plan D for Democracy, Dialog, and Debate" (Commission Press Release, October 13, 2005).

33. "Eurocrats to Splash Out Millions on 50-day Golden Jubilee Party," *Daily Telegraph*, October 29, 2005.

34. EUreferendum.blogspot.com, December 22, 2005.

35. "Barroso Sets Up Advisory Group on Transparency," *European Report*, May 19, 2005; "EU Lobbyists under Attack" *The Guardian*, May 30, 2005; "Olaf Faces Increased Supervision," *Accountancy Age*, July 21, 2005.

36. "Kallas Sees Deal on Audit Reform in November," *European Report*, October 5, 2005; "Setback for Brussels Transparency Drive," *Financial Times*, October 21, 2005.

37. "Brussels Stutters over Transparency Text," EUObserver.com (October 24, 2005).

38. John Peet, "The EU Budget: A Way Forward" (Center for European Reform, September 2005).

39. Martin Wolf, "The World Has Everything to Lose if Trade Liberalization Fails," *Financial Times*, November 2, 2005; Pierre A, Meserlin, "A European Economic Agenda after the NO Votes" (35th Wincott Lecture, October 3, 2005).

40. David Kernohan, Jorge Nunes Ferrer, and Andreas Schneider, "The EU Budget Process and International Trade Liberalization," Working Document 230 (CAPS, October 2005), 1–39; Martin Wolf, "To Improve Policy Brussels Must Scrutinize Its Failures," *Financial Times*, October 5, 2005; Jagdish Bhagwati, "From Seattle to Hong Kong," *Foreign Affairs*, December 2005 (WTO Special Edition).

41. Gillingham, *European Integration*, op. cit., 4, 444–445.

42. "The Doha Trade Talks," *The Economist*, November 5, 2005.

43. Philip Bowring, "The Rest of the World Needs to Look at New Ways of Dealing with Europe on Trade Issues," *The International Herald Tribune*, November 2, 2005.

44. Bhagwati, op.cit.; Peter Sutherland, "Correcting Misperceptions," *Foreign Affairs*, December 2005 (WTO Special Edition).

45. "The Harnessing of Nature's Bounty," *The Economist*, November 3, 2005.

46. Gillingham, *Superstate or New Market Economy*, op. cit.
47. "In the Rough. The Doha Trade Round Needs Some Bold Strokes to Get Back on the Fairway," *The Economist*, November 3, 2005.
48. "French Farmers Holding the World to Ransom," *Financial Times*, November 3, 2005; "World Trade Talks on the Brink of Collapse," EUObserver.com (November 4, 2005); "New Offer by Europe on Trade is Assailed," *New York Times*, October 29, 2005.
49. Bowring, op. cit.
50. "EU Will Not Open Farm Markets Further," *Financial Times*, November 8, 2005; Jean-René Fourtou and Marcus Wallenberg," Last and Best Chance to Move Doha Round to a Successful Conclusion," *Financial Times*, November 8, 2005.
51. Jagdish Bhagwati, "How to Resolve the Deadlock Holding Back World Trade Talks," *Financial Times*, November 15, 2005; C. Fred Bergsten, "Rescuing the Doha Round, *Foreign Affairs*, December 2005 (WTO Special Edition).
52. "Discussion with Prime Minister of Turkey" (transcript of Charlie Rose Show, September 15, 2005).
53. Yueksel Soeylemez, "The EU Morning after Luxembourg," *Turkish Daily News*, October 9, 2005.
54. Guel Demir, "Baydarol: Turkey Won't Become a Full EU Member Quickly," *Turkish Daily News*, September 21, 2005.
55. Ibid.
56. Richard H. K. Vietor and Emily J. Thompson, "Turkey: Securing Stability in a Rough Neighborhood" (Harvard Business School, May 24, 2004), 704–745.
57. John Gillingham, *Europe at the Tipping Point* (Telders Lecture, March 2005).
58. David Judson, "The Start of a Painful Journey: The Approval of Turkey's Candidature for EU Membership is just the Start of a Decade Long Process," *Euromoney* 36, no. 1430 (February 2005).
59. Vietor and Thompson, op. cit.
60. Arjan M. Lejour and Ruud A. de Mooij, "Turkish Delight: Does Turkey's Accession to the EU Bring Economic Benefits?" *Kyklos* 58, (2005): 87–120.
61. *"Giant Underground Economy Casts Pall over Turkey's Progress"* (Agence France Presse, October 28, 2004); Katinka Barysch, "Slow Train from Istanbul," *Wall Street Journal*, September 27, 2005.
62. "Turkey Is Just Beginning to Reap Economic Benefits Says Babacan," *Turkish Daily News*, November 9, 2005.
63. Lejour and de Mooij, op. cit., 90–93.
64. "Turkey is just Beginning to Reap Economic Benefits," op. cit.
65. Timothy Garton Ash, "How the Dreaded Superstate Became a Commonwealth: The Question to Ask Now Is Not What Europe Will Do for Turkey, but What Turkey Has Done for Europe," *The Guardian*, October 6, 2005; John Gillingham, "Neither Superstate nor New Market Economy: The Impact of the Constitutional Referenda – A Preliminary Assessment," *Merkourios*, December 2005 (forthcoming).

66. Martin Wolf, "A Union with Turkey Would Be a Prize for a Divided World," *Financial Times*, October 12, 2005; "Expert Hail Start of Turkey, Croatia Talks as 'Good Sign' for Macedonia," BBC Monitoring Euro-Political, October 10, 2005; "What's the Status of Kosovo?" (UPI, October 7, 2005); Misha Glenny, "A Balkan Success Story: Observations on Macedonia," *New Statesman*, September 26, 2005; "Serbia-Montenegro Hails EU Decision to Open Entry Talks," Xinhua News Agency, October 3, 2005.

67. Christopher Caldwell, "The East in the West," *New York Times*, September 25, 2005; "If Blair Wins, the Odds for Turkey Increase," *Turkish Daily News*, June 21, 2005.

68. Igor Torbakov, "Russia and Turkey Forge New Ties on Security, Trade," Eurasianet.org (August 8, 2005); "Russia Plans to Use Turkey as Hub for Gas," *New York Times*, November 18, 2005; Daniel Howden and Philip Thornton, "The Pipeline That Will Change the World," *The Independent*, May 25, 2005.

69. Mark Leonard and Charles Grant, "Georgia and the EU: Can Europe's Neighborhood Policy Deliver?" (Centre for European Reform, September 2005); Mevlut Katik, "Turkey Promotes Stability in the Caucasus," Eurasianet.org (July 18, 2005).

70. Caldwell, op. cit.

71. "Thirteenth Birthday of Black Sea Economic Cooperation," *Turkish Daily News*, June 26, 2005.

72. Leonard and Grant, op. cit.

73. Tatiana Korobova (Interview) www.obozrevatel.com.ua, October 29, 2005.

74. Timothy Garton and Timothy Snyder, "The Orange Revolution," *New York Review of Books*, April 28, 2005.

75. Ibid.

76. Central Intelligence Agency, *The World Factbook* (May 17, 2005).

77. Volodymyr Dibrova, "Mapping out Ukrainian Identity," (Speech, Stanford University, June 2005).

78. Neil Buckley and Stefan Wagstyl, "Orange Alert: Putin Turns Populist as Fears of a Ukraine-Style Revolt Haunt the Kremlin," *Financial Times*, September 26, 2005.

79. Anders Aslund, "Why Tymoshenko's Figures Didn't Add Up," *Moscow Times*, September 14, 2005; "Ukraine's Orange Revolution Can Still End in Success," *Financial Times*, September 26, 2005.

80. Korobova, *op. cit.*

81. Tammy Lynch, "Viktor Yuschchenko: Patterns of a Political Life" (manuscript, November 2005). Forthcoming in *Journal of the Institute of Politics*, Ukrainian Academy of Sciences.

82. Robert S. Kravchuk, *Ukrainian Political Economy: The First Ten Years* (New York, 2002), 37–63.

83. Ibid., 66; Robert Kravchuk, "Kuchma as Economic Reformer, 1994–2004," *Problems of Post-Communism* 52, no. 5 (September–October 2005): 1–11.

84. "Ukraine's Best-Known Tycoons" (Agence France Presse, October 11, 2005).

85. Kravchuk, *Ukrainian Political Economy*, op. cit., 82–92.
86. "Full Text of Interview with Ukrainian President," *Financial Times*, October 14, 2005.
87. "Yulia Tymoschenko: 'Ich bereue nichts," (interview) *Die Welt*, December 5, 2005.
88. Kravchuk, *Ukrainian Political Economy*, op. cit., 86f.
89. "Key Dates in the Gongadze Affair" (Agence France Presse, March 4, 2005); "Interview: Olena Prytula, Ukrainskaya Pravda," PBS Frontline Web site (Ukraine: A Murder in Kyiv, October 2005).
90. "President's Aides in Murder 'Cover Up'," *Sunday Times*, September 18, 2005; "Interview: Olena Prytula," op. cit.; Boris Volodarsky, "Getting the Reds Out of the Orange Revolution," *Wall Street Journal*, October 14, 2005.
91. "Yuschchenko Rocks Ukraine but Can It Roll?" *The Business*, July 3, 2005.
92. "Russian Adviser to Ukraine's Leader (Boris Nemtsov) Applauds Dismissal of Premier," BBC Monitoring Former Soviet Union, September 14, 2005.
93. Aslund, "Orange Revolution," op. cit.
94. "Yulia Tymoshenko Strikes a Pricing Blow at Russia," *Kommersant*, April 13, 2005; "Ukrainian Parliament Sabotaging WTO Entry," *Delovaya Stolitsa*, October 29, 2005; " First Defeat for Ukraine's New Leader Raises Doubts on Reforms" (Agence France Presse, July 10, 2005); Tammy Lynch, "Time for Yushchenko to Step Up" (Briefing, Institute for the Study of Conflict, Ideology and Policy, June 28, 2005).
95. "Turchanov's Sensational Statements. Kuchma's Schemes Taken Care of by Tretyakov. Yushchenko's Poisoning not yet Confirmed," *Ukrains'ka Pravda*, September 13, 2005; "It Is Tymoshenko Who Is Copying Kuchma" (interview of Poroshenko), *Gazeta Wyborcza*, September 15, 2005; "Rybachuk: The List of Crooks Will Be expanded," *Novaya Gazeta* 1094, September 19–21, 2005; "And then They Woke Up. The Dream of a Democratic, Non-Corrupt Ukraine May Die," *The Economist*, September 15, 2005; "Deal for Ukraine Company Renews Charges of Abuse," *New York Times*, September 15, 2005; "Yulia Tymoschenko: 'Ich bereue nichts'," op. cit.
96. "Former Ukrainian Security Supremo Says Ex-Premier Ruined Economy," BBC Monitoring International Reports, September 25, 2005; "Corruption Scandal Aims to Distract People's Attention – Proshenko," ITAR-TASS, September 25, 2005; "Former Ukrainian Premier Talks About How She Was Sacked," BBC Monitoring Former Soviet Union, September 19, 2005.
97. "Berezovsky: 'I Can Show You Payment Instructions for Another 6 Million Dollars," *Ukrains'ka Pravda*, October 11, 2005; Oleg, Varfolomeyev, "Ally Cleared of Criminal Charge – A Trap for Yushchenko?" *Eurasia Daily Monitor*, October 26, 2005; Oleg Varfolomeyev, "Did Berezovsky Finance Ukraine's Orange Revolution?" *Eurasia Daily Monitor*, September 19, 2005.
98. "Yuschchenko Extended His Hand to Yanukovich," RusData Dialine, Kommersant 176, September 20, 2005; "Memorandum of Understanding between the Government and the Opposition," *Ukrains'ka Pravda*, September 22, 2005.

99. "Ukrainian President's Adviser Warns of Economic Crisis," BBC Monitoring Former Soviet Union, September 7, 2005; Craig Mellow, "The Orange Evolution," *Institutional Investor* 39, no. 5 (May 2005); "Ukraine President Restructures Administration," BBC Monitoring Former Soviet Union, September 22, 2005.

100. Charles Paul Lewis, *How the East Was Won, The Impact of Multinational Companies on Eastern Europe and the Former Soviet Union* (New York, 2005); "East, West and the Gap between," *The Economist*, November 24, 2005.

101. "Ukrainian President's New Chief of Staff Vows to Keep Revolution Promises," BBC Monitoring Former Soviet Union, September 12, 2005.

102. "Proposed Measures to Revive Investments and Growth," SigmaBleyzer and Blyzer Foundation, November 2005.

103. "An Exemplary Start," *Financial Times*, October 26, 2005; "Sale Ends Ukrainian Re-Privatizations," *Financial Times*, October 25, 2005; "Sins of the Fathers," *The Economist*, October 27, 2005; "The Long and Winding Road West: One of Ukraine's Richest Men, Viktor Pinchuk, Pops into Brussels," *Guardian Unlimited*, November 10, 2005.

104. Anders Aslund, "Russian-Ukrainian Gas War: Munumental Russian Mistake," (Action Ukraine Report 635, 5 January 2006).

105. "Russia-Ukraine Gas Deal Too Murky for Comfort," REUTERS, January 5, 2006.

106. "Awash with Petrodollars, Russia Frets About the Paradoxes of Bounty," *The New York Times*, November 15, 2005; "Recycling the Petrodollars," The *Economist*, November 10, 2005; "Oil Prices and Russia's Return to Superpower Status," RIA Novosti, October 13, 2005.

107. Sergei Blagov, "Russia Outmaneuvers Ukraine for Turkmen Gas – for now!" Eurasianet.org (April 21, 2005); "Putin Ally in Prime Position to Take Over," *Financial Times*, November 15, 2005.

108. "EU Should Separate Energy Disputes from Russia," *Moskovskie Novosti*, October 7, 2005; "EU 'Over-Dependent' on Russian Gas Supplies," *Financial Times*, December 2, 2004; "Russia – EU Energy Relations the Ultimate 'Common Space'," RAI Novosti, October 5, 2005; "Russia Covers 90 Percent of EU Natural Gas Needs, Putin," RAI Novosti, October 4, 2005.

109. Keith C. Smith, "Ukraine between a Rock and Hard Place" (Speech, Washington DC, November 4, 2005); "Ukrainian Fuel and Energy Minister Sets Out Strategy for Sector," BBC Monitoring Former Soviet Union, May 19, 2005.

110. Roman Bryl, "Navtogaz Attracts Huge Credits with Hidden Purpose," IntelliNews, Kyif, October 25, 2005; Margarita M. Balmaceda, "Energy and the Rise and Fall of the Orange Revolution Coalition," HURI, Ukrainian Study Group, November 3, 2005; John E. Herbst, "Energy Sector Reform and European Integration" (Speech, Kyiv, November 9, 2005); "Europe's Gas Supply at Risk," *Financial Times*, November 24, 2005.

111. "Russia's Energetic Enigma," *The Economist*, October 6, 2005.
112. "No More Cheap Gas, Russia Tells Neighbors" (Associated Press, Moscow, November 28, 2005); " Ukraine Urges Compromise in Latest Gas Dispute with Russia" (Associated Press, Kyif, November 24, 2005); "Europe's Gas Supply 'at Risk' Because of a Stand-Off between Russia and Ukraine," *Financial Times*, November 24, 2005; "Ukraine Looking for Support on Oil Pipeline," *Ukrainian Journal*, November 24, 2005.
113. "Advisor Says Putin's Government Slowed Russian Economic Growth by 9 Percent in 2005," Mosnews.com (September 24, 2005).
114. Dmitri Tremin, "Russia, the EU and the Common Neighborhood" (Centre for European Reform, September 2005).
115. "Russian Commentator Decries Russia's Gloating at Ukrainian Political Crisis," BBC Monitoring International Reports, September 25, 2005.
116. James Sherr and Zerkalo Nedeli, *Mirror-Weekly*, October 29–November 5, 2005; "NATO Parliamentary Secretary Says Door Open to Ukraine," November 11, 2005; Yulia Mostovaya and Zerkalo Nedeli, "Interview with Zbigniew Brzezinski: 'Europe from Cabo de Roca to Kamchatka'," *Mirror-Weekly*, December 3–9, 2005.
117. "NATO Chief Urges Free Elections, Democratic Reforms in Ukraine," BBC Monitoring Former Soviet Union, October 19, 2005; "Ukrainian Sees No Russia Block in NATO Entry," *New York Times*, October 24, 2005; "Ukraine's Security Chief Plans to Reform His Agency," BBC Monitoring, Former Soviet Union, October 15, 2005.
118. Tom Warner, "EU Grants Ukraine Market Economy Status," *Financial Times*, December 1, 2005; "Viktor Yuschencnko's Radion Address," Kyif, December 3, 2003.
119. Vaclav Klaus, *On the Road to Democracy* (Dallas, 2005), 115.
120. Quentin Peel, "A Presidency in Danger of Irrelevance," *Financial Times*, November 24, 2005; "Barroso's Anniversary (from Alexandrine Bouilhet, *Le Figaro*, November 17, 2005)," *European Foundation Intelligence Digest*, November 23, 2005.
121. Glyn Morgan, *The Idea of a European Superstate* (Princeton, 2005).
122. "Interview with Zbigniew Brzezinski," op. cit.
123. "Ukrainian President Yushchenko Rallies Supporters on Anniversary of Orange Revolution," November 23, 2003.

POSTSCRIPT: NEITHER SUPERSTATE NOR NEW MARKET ECONOMY

1. Open Europe Bulletin 12, November 29, 2005.
2. "EU Agrees to Give Ukraine Market Economy Status" (AP Worldstream, December 1, 2005).
3. John Peet, "Wider not Deeper: The European Union Searches for a Sense of Direction," *The World in 2006* (*The Economist*), December 2005.

4. "EU Leaders Still Want to Press on with EU Constitution" (Open Europe Bulletin, November 12–29, 2005).

5. "Gloom Casts a Shadow on Chirac's Presidency," *Financial Times*, November 29, 2005.

6. "Blair Seeks Smaller EU Budget," *Reuters*, December 1, 2005.

7. Ambrose Evans-Pritchard, "Bonfire of Diktats Has 'Failed to Ignite'," *Daily Telegraph*, November 29, 2005.

8. Vaclav Klaus, *On the Road to Democracy*, op. cit., 143.

9. Timothy Garton Ash, "Can Hampton Court Be Europe's Great House of Easement?" *The Guardian*, October 27, 2005.

10. (New Great House of Easement).

11. Anne-Marie Slaughter, *A New World Order* (Princeton, 2004).

12. Friedrich A. Hayek, "The Economic Conditions of Interstate Federalism" (reprinted in *Individualism and Economic Order*, Chicago, 1948).

13. John Gillingham, *European Integration: Superstate or New Market Economy?* xi–xv,487–497.

14. Klaus, op. cit., 120.

Index